# Counter-Hegemony and Foreign Policy

For Your Excellency
The Vice President
of Nigeria.

Towards The freedom of
Our peoples

*[signature]*

April 01, 2001

*SUNY series in Global Politics*
*James N. Rosenau, Editor*

*Counter-Hegemony and Foreign Policy*

## THE DIALECTICS OF MARGINALIZED AND GLOBAL FORCES IN JAMAICA

*Randolph B. Persaud*

*State University of New York Press*

Published by
State University of New York Press, Albany

For information, address State University of New York Press,
90 State Street, Suite 700, Albany, NY 12207

Production by Diane Ganeles
Marketing by Fran Keneston

**Library of Congress Cataloging-in-Publication Data**

Persaud, Randolph B., 1959–
    Counter-hegemony and foreign policy : the dialectics of marginalized
and global forces in Jamaica / Randolph B. Persaud.
        p.   cm. — (SUNY series in global politics)
    Includes bibliographical references and index.
    ISBN 0-7914-4919-X (alk. paper)—ISBN 0-7914-4920-3 (pbk. : alk. paper)
    1. Jamaica—Foreign relations.   2. International relations—Political
aspects.   I. Title.   II. Series.
    JZ1541.P47 2001
    327.7292'009'046—dc21                                          00-041297

10 9 8 7 6 5 4 3 2 1

*For Thea Vandana and B. K.*

# Contents

Contents                                      ix

# Foreword

This book has meaning at several levels. At one level, it is a study of foreign policy in a small Third World country, in this case Jamaica. At another, it is a critical reconsideration of the very notion of foreign policy as a struggle between local social forces and global economic, political and ideological hegemony with the state playing an intermediary role. At yet another, it is an examination of race as the subjective way in which oppression is experienced and as the basis for the formation of a culture of resistance.

Randolph Persaud argues that hegemony always implies resistance. The two are a dialectical pair. Hegemony looks at the world from the top down in the perspective of dominant power acquiring consent or acquiescence from the subordinate. Resistance seeks to remake world order from below a civil society that becomes conscious of its own subordination and creates the means of envisaging and struggling for emancipation—for the formation of a counter-hegemony. Although resistance arises in a national setting, it is implicitly as global as the hegemonic force itself. The principle vehicle arousing the will to struggle is culture. Culture gives people a sense of affinity and purpose, and it marks a cleavage from the hegemonic ideology. Persaud cites the music of Bob Marley as a vital source of resistance, in Jamaica in the first instance, but in the world beyond as well, wherever the spirit of resistance is aroused.

One fascinating part of Persaud's account is his analysis of how the culture of resistance took form through the Rastafarians and the black urban poor. Jamaica is a stratified society with a dominant white elite, a "brown" intermediate group including professionals and political leaders—a group ambivalent between preserving the status quo and mobilizing resistance—and the black populace with its racial memories of slavery. The cultural movement from below made race and color the subjective expression of rebellion and gave it a meaning transcending the geographical boundaries of Jamaica. Here is a particular instance of the articulation of voices from below, voices seldom heard with emphasis in discussions about world political economy.

The story told in this book is one of political failure. Michael Manley's government made a noble effort to challenge the dominant world economic order. His government was a leader in the demand through the United Nations for the New International Economic Order. It attempted to turn the bauxite industry to the benefit of Jamaicans and internationalized this effort through the formation of the International Bauxite Association which was perceived by the major economic powers as only slightly less threatening than the oil cartel OPEC. He cultivated good relations with Castro's Cuba and envisaged the formation of a socialist grouping of Caribbean countries (Jamaica, Guyana, Grenada, Cuba) under the nose of U.S. power. It all fell apart as Jamaica's economy verged on catastrophe and a less permissive global environment emerged with the political victories of Thatcher and Reagan assisted by Kissinger and the ideology of neoliberal capitalism. In this new context, Manley about turned to seek aid from the International Monetary Fund as a way out of the economic impasse with all the restrictions on the domestic economy that would imply. He lost the next election to Edward Seaga, a reversal comforting to Jamaica's elites and to American views about desirable political and economic behavior.

The nagging question to which Persaud's analysis points is: Why did Manley seemingly renounce his project of Jamaican independence and capitulate to the forces of world economy embodied in the IMF? In the top-down perspective of global hegemony, political realism would dictate compliance to superior economic and political power in a climate of lesser tolerance for deviance. That would be the simple and perhaps the correct answer. In the bottom-up perspective of resistance the answer would appear more complex. The government was confronted by the certainty that its reformist democratic socialism at home and diplomatic efforts to build a sustaining group of countries abroad would leave Jamaica in economic collapse. The alternatives would be *either* compliance with world-economy demands administered through the IMF and obedience to U.S. political imperatives in abandoning the project of closer relations with Cuba and the socialist bloc, *or* making a radical break with the world economy though revolutionary mobilization of the Jamaican resistance forces toward a self-sufficient economy (what Persaud calls "decommodification"). Was the option for compliance determined by the realist assessment that mobilization would not succeed, or by a "brown-man's" hesitation to make the fatal break with the erstwhile leading strata of Jamaica society?

However you may answer, there is no finality to this story. The world political economy on the threshold of the twenty-first century shows signs of renewed instances of resistance to the hegemony of globalization. These signs come from within the economically dominant countries as well as from those more economically dependent. The collapse of trade negotiations at the World Trade Organization meeting in Seattle toward the end of 1999 gave a vivid illustration of popular forces of protest in the streets, diplomatic differences among the major economic powers, and refusal on the part of poor country governments. A culture of resistance appeared to be building again with a variety of component elements. Race is still a component, as is class, ethnicity and religion. Concern for ecology is a newer element. The open question is whether these distinct forms of subjectivity can be transcended in a broader counter-hegemonic perspective with coherent political aims. Randolph Persaud's book is an introduction to the problematic of the formation of such a movement and such a perspective.

ROBERT W. COX

# Preface

This is a book about the doubly marginalized. It is about the small island of Jamaica, which, by any measure of material power, would render it insignificant in the international system. And if indeed Jamaica exists at the margins in the interstate system, the civil society groups and social forces within the country are even further removed from the theater of global politics. Yet, these are precisely the types of "actors" I consider vital in arresting the historicity of the postwar hegemonic world order. How could this be? I offer three general arguments in this book.

First, a hegemonic world order is not a pregiven reality. Hegemonic orders are deliberately and methodically constructed through (a) the global institutionalization of the preferences of the state(s) and social forces that seek hegemony, (b) the articulation of an ideology which establishes the ontological and operational foundations of the particular world order, (c) the constitution and diffusion of legitimacy by the hegemonic "leaders," and (d) the construction of followership. Two things are obvious: a hegemonic order is the result of a process of *hegemonization*, and correspondingly, hegemony is a *relational encounter* with followers. On account of the relationality of hegemony, the objects of hegemonization must be an integral part of the theoretical and historical problematization of a hegemonic world order. The modalities and conditions of entry by the followers, or the latter's resistance to enter the hegemonic space, is generative of the specific form of the hegemonic order. For this reason, the story of the hegemon's logically necessary "Other" is required.

Second, to the extent the question of followership has been explored in global politics, it has been confined to the activities of states. Civil societies within hegemonized states are routinely ignored. The success of a global hegemony, however, is ultimately dependent on the extent to which the hegemonic forces penetrate the civil space of the hegemonized. More often than not, the resistance to such hegemonic interpellation comes from forces within the civil society of the latter. In this book, I demonstrate how influential these forces in Jamaica were, in countering the hegemonic designs of powerful actors in the global political economy, and of the United States. Ironically, the "marginalized within the marginalized" became influential in questions relating to such diverse international issues such as the liberation of southern Africa; the policies of the IMF; the suitability of American world leadership; strategies of economic development; the NIEO; institutionalized global racism; and not the least, the cultural dimensions of the Cold War.

The global democratization of knowledge about world politics must systematically incorporate the "voices from the margins." Reliable knowledge cannot only come from the experience of the Great Powers. The marginalized, after all, make up the bulk of the world. Yet, it is not simply a matter of numbers. Nor is it an issue of accommodating authentic subaltern perspectives, for the sake of "giving voice." The real problem is, rather, one of epistemology. The fact of the matter is that the Third World does not *merely respond* to the actions of Great Powers, or the hegemonic power. To conceive of global politics thus would have no other consequence than relegate the great mass of humanity to mere appendages in the making of history. A more innovative approach might focus on capturing the historical dialectic of world order through what Antonio Gramsci called absolute historicism. This book is a step in that direction. It shows that Jamaican foreign policy, and forces within the civil society of that country, figured a great deal in the *making* of the post-war world order. In short, this work is about the historical formation of world order "from below."

One specific aspect of this book sets it apart from the emerging critical literature on hegemony in world order. While critical political economy approaches have indeed gone beyond state-centric analysis and other pitfalls of the "mainstream," there seems to be hesitancy in understanding the generative capacity of race in the configuration and reproduction of domestic social formations, and global structures of accumulation. Hegemony, in my view, cannot be adequately theorized without careful consideration of the ways in which processes of racialization have been imbricated in the making of hegemonized "common sense." Moreover, counter-hegemonic practices emanating from outside the West, invariably frame dimensions of their discourses in terms of liberation from racial supremacy. Part of the problem is that we do not definitively know what race is. The fact of the matter is that it has no "isness." For now, let me suggest that in the making of historical structures, race may shed old meanings; take on new ones; be called upon to delineate inside from outside; be employed in the contestation of what is good and evil; be combined with other artifacts to produce identity and mark difference; become the nodal point of cultural or national unity; act as a fulcrum for political mobilization; serve as a principle of justifying class exploitation, inequality, and the structure of the division of labor; function as an explanatory concept in the development of civilizations; be used as an instrument to inscribe status; and be drawn into movements of resistance. This book makes an explicit and determined attempt to connect the dialectics of race at the domestic and international levels. Particular emphasis is placed on the constitutivity of race in the inscription of hegemony and the sustained "war of position" against this common sense from above.

I am indebted to a large number of people and organizations for bringing this book from an idea to final form. First, I would like to express deep appreciation to Robert W. Cox (my dissertation supervisor at York University), who gave so much of his theoretical rigor and great intellect through the years. Stephen R. Gill allowed me to exploit his vast knowledge of international relations, and provided extensive commentary on all aspects of this work. David-Leyton Brown, Rudy Grant, and Craig Murphy also provided extremely useful comments, for which I am thankful. While on research trips in Jamaica, I stayed with the Beepat family (at Mico College). They were exceptionally kind to me, a virtual stranger, and for all they gave and the little I have managed to return, I wish to record my gratitude. Thanks also to Mrs. Hammond, Head Librarian of the PNP Archives, and all the other staff at this excellent library, who spent so much of their valuable time digging out and photocopying dozens and dozens of documents. Claudette Aldred at the Ministry of Foreign Affairs' Library also provided some key sources and provided some good leads for me to follow. The staff at the International Bauxite Association, Jamaica Bauxite Association, Institute of Jamaica, National Planning Agency, and the Mona Library at the U.W.I. were all cooperative and efficient. My thanks also to Ambassadors Don Mills and Herbert Walker who gave me important insights into Jamaica's multilateral policies. The personnel at Jamaica's Mission to the United Nations (New York) and that of the consulate in Toronto, were very helpful as well. The staff at the New York Public Library also provided competent advice on accessing United Nations "roll call" votes.

Walter Persaud, Dr. Rishee S. Thakur, and Dr. Arnold Itwaru allowed me to run obscure and often incoherent ideas by them for years. They, along with Elarick Persaud, S. Hydaralli, Atul Bahl, and L. Singh, provided a rich intellectual context for me to think seriously. I owe them all a great debt for this happening. Samantha Arnold edited the first draft of the manuscript with care, and Rebecca DeWinter provided valuable service as a Research Assistant. Marios Vassiliou, Jennifer Douglas-Abubakar, Huong Nguyen, and Chandra Dunn gave generously of their time in preparing the index. James N. Rosenau was also very encouraging through the final preparation of this work, and I thank him for that. Michael Rinella and Diane Ganeles of SUNY Press were unfailing in their patience and support and, for that, I thank them sincerely. I would be remiss if I did not single out Dolly Persaud for her understanding through the years.

Randolph B. Persaud

# Abbreviations

| | |
|---|---|
| ACP | African, Caribbean, and Pacific Countries |
| BITU | Bustamante Industrial Trade Union |
| CBI | Caribbean Basin Initiative |
| CEO | Community Enterprise Organization |
| CIA | Central Intelligence Agency (U.S.A.) |
| CLC | Caribbean Labour Congress |
| CMEA | Council of Mutual Economic Assistance |
| EFF | Extended Fund Facility |
| EPP | Emergency Production Plan |
| FIU | Financial Intelligence Unit |
| IBA | International Bauxite Association |
| IBRD | International Bank of Reconstruction and Development |
| IDB | Inter-American Development Bank |
| IMF | International Monetary Fund |
| JAMAL | Jamaica Adult Literacy |
| JAS | Jamaica Agricultural Society |
| JBC | Jamaica Broadcasting Corporation |
| JBI | Jamaica Bauxite Institute |
| JCC | Jamaica Council of Churches |
| JDF | Jamaica Defense Force |

| | |
|---|---|
| JDP | Jamaica Democratic Party |
| JLP | Jamaica Labor Party |
| JMA | Jamaica Manufacturers' Association |
| JNH | Jamaica Nutrition Holdings |
| JNIP | Jamaica National Industrial Promotions Ltd. |
| JOS | Jamaica Omnibus Service |
| JPL | Jamaica Progressive Party |
| JPS | Jamaica Public Service Company |
| JTC | Jamaica Telephone Company |
| JWTU | Jamaica Workers and Tradesman's Union |
| MPLA | Popular Movement for the Liberation of Angola |
| NIEO | New International Economic Order |
| NPA | National Planning Agency |
| OPEC | Organization of Petroleum Exporting Countries |
| OPIC | Overseas Private Investment Corporation |
| PNP | People's National Party |
| PNPYO | PNP Youth Organization |
| PSOJ | Private Sector Organization of Jamaica |
| RJR | Radio Jamaica Rediffusion |
| SEC | Special Employment Program |
| STC | State Trading Corporation |
| TUC | Trade Union Council |
| TUEI | Trade Union Education Institute |
| UWI | University of the West Indies |
| WPJ | Workers' Party of Jamaica |
| YSL | Young Socialist League |

# 1

## Introduction: The New Historical Materialism

In January 1972, the People's National Party (PNP), led by Michael Manley, won the general elections in Jamaica and replaced the Jamaican Labor Party (JLP) which had been in office since 1962. Between 1972 and 1980, the PNP undertook a significant number of domestic reforms aimed at bettering the lives of Jamaicans, and these reforms were accompanied by a determined effort to reorient Jamaica's linkages with the outside world. The PNP held the view that meaningful change within the country was possible only if Jamaica modified its traditional ties with the North Atlantic (mainly the USA, Canada, and Great Britain), multinational capital, and multilateral institutions. Instead of "dependent capitalist development" which the JLP had hitherto pursued through various foreign investment strategies, and a close relationship with the West, the PNP felt the need to move Jamaica in the direction of "self-reliance" through "Democratic Socialism," and closer relations with socialist and Third World states. Moreover, whereas the JLP had accepted the basic assumptions and practices of the extant Bretton Woods world economic order, the Manley administration felt it was necessary to change that order and replace it with a New International Economic Order. The democratic socialist government was of the firm view that the underdevelopment of Jamaica and the Third World were directly related to the structure and operation of the capitalist world economy and the imperialist policies of major capitalist states. Given the distribution of economic and military power in the world, real change could only come about by the collective action of Third World states, vis-à-vis the West/North, as well as increasing South-South cooperation. Accordingly, the PNP embarked on reorienting Jamaican foreign policy from a position of deference to the West—and passive acceptance of the extant world order—to one of bringing about change in the world economy through Third

1

World solidarity. In contradistinction to Kenneth Waltz's sardonic little aphorism—small states do not matter—Jamaican foreign policy during the 1970s demonstrated that at a particular conjuncture of world history, this small state was able to play a role far more significant than traditional power politics would predict.

Three major factors relevant to the international relations of Third World countries, but often ignored, need elaboration. First, despite the overwhelming strength of the Great Powers, small and/ or poor states *do have options* for independent action in the international system. It is indeed the case that weaker states are generally defensive and acquiescent in their external behavior and, more often than not, would follow "the lead" of larger powers (as the JLP did from 1962–1971). Yet, there have been occasions, and more importantly historical conjunctures, when small underdeveloped countries, such as Jamaica in the 1970s, pursued policies which were deliberately intended to challenge key aspects of the international system, even if that meant incurring penalties from one or more of the Great Powers, and some multilateral organizations. While individual small/ poor states may not have the power to influence system wide change, their *collective action* may, and have, resulted in substantial adjustments to global institutions or even Great Power behavior.

Secondly, states per se, do not have pre-given national interests (upon which foreign policy is constructed). On the contrary, what emerges as the accepted national interest is very much a consequence of political, cultural, ideological, and economic struggles among competing social forces in a particular social formation. For this reason, a good portion of this book is devoted to understanding the social forces themselves and the way in which particular configurations of them influence the emergence of "core values." Further, while economic and security questions often inform the making of national interests, it is the case that culture and ideology also play critical roles. In fact, as will become evident, sometimes cultural interests inspire the central questions around which the core interests of a nation are negotiated. If we accept the proposition that states do not have *inherent* interests (apart from basic survival), then whatever foreign policy objectives are pursued at any given time could, alternatively, be understood as an historical question grounded in the material conditions of that society and the existing world order.

Thirdly, throughout this book, it is assumed that foreign and domestic policies are not mutually exclusive, but are different dimensions of the same correlation of forces and structural conditions. This assumption of reciprocal co-implication allows for easy movement between the two realms of policies, without having to make a prior announcement as to which one is antecedent or consequent. Instead of the usual bifurcation of the domestic and foreign, a holistic and recursive view allows for careful examination of the reciprocity of the two areas, and facilitates the analysis of relevant national and transnational conditions.

The three factors just described are themselves situated in a larger whole, namely, a framework aimed at the development of a social forces and new historical materialist approach to international relations in general, and foreign policy analysis in particular. In this reconstructed historical materialism, considerable emphasis is placed on the ways in which the material conditions of life, the institutionalization of these conditions, and the intellectual frameworks in which these are understood and explained, combine in specific historical conjunctures and, through such combination, give rise to different structures and generate new forces. It is assumed that it is the contestation and/or coalition of social forces that "moves history." Accordingly, the explanation of "foreign policy" undertaken here is grounded in a thorough examination of the social forces underpinning state behavior.

## Why Jamaica 1962–1980?

The period covered here represents a conjuncture, when historic blocs and the form of state in Jamaica started to undergo substantial transformation. These latter corresponded to the emergence of new transnational social forces, a sustained "war of legitimacy" between global hegemonic and counter-hegemonic forces and, eventually, the configuration of new sets of material and ideological factors which changed key aspects of the post-war world order. More concretely, the opportunity arises to demonstrate the ways in which different configurations of domestic social forces underpinned particular orientations to economy and society, and to the external world. In the 1960s, for example, a historic bloc welded together by what Obika Gray has called an ideology of "exceptionalism" (and led by the Jamaican Labor Party) displayed considerable deference to the West, while excluding significant sections of Jamaicans from the benefits of development.[1] In the 1970s, however, the Peoples National Party became part of a reconfigured correlation of social forces, and articulated quite a different orientation. Apart from the policy reversals which occurred between the two decades, important questions about the development of hegemonic and counter-hegemonic practices present themselves for investigation.

A study of Jamaica also allows a unique opportunity to examine the impact on developing states of the shift in the center of economic gravity and military power from Great Britain to the United States of America. What is interesting here from the perspective of understanding global politics, is the manner in which the instruments of hegemonic domination had to be retooled. It will be shown that while British hegemony operated in the context of formal colonialism, American neocolonial hegemony has functioned through more complex and diffuse mechanisms.

While the *typical* Third World country is very much a conceptual construction, Jamaica does have the structural socio-economic composition usually associated with those countries categorized as developing. The case becomes even more *sociologically interesting*, to borrow a phrase from C. Wright Mills, once it is recognized that the country's policies during the 1970s (both domestic and foreign) were geared toward transforming these structures. Because of this, the efforts to influence this transformation from abroad, but from a different perspective, brought Jamaica and these external forces into situations of *antagonism*. These antagonisms were symptomatic of some of the tensions and contradictions in the postwar order, and the book examines the manner in which they were "resolved" or at least rearticulated.

## Historicism and the New Historical Materialism

In very broad terms, this work employs an historicist approach in the specification; interrogation; and analysis of the objects of inquiry. Although definitions can often be restrictive and artificial, Antonio Gramsci's notion that things "must be known genetically in the movement of their formation" does capture the basic epistemological point of departure adopted here.[2] This emphasis on the genetic flux of global politics and, specifically, the place of Jamaican foreign policy in the making of world order, will be analyzed through the method of "historical structure" which focuses not only on structures and agency but, very importantly, on the historicity of structures. The method of historical structure develops diachronically within the text; that is to say, it is embedded in the narrative construction/deconstruction of the problematized objects.

The notion of "problematized objects" is important and needs elaboration. An object of inquiry cannot exist in and of itself; that is, an object is not merely an empirical instance, which by the very fact of its existence, is capable of revealing *theoretical knowledge*. The axiomatic transposition of empirical instances into objects of analyses is nothing other than empiricism. It is precisely this kind of empiricism which, when combined with the positivism of what is called here *fixed-universals* (interest, state, and power), that produces static and ahistorical concepts/theories and, ultimately, explanations for which much of international theory has been justly criticized.

The first step in the movement away from methodological individualism and positivism which underpin problem-solving theory, is to develop a critical ontology. According to Stephen Gill, the particular ontology used by critical theory is not "self-evident"; rather it must be a "theorized one."[3] Consistent with the Gramscian historical materialist ontology employed by Robert W. Cox, Stephen Gill, Craig Murphy, Mark Rupert, William Robinson and others in this tradition, this study assumes an ontology ". . . founded upon the idea of a global social formation constituted in part by the degree of integration/disintegration of basic social structures, social forces and . . . forms of state."[4] Individual states, and individuals, groups, and institutions within states, are seen as constituent properties of a global ensemble of structures and forces, which *in their movement*, make up the object known as the global political economy. It is these movements and the relations among the relevant social forces that form the objects of investigation in this study.

Gill also points out that the Gramscian approach places particular emphasis on the ". . . ethical dimension to analysis, so that the questions of justice, legitimacy, and moral credibility are integrated sociologically into the whole and to many of its key concepts."[5] This author assumes that such an "ethical dimension" is indeed central to both a critical approach to international relations, and a meaningful framework for global structural transformation. With respect to the former, the positioning of resistance/counter-hegemony as key historical components in the making of world order seeks to redress the inadvertent civilizational bias which sees Euro-America as *the maker* of world history. As such, Jamaica is one of the many poor countries which, in the moments of its struggle for a just international order, has contributed to the making of the world as we know it. In part it is in this deprivileging of Euro-America, as the leitmotiv of world history, that critical theory needs to take seriously. The analysis of Jamaica's international relations can be used, therefore, to explore broader changes in world order, and to do so from a perspective of the doubly marginalized. It is a means, to follow Fernand Braudel, of elaborating one or more dimensions or vantage points in the "perspective of the world." It is an exploration, materially, politically, and culturally, of the making of the postwar world.

## The Organization of the Study

Having identified the broad themes in chapter 1, chapter 2 provides a critical examination the literature on Third World foreign policy. The critique is focused on the quest for nomothetic generalization which characterizes the bulk of theorizing on Third World foreign policy. Chapters 3 and 4 are concerned with a detailed elaboration of a framework for the study of Third World foreign policy. With respect to the latter, the author holds the view that an approach to the subfield of foreign policy analysis cannot exist outside of a larger framework of international theory as a whole. Accordingly, chapter 3 outlines the framework of historical structure as an alternative approach to both I.R. and foreign policy.

Chapter 4 continues with the process of developing an alternative framework by sharpening and extending the concepts of reality and hegemony. This is done through an analysis of ideological practices as functionally constitutive in the making of known reality and culture. The framework developed here rejects the notion of floating signifiers. Nonetheless, an attempt is made to (re)produce identity and socio-political agency beyond the domain of social classes.

Chapter 5 traces in detail the making of modern Jamaica, as well as the emergence of hegemonic social forces. The task here is not simply to describe these forces, but to demonstrate how particular configurations of them constitute a particular historical structure. In doing this, the Braudelian method of historical time is employed. First, the *longue durée* elements of the social structure are mapped, with emphasis on the function of race as a social category in the making of the broad outline of the social structure. Associated with the latter, is the way in which socio-economic and cultural differentiation become embedded in the political economy through political struggle.

In chapter 6, the focus is on those forces in Jamaican society dedicated to the disestablishment of "exceptionalism." Among the ones examined here are the Black Power movement, the Abeng Group, academics and students, the Youth movement known as "Rude Boys" or "Rudies," and the Rastafarian movement. The considerable space devoted to the Rastas is a way of entry into the complexity of counter-hegemonic disarticulation, especially given the diffusion of "Rasta ideology" among the other antiexceptionalist social forces. In this chapter, the central importance of cultural nationalism and racial consciousness in the making of "democratic socialism" (which the PNP adopted in 1974) are adumbrated.

Chapter 7 examines the attempt by the dominant classes in Jamaica to consolidate their hegemony by continuing with the process of capitalist modernization through heavy reliance on foreign capital. This attempt which is called "passive revolution," however, is fiercely resisted by large sections of the society which begin to emerge as coherent and organized social forces. During this period, deep cleavages in the society are opened and the antiexceptionalist social forces begin to gain ground. As the cultural "war of position" moves through the 1960s, the hitherto marginalized social forces begin to articulate complex and overdetermined positions, indicating historical progress from "resistance" which is reactive in motivation and refractory in consequence, to counter-hegemony which is more deliberate as action, and comprehensive in terms of its transformative potential.

In chapter 8, the 1972 defeat of the JLP by the PNP is analyzed. The change in government also brought major changes in domestic and foreign policy. On the domestic front, there were important continuities, but also the introduction of a number of policies which the JLP and dominant classes found anathema. These new policies very much reflected the importance of the newly emergent social forces in the society. The declaration of Democratic Socialism by PNP signaled a change in philosophy and direction, and is examined. In the area of foreign policy, notable shifts in conception and practice are discerned.

The 1976 general elections in Jamaica was the occasion through which a fundamental realignment of social forces was expressed. On account of this, chapter 9 begins with a thorough analysis of this reconfiguration. The advance of the Left within the PNP in conjunction with the broader societal leftward shift set the conditions for the retrieval of the socialist tradition of the PNP. The disarticulation of the Anglo-Christian hegemonic ontology which had begun since the 1960s now asserted itself with greater force. This counter-hegemonic push, however, became tempered by the local ruling classes; the structural power of international capital; and by an increasingly malevolent posture from the United States, vis-à-vis Jamaica. Jamaican society and its foreign policy was buffeted by these opposing forces.

Chapter 10 concludes with an assessment of the method of "historical structure" as applied to Jamaica, and as it pertains to the study of global politics. The condition for a global praxis of counter-hegemony is also adumbrated.

# 2

---

# Approaches to Third World Foreign Policy

## The Will to Classify

Some forty years ago, the French structural anthropologist Claude Levi-Strauss noted that any "classification is superior to chaos and even a classification at the level of sensible properties is a step towards rational ordering."[1] While all problems of science begin with a puzzle, the first step in the scientific enterprise begins at the level of taxonomy. Whether one is rationally ordering plant species or states, intelligent statements about the *theoretical object* of research can only be made if seemingly disparate properties/ phenomena are parsimoniously categorized on the basis of an explicit principle of delineation. Without a taxonomic schema, generalization would be groundless and there would have to be a "theory" for everything existing, by everyone. In this case scientific knowledge would be impossible excepting in the near infinite spectrum of "right pending disproof[s]."[2] It is for these reasons that scientists, including social scientists, begin with classifying things. The subfield of foreign policy in particular, and the field international relations in general, are no different. The general thinking is that by classifying states one could proceed to make general descriptive and theoretical statements about the foreign policy behavior patterns of an entire *class* of states.[3]

This combination of positivism and realism has resulted in two things. Firstly, there is considerable over-generalization and, secondly, the assumptions of power politics have marginalized the Third World in the making of world order. The "international relations" of Great Powers have been privileged, since according to the logic of power politics small, weak, or poor states cannot affect the balance of power. It is precisely on this basis that Waltz came to the rather bold conclusion that "Denmark doesn't matter." Of course, the judg-

9

ment of the arch neo-realist was not based on prejudice against the little European nation. Rather, it was based solely on a taxonomic extrapolation, namely, that Denmark belongs to *a class of states* which cannot, by itself alter the conduct or properties of the "international system." The general problem with producing knowledge for whole classes of states is that there is a tendency to posit nomothetic propositions, and by so doing, there is repression of specificity and historicity. It is important to keep in mind that generalizations based on cross-national comparisons is only one form of knowledge.

This chapter explores the procedures of classification in the foreign policy literature on Third World states. Considerable emphasis is paid to the ontological, epistemological and methodological grounds on which various explanations and theories stand. It is on these bases that seemingly unconnected intellectual practices are brought into relation, defined as it were under the rubric of "approaches." The aim here is not simply to put theories in general categories, but to demonstrate the epistemological problems with the quest for a "physics" of international politics.

## Groping for Categories

Three distinctive perspectives on the foreign policies of countries not classified as "Great" or "Middle" powers may be identified.[4] We may specify these as follows: (a) the small/weak state school; (b) situation—role analysis; and (c) the dependence/compliance/dependency school.[5] Although significant overlaps exist among these perspectives there are sufficient differences which may form the basis for delineation and classification.

The taxonomic gyrations in Third World foreign policy, combined with theoretical generalizations of foreign policy as a whole, have not gone unnoticed by some scholars in the field. First, some theorists have rejected the position that generalizations extrapolated out of the history of Great Powers are adequate, or for that matter relevant, to the analysis of small and/or dependent states foreign policies. Bhagat Korany observes that "students of foreign-policy analysis . . . still elaborate (supposedly universal) models to explain the foreign policies of Ghana as well as Sweden, Indonesia as well as the Federal Republic of Germany—with the implicit assumption that all these actors are interchangeable."[6] Michael Handel is suspect of universal applicability of "small states" noting that "while most of the existing theories of international relations can be readily applied to the behavior of weak states in the international system, the overall weakness of these states must be taken into consideration."[7] The real problem, of course, is that all these states are deemed to belong to the *same universal class* of states, or if not, attempts are made to produce more scientific categories.

This skepticism notwithstanding, there is only a modicum of consensus about alternative ways of understanding the foreign policies of non-great/middle powers. To begin with, there is no agreement on an appropriate categorization of these states. Among the more popular ones currently in use are: weak, small, secondary, dependent, Third World, underdeveloped or developing, and occasionally, mini or micro states.[8] The term "emerging" has been recently added. As will be seen presently, the debate about *naming* is more than a matter of semantics. The terminological difficulty with these categories is in fact symptomatic of the failure to agree on the taxonomic criteria which should govern classification. After all, "Great Power" and "Middle Power" are conceptual constructions themselves.[9]

## The Small/Weak State School

Size is the single most important variable in this attempt to specify the uniqueness of this class of states.[10] Neil Amstrup notes that "in the greater part of the literature, it seems to be assumed that given a satisfactory definition of an independent variable, viz., size, it is also possible to predict something about some dependent variable, viz., the behavior of small states."[11] But size of what—territory, population, Gross National Product? Further, specifically what criteria should be used to determine the points of demarcation in each of these indicators?

The classification by the United Nations Institute for Training and Research (UNITAR) is symptomatic of the difficulties that have dogged the quest for taxonomic neatness.[12] Using an upper population ceiling of one million and combining that with political status, the study identified fourteen categories of states and territories. The one million upper limit has other adherents. Colin Clarke and Tony Payne, for example, adopt this definition in their volume, *Politics, Security, and Development in Small States*.[13] There is hardly consensus, however, on this one million limit.

Ronald P. Bartson uses a definition of ten to fifteen million but immediately admits to loopholes.[14] Masarky and Marriot set an upper limit of twenty million, but this applies only to European states.[15] More ambitious schema have been attempted by Vellut and Vital. Vellut combines population with Gross National Product and suggests the three following categories: (1) ten to fifty million population and/or two to ten billion GNP; (2) five to ten million population and/or one to two billion GNP; and (3) below five million population and below one billion GNP.[16] In a similar vein, David Vital specifies two groups of small states based on population and level of economic development, namely: (1) a population of ten to fifteen million for advanced countries, and (2) twenty to thirty million for underdeveloped countries.[17]

There are two recurrent problems with these attempts to delineate classes of states on the basis of population size and/or economic attributes. To begin with, there is the problem of arbitrariness. This is revealed in two ways. First, the difference in the size of the population used to specify limits is considerable. Recall that the comprehensive UNITAR study as well as the more recent volume edited by Clarke and Payne use a one million upper limit. By comparison, Vital's highly respected *The Inequality of States* specifies upper limits of fifteen and thirty million for developed and underdeveloped countries respectively. We can see that the figures offered by Bartson and Vellut are generally consistent with Vital's.

What is immediately evident here is that the entire class of states which Vital, Bartson, and Vellut classify as "micro-powers" or "mini-states" fall into the category of "small states" for UNITAR, Clarke and Payne, and others. Vital, in particular, is insistent that micro-powers ". . . constitute yet another class of states with reasonably distinct and characteristic problems of their own."[18] On the other hand, according to the definition offered by UNITAR and Clarke and Payne, the class of states identified by Vital, Vellut, and Bartson as small states are closer to middle powers. Where is the objective basis for "science" here?

The second symptom of arbitrariness is decipherable through the extensive qualifications which accompany the various definitions. Despite UNITAR's sweeping one million limit and fourteen subcategories, it was necessary to create an exceptional category for "States and Territories with a Population Over One Million, but with an Exceptionally Small Land Area, and a Resultant Very High Density of Population." This was necessary to accommodate Singapore and Hong Kong which would otherwise have been excluded from the class of "small states and territories."

It should be evident that the specification of a class of states, viz., small states through size variables, has only been accomplished via methodological fiat. This is further exacerbated when we examine the constituent properties, that is actual units, which form the class of small states. Here we find staggering incongruity with respect to the countries which belong to the same class.

The UNITAR study includes such diverse states/territories as Gibraltar; Namibia; Luxembourg; Lesotho; Iceland; Trinidad and Tobago; Swaziland; and Monaco. Clearly the only principle of comparison here is the one million population limit. Many of the ninety–six states/territories included here have far less in common than with states excluded. Thus, although Jamaica and Guyana (for example) have similar colonial pasts; social and economic structures; and regional and global interests, the former is excluded and the latter included in the class of small states.[19] Some of the poorest African and Caribbean countries such as Swaziland and Guyana are compared to European states like Luxembourg and Iceland.

The question at issue here is not so much the *formal units* such as Lesotho or Finland. Rather, it is the methodological basis on which a *system of equivalence* is established in order to compare. This is particularly important given the tendency of the small state school to posit nomothetically derived generalizations based on cross-national comparisons.[20]

It is perhaps worthwhile to recall A. Przeworski and H. Teune's suggestion that "the critical problem in cross-national research is that of identifying "equivalent" phenomena and analyzing the relationship between them in an "equivalent" fashion."[21] Instead, the small state school (outlined below) formalizes these relationships into static categories which are assumed to operate identically and with the same effects in all small states. On the contrary, a more historically oriented approach would accept that the size of population is significant but that the consequences of this is contingent rather than necessary.

## "Small" or "Weak" State

The concept of small state has been widely criticized, and justifiably so. The grounds for such criticism range from the concept being imprecise, to useless. Consequently, while some completely reject this concept others accept its intellectual trajectory but insist on further refinement. The latter process gave rise to the concept of weak state.

The reformulation of the concept small state into weak state stems from two theoretically distinct sets of considerations. First, there are those who argue that the international position and consequent behavior of Third World states is less a matter of their strength defined in terms of quantitative attributes, and more a function of economic and political underdevelopment that condition their behavior. Economic backwardness generates weakness and it is this, not size per se, that informs the foreign policies of Third World states. The second version of weakness takes security as its point of departure. In this case, it matters little whether a state is small or not, or whether it is advanced or underdeveloped. The fundamental concern here is the degree to which a state is self-reliant in terms of its protection of core interests and values.[22] The less self-reliant a state is, the more vulnerable it is to foreign penetration. In this scenario, the concept of weakness problematizes the degree of vulnerability and lack of self-reliance. M. Handel summarizes this line of thinking as follows: "Whereas one of the most important characteristics of the great powers is their military strength and capacity for self-defense, the weak states are continually preoccupied with the question of survival."[23]

Handel, who is probably the chief exponent of the security version of the weak state concept, argues that the idea of small powers is "self-contradictory." Small states are characterized by a lack of power, hence their weakness.[24] Moreover, it is not the size of a state that determines its place and role in the international system; rather it is its relative strength. For him, the appellation small power, should be restricted in its application to concrete cases. A good case might be Israel. Only those states which are small in size and lack strength should be described as, and included in, a category of small states.[25] Alternatively, the category weak state allows for a larger inventory of states. Hence a state could be small or large in territory and yet be included in the same class, provided that it is weak.[26]

Now, despite his concerted effort to establish a conceptual distinction between small and weak states, Handel fails to go beyond simple definitional issues. This becomes evident once we examine the typical behavioral patterns of weak states as defined by Handel. Indeed a comparison of his *Weak States in the International System* with works by R. L. Rothstein, Annete Baker Fox, and David Vital, all of whom use the concept small state/power, demonstrates that the substantive theoretical questions are virtually identical.[27] In particular, all of these studies, Handel's included, analyze the conditions under which non-great powers are able to secure their national sovereignty, narrowly defined as territorial integrity. Moreover, the distinctions notwithstanding, there is clearly an effort to construct a general category in which all Third World states can fit into.

With respect to the first version of the weak-state concept, there is a clear attempt to separate developed small states from Third World countries. This is sharply revealed in two books by Rothstein. His *Alliances and Small Powers* accepts the concept small-state/power as the title suggests.[28] The key concern here is with the security position of "satisfied small states," viz., small European states. Rothstein makes his intentions abundantly clear. He points out that generalizations derived from this study are only relevant ". . . to those small states that are either directly involved, politically and geographically, in relations with Great Powers. . . ."[29] This is, of course, yet another qualification regarding a whole class of states.

Rothstein's dilemma does not end there, for he finds it necessary to write *The Weak in the World of the Strong* which is solely devoted to Third World states. Instead of the preoccupation with security issues as in the case with European small powers, Rothstein analyzes a wide spectrum of questions pertaining to development, international organizations, as well as supposedly intrinsic Third World attributes which impact on foreign policy. "Weakness" in this case is synonymous with being poor and underdeveloped. Size is thus displaced by other attributes in the quest for taxonomic neatness.

Marshall Singer's *Weak States in a World of Powers* may be delineated as a third version of the weak-state concept.[30] In this comprehensive study, Singer analyses the psychological relationship between five major Powers and weak states associated with the former. Weak states, as used here, may be understood in a dual sense. Firstly, it is purely descriptive of Third World countries and, more especially, recent ex-colonies. Secondly, weak states may be taken to mean those which are psychologically dependent (with regard to their national identity), on another country. The thrust of Singer's argument reasonably leads one to conclude that psychological dependence has far-reaching ramifications for the international conduct of the "afflicted" state. This focus on identity and dependence forms yet another attempt to find the correct general category, the logic in this instance being that a common history led to common pathologies and, consequently, the behavior in the post-colonial period must be equally common!

## Power and Capability

The various attempts at producing general categories are in fact united by a subtext, viz., political realism. This connection requires further interrogation. The central analytic and articulating concept of the small/weak state perspective is *capability*. As used here, capability refers to the degree/ability of states, defined in terms of scope and effectiveness, to act independently in the international system. If we accept this, then it is also necessary to specify the constituent properties of capability. Further, how is capability organized and measured? In other words, there must be some general equivalent through which capability is expressed.

Methodologically, the concept of capability is not autonomous and free-floating. Rather, it belongs to a *system of concepts* which in their articulation constitute a coherent theoretical system. What is more, a theoretical system rests on specific ontological premises.[31] In view of these considerations, it is not sufficient to merely specify capability and show how it relates to the small and weak state schools. We must go one step further and locate capability in the general theoretical system to which it belongs. When this is accomplished, we would be in a position to make clear the relationship among the small/weak state school and the theoretical system to which it properly belongs, viz., political realism. More than that, the relationship between the quest for "scientific" (taxonomic) categories, and generalizations about foreign policy behavior should be clearer.

At this juncture, we are not interested in a comprehensive overview of political realism. The intention is restricted to a synoptic view which allows us to understand the role of capability within the theoretical system.

Realism, says R. Gilpin, is a "philosophical disposition" which, notwithstanding divergent trajectories, contains three fundamental assumptions. These are as follows: a) that international affairs are essentially conflictual; b) ". . . that the essence of social reality is the group," and that in the modern world the nation state is the highest expression of all groups; and c) that power and security are the primary human motivation of all political life.[32] These latter are, of course, themselves classifications of the human condition and political behavior. It might be useful to combine these assumptions into a coherent descriptive statement in order to get a better picture of the philosophical disposition of realism. By doing this, we would be better equipped to appreciate the theoretical concerns of realists and the way in which these concerns inform the production of the concepts small and weak states. Thus, we may state the following: in the modern world individuals have traded their natural rights for political rights through the formation of political communities. The state has a monopoly of legitimate coercive powers and is thus responsible for the security of citizens and the political arrangements, namely national sovereignty, through which such rights are guaranteed. States define and pursue the values which are necessary for the security of the nation. These values may be called national interests. Now, since the international system is anarchic (defined as the absence of a legitimate political body which can enforce rules), the pursuit of one state's national interest may threaten that of other states. In fact this has always been the case.[33] The ability of a state to pursue its national interest or to withstand the same from another state, which by so doing threatens its core values, is dependent upon its power. Power, therefore, is the basis on which all interest is pursued and/or protected. This brings us back to capability.

Having arrived at the conclusion that power is the raison d'etre of realism, we must establish its theoretical relationship with capability. At one level, power and capability are synonymous. This is easy to establish if we compare Hans Morgenthau's concept of national power with Kenneth Waltz's concept of capability. In his analysis of (national) power, Morgenthau identifies various "elements of power." Among the principal elements are: geography; natural resources; industrial capacity; military preparedness; and population, as well as a number of intangible attributes.[34] Waltz uses the identical factors in his assessment of national capability.[35] However, he adds a systemic component to his definition thus going beyond a purely national calculation of power. The argument is summarized as follows:

> Power is estimated by comparing the capabilities of a number of units. Although capabilities are attributes of units, the distribution of capabilities across units is not. The distribution of capabilities is not a unit attribute, but rather a system-wide concept.[36]

The concept capability, therefore, has three dimensions. Firstly, there are various disaggregated sectorial capabilities within each unit; this is the equivalent of Morgenthau's "elements of national power." Secondly, when these sectorial capabilities are merged they form a combined capability; this is what Morgenthau calls "national power." And thirdly, there is the distribution of capabilities within the system. It is this third component that separates the concepts power and capability within realist thinking. Waltz makes this point cogently when he writes, "to be politically pertinent, power has to be defined in terms of the distribution of capabilities. . . ."[37]

Now that the concept of capability has been specified and located in the general theoretical system of realism, we can proceed to demonstrate the way in which it unifies the seemingly disparate tendencies of the small and weak state schools which are so influential in theorizing Third World foreign policy.

A good point of departure is to ask the questions as to why they are both keen on delineating a class of states and how they go about doing this? The answer to the second part of the question is obvious. Virtually all the scholars use one of the three dimensions of capability outlined above to classify states. Hence, while some use size of territory, population, or level of economic development, others use various combinations of these variables. Those who approach the problem from Waltz's "third image" use the *distribution of capabilities* across the system in their classification. The crucial point here is that capability is the basis of classifying states. Whether they are called small or weak is decidedly irrelevant.

The answer to the first part of the question, namely why the keenness on classification, is more complex. This is so because the classificatory schema rest on certain theoretical assumptions which are not always made explicit.

Firstly, to divide up the international system into classes of states one must first accept that states are the dominant actors and by implication the legitimate units of analysis. Secondly, if by virtue of the principle of national sovereignty all states are equal, then the only basis of differentiation is capability.[38] Thirdly, therefore, "relations defined in terms of groupings of states do seem to tell us something about how states are placed in the system."[39] If we further assume that "capability tells us something about units," especially their capacity to act in the system, we can reasonably conclude that intelligent statements about the behavior of states could be made on the basis of their grouping.[40] Another way of stating this is that different classes of states have different foreign policies and patterns of behavior.

## Core Generalizations

Notwithstanding the geographical; historical; socio-economic, and cultural differences among small states, and specifically between developed and underdeveloped states, a number of general propositions have been advanced about the foreign policy behavior of the *class* of small states. The most salient of these are as follows: (a) low level of participation compared to large states; (b) their basic preoccupation is with survival defined in terms of security; (c) small states rely on external sources of security; (d) the scope of their behavior is narrow and geared toward the short term; (e) they rely heavily on international and regional organizations; (f) they prefer multilateral to bilateral diplomacy; and (g) (consistent with (e) and (f)) they attach considerable importance to world public opinion and international morality.

Virtually all of these behavioral patterns are explained by small state theorists as direct consequences of low capability. The next few paragraphs examine these generalizations.

Although some argue that the weakness of small states is exaggerated, it is received wisdom in the literature that the foreign policy and behavior of these states are geared toward self-preservation.[41] Thus Vital writes, "it is the peculiar and characteristic quality of the external affairs of the small state that fundamentally, and in the long run, it leads a defensive life."[42] Since they do not have the capability to defend themselves, small states must rely on external sources of protection. The specific strategy that is adopted, however, is dependent on the nature of the international system.[43] For Handel, weak states can find themselves in two ideal type situations in the system. In a competitive system they have greater freedom of maneuver and can align with any other country. This is not the case in a "hegemonial" system where such freedom is circumscribed by definitions of spheres of influence by the great powers. While low capability forces the small state toward external protection, it is the dynamics of the system that ultimately define the patterns of alliance. Nonalignment, for example, is specifically the result of both weakness and a bipolar international system:

"Lesser states" for some align with great powers in order to achieve security, status and stability.[44] Apart from aggregating capability, alliances also enhance the reputation of small states.[45] If a small state is known to have a credible "backer" it reduces its vulnerability in the eyes of potential aggressors. Also in return for aligning the small state may procure economic assistance necessary for internal political stability.

Further, low capability defined in terms of lack of resources, forces small states to concentrate on a narrow range of issues. This leads to more selective external relations and ultimately to lower levels of international participation. The *scope* of foreign policy behavior is, for some theorists, the major difference between small and Great Powers. Historically, for the small developed states of Europe, the central preoccupation has been to withstand the expansionist designs of continental Great Powers.[46] In the European case, territorial integrity and national sovereignty have been the most salient values. For Third World states the focus is overwhelmingly on economic control and development at the domestic level, and the pursuit of a more equitable distribution of global wealth at the international level.

The lack of capability also generates identifiable patterns of diplomatic behavior. Usually, multilateral diplomacy is preferred and is most often pursued through regional and international organizations. The primary reason for this strategy seems to be that since these organizations are the bastions of rules, norms and principles of *international society*, small states have a greater chance of being listened to there.

The generalizations examined thus far pertain to the foreign policy behavior of small states in general. As was pointed out earlier, however, certain distinctive features of underdeveloped small states have been isolated through national attribute analyses. Of these, institutional underdevelopment, personalism, and ideology are the most important.

It is received wisdom among small state theorists that institutional underdevelopment has specific negative consequences for foreign policy formation in Third World states. Generally, the decision making process is thought to be irrational. Economic constraints first affect the gathering of information. Due to minimal research and small or nonexistent intelligence networks, policy makers are usually uninformed or work with second-hand information.

Instead of a rational, impersonal bureaucracy with mechanisms for the collection, classification, and storage of data, the standard operating procedures and other elements of a modern bureaucracy, underdeveloped states languish under the might of corruption, incompetence, and personalism.[47] Sluggish bureaucratic input leaves foreign policy an open field to the leader. Thus, rigorous cost/benefit analysis of various foreign policy options is absent and instead it is the leader's personal orientation that counts the most.

The absence of bureaucratic input leads, therefore, to highly personalized foreign policy decision making. Combined with improper channels of feedback from the public, foreign policy becomes the exclusive preserve of the leader. In fact, many small state theorists argue that foreign policy is largely a mechanism of diverting the attention of the public from excruciating domestic hardships. While often true, this is a rather cynical generalization.

These typical foreign policy/behavior patterns have, perhaps, been most comprehensively theorized by McGowand and Gottwald. Drawing on Rosenau's notion of adaptive behavior, they examine two behavioral tendencies pertinent to all states—participatory and affective behavior and two ". . . behavioral patterns that may be unique to tropical Africa, but that are probably shared with other small, less-modern states of the Third World—political dependence and economic dependence."[48] The central argument is this: external demands exert pressures on domestic structures which forces the elite to respond. This response, which takes the form of foreign policy, is geared at ". . . adapting to external events in order to secure satisfactory performance of domestic structures."[49]

There are four typical forms of adaptive behavior: acquiescent, intransigent, promotive, and preservative. Acquiescent and intransigent foreign policy behavior are defined as responses to international and domestic demands, respectively. And whereas promotive refers to ignoring demands from the external and internal environments, preservative refers to an attempt to bring the two into equilibrium.[50] McGowand and Gottwald modify these categories on the basis of the typical aims of policy. Further, they introduce the concepts *influence capability* and sensitivity formulated by Hansen. The former is defined as ". . . the degree to which a state can afflict the international environment."[51] Stress sensitivity represents the impact of external pressures on "domestic state-society structures."[52] Next, two assumptions are stated: 1) "the bigger the state, the greater its stress sensitivity," and 2) "the more modern the state, the greater its stress sensitivity."[53]

McGowand and Gottwald then turn to the elite perception of itself and its environment. Perception is defined in terms of orientation and attitude. Thus elites may have an attitude of "active involvement or passive withdrawal and an 'inner directed' or 'other directed' attitude."[54]

By assuming that size and modernization are orthogonal, and by incorporating the perceptual, influence, and sensitivity categories, McGowand and Gottwald specify the following (adaptive) conception of foreign policy for all states: (a) large modern states will display intransigent or preservative behavior and show active involvement in the international system; (b) large less-modern states are expected to be promotive or intransigent and inner-directed; (c) small modern states will be acquiescent or preservative and other directed; and (d) small less-modern states will display either promotive or acquiescent foreign policy behavior and demonstrate passive withdrawal from the system.[55]

While many of these generalizations are useful, it must be acknowledged that what one has in actuality, is general knowledge about a general category of states, but not much specificity about any one of them. Is this really satisfactory?

### Situation Role Analysis

The quest for reliable knowledge based on a whole class of states continues even with theoretical approaches which have different assumptions, and ultimately different explanations. This is quite evident in what can be called the situation-role school. Again, the common denominator here is the quest to make statements purporting generalized behavior of a whole class of states.

The intellectual precursor of situation role analysis is to found in a seminal essay by K. J. Holsti entitled "National Role Conceptions in the Study of Foreign Policy."[56] Holsti argues that "national role conceptions" as a concept has the descriptive and explanatory capacity to give more precision to studies of foreign policy and international systems.[57] Moreover, since the relevant data for role analysis is easily accessible for all types of states, comparative foreign policy is strengthened.

Holsti's point of departure is that recognizable patterns of foreign policy behavior may be attributed to *classes of states*. Such classes include "nonaligned," "bloc leaders," "balancers" and "satellites," among others.[58] He explains:

> When we classify a state as "nonaligned," we imply that in
> a variety of international contexts and situations, its

diplomatic-military actions and decisions will be consistent with the "rules" subsumed under the general category or class of states called "nonaligned." The term summarizes a broad but typical range of diplomatic behaviors and attitudes.[59]

This is a lower level of taxonomy. It is more historical than logical. That, however, does not make it less positivist—in the productive sense of that term.

The general categories advanced are more heuristic devices and "do not reveal all the behavioral variations observable in the different sets of relationships into which states enter."[60] To be analytically useful these categories need conceptual refinement. Seen this way, the various categories of state alluded to above may be understood as national role conceptions.

The fundamental problem that role analysis is concerned with is the definition of the nation's role in international affairs. For theorists who privilege the "policy makers views" in the determination of national role conception, the individual level of analysis is assumed. If this is accepted, role theory suggests that the analyst focuses on the sources of the policy makers *perception*. In this case, the personality of decision-makers and the consequent effect upon the decision-making process are seen as integral to foreign policy formation and behavior.

In a self-critique of his seminal article "Pre-Theories and Theories of Foreign Policy," James Rosenau argues that the incorporation of individuals in International Relations analysis is desirable.[61] He sees this as a good way of linking up "micro-units" with "macro-theories." Importantly, his idea of the individual goes beyond a narrow and atomistic conception of "person." He suggests that there may be utility in treating:

> [I]ndividuals not as concrete, identifiable persons, but as complexes of roles and statuses, as members of a variety of systems that so fully account for the expectations to which they respond that nothing meaningful is left over as the quintessentially unique person.[62]

As such, policy makers are like "pastiche combinations" of the nation's social, political, and cultural attributes; they are "role composites." At this level of analysis, the sources of role conception is sought in various aspects of the national character as embodied in the policy maker.

National role may be defined through the mechanics of the international system. On the basis of certain distinguishing features, such as size, states occupy such a place in the hierarchy of nations that prescribe what their roles should be. A good example of this is Annete Baker Fox's proposition that all small states are "anti-balance" in their foreign policy behavior. Domestic structures and especially the decision-making process are viewed as only partly consequential upon foreign policy behavior. Nonetheless, there is a problem here of establishing the relative weights of the international and the domestic in the making of policy, and in the behavior that follows. The theoretical resolution of this problem is to take cover under taxonomy. No less a figure than Robert Jervis succumbs to the temptation. Here he is:

> [T]o argue that the international environment determines a state's behavior is to assert that all states react similarly to the same objective external situation. Changes in the state's domestic regime, its bureaucratic structure and the personalities and opinions of its leaders do not lead to change of policies.[63]

There is real sense in which role is employed as a pre-analytic category to account for behavior. How else is it possible to arrive at the conclusion that the domestic does not really matter. What is role theory? Four essential concepts of role theory are relevant to foreign policy. Firstly, *role* or *role performance* refers to the attitudes, decisions, and actions of governments, or in other words, to behavior. Secondly, *role prescription* is generated internally in culture, social institutions, organizations, and laws. As a complex totality these underpin norms and expectations. In addition, *role prescription* is determined by the external environment, that is, the international system. Thirdly, the policy maker occupies a *position* from which he views the world. "Position" refers to "a system of role prescriptions." And fourthly, *national role conceptions* are defined by policy makers. From a theoretical standpoint role analysis "emphasizes the interaction between role prescription of the alter and the role performance of the occupant of a position (ego)."[64]

In the application of role theory to foreign policy behavior, Holsti suggests that while domestic organizational, social, and cultural forces in conjunction with external pressure may be critical, in the end it is the policy makers *perceptions* of those forces and pressures that inform behavior. Objective structures, both domestic and external, therefore, may define the parameters of policy but actual behavior "of governments may be explained primarily by reference to the policy makers *own* conceptions of their nation's role in a region or in the international system as a whole."[65] Notice how nonchalantly domestic specificity is jettisoned.

The empirical application of role theory has, thus far, been mostly focused on the foreign policy of Third World states. In part, this may be due to the (supposed) peculiar relevance of the approach to less developed countries. For it is generally assumed that one of the key attributes of these states is the dominance of personalism. Decision making is highly centralized and most often dominated by a charismatic leader (so called), who is hardly responsible to an electorate. As such, the idiosyncratic views of the leader "has the potential of influencing both his government's domestic and foreign policy behavior."[66] The leader's perception is thus critical, which makes role theory especially relevant given its stress on this factor.

The most elaborate application of role theory to foreign policy behavior of Third World states has been done by Bhagat Korany.[67] The Korany model is actually a reformulation of role theory defined in terms of national role conceptions. His point of departure is the *situation*. "Simply defined "situational analysis" stipulates that the action or behavior of an actor is a function of the situation he confronts."[68] The combination of the "situation" and "national role conceptions" form the basis of the situation-role model.

The model is based on two fundamental assumptions.[69] Firstly, the *situational component* must incorporate all three levels of analysis, namely, "the domestic political subsystem, the international, as well as the personality variables of the policy maker."[70] Secondly, the situation-role model must emphasize "psycho-societal" key attributes. In this case personality characteristics of the policy maker, as well as domestic factors, are critical in the definition of the situation.

The model is similar to the small state school with respect to the *international component*. They both suggest that the structure of the international system (i.e., whether it is unipolar, bipolar, multipolar, etc.), has definite consequences for the foreign policy strategy of Third World states. Generally, the system defines the nature and range of constraints and opportunities within which states act. Further, the situational-role model posits that the broad foreign policy *orientation* of Third World states is substantially defined by the international component. In his examination of non-aligned states, for example, Korany found that "policymakers perceived major structural characteristic of the external environment in approximately the same way and adopted strategies and policies that orient their states' policies to fit this systemic structure.[71] Non-aligned states share this common foreign policy orientation because, on the whole, they occupy the same position in an internationally stratified system. According to Korany, "theirs is a position of 'demanders of aid,' of economic dependence and frequently of political subordination."[72]

Apart from its structure, the international system also generates norms which impact on the foreign policy objectives of states. This is a critical argument but remains undeveloped in the situation-role model. No attempt is made to analyze the power configurations that underpin the production and socialization/consolidation of norms in the international system. Rather, Korany merely acknowledges their presence and proceed to specify the systemic norms of non-aligned states. In this model, therefore, norms are treated as givens of the international system.

While the international component may condition foreign policy orientation, national and personality components are more directly related to behavior. The model actually privileges the latter.

The analysis of national components is essentially an analysis of national attributes. The level of economic development, political stability, social mobilization and cultural definition, among other national values, are critical in shaping national role conceptions. Is this not remarkably similar to the small state school which suggest a close relationship among national attributes, capability, and foreign policy? All the situation-role model does here, it appears, is add a perceptual category. In this case the objective is to establish the relationship among national attributes, role conception, and behavior.

In fact, Naiomi Wish, who employs role theory, suggests exactly that. She notes the national attribute-national role conception model:

> [P]ostulates that a nation's foreign policy behavior is in large measure a product of its national capability or attributes and that its decision makers' national motivations are expressed as national role conceptions. The latter are defined as foreign policymakers' perceptions of their nations' position in the international system.[73]

Again, like those explanations which give considerable weight to size-related variables, role theory suggests that national attributes, (a key factor in the national component), is a determinant instance of foreign policy behavior. National attribute affects the amount of resources available for foreign policy, provides guidelines based on capability analysis and acts as "... a major source for the formulation of national role conceptions."[74]

Korany introduces a more structural version to the national component and foreign policy behavior of Third World states. For him the problem is " a characteristic of the domestic component of the situation of these actors is the pressure of social change, leading to strain not only in the political subsystem but in the social system as a whole."[75] The argument is that the disjuncture between social expectations and social satisfactions leads to systemic frustration.[76] The principal cause of the disjuncture lies in the rate and nature of social change in the Third World countries. The rate of modernization in these states is much more rapid than that of earlier modernizers. In addition, "... these countries meet the problems of social change, national integration, centralization of authority, or social welfare simultaneously rather than sequentially."[77] Assuming a positive correlation between social mobilization and political instability, or between social change and systemic strain, the situation-role model asserts the primacy of the national component in defining the situation. This represents a movement away from the tendency to ignore the internal, and to grope for general statements based on "objective attributes" such as size, role, and so on. But this healthy diversion lasts for only a while.

For despite the considerable weight given to the national component, in the end, the situation-role model succumbs to the personality component in the explanation of foreign policy behavior. Thus, "if men define situations as real, they are real in their consequences." Further, it matters little what the objective situation is. What is crucial is policymakers' interpretation and the way in which this interpretation influences behavior. The second justification lies in a supposedly peculiar attribute of Third World leaders, namely, their "charismatic personality." The object of analysis in the situational-role analysis is thus the personality of the policymaker. Despite efforts to refine personality analysis such as offered by Margaret Herman, this attempt to theorize decision making fails to go beyond behavioral attributes. Most importantly, the structural attributes which seem to form the point of departure for this class of states in the first place, is summarily abandoned.

## The Dependence/Compliance-Dependency Approach

Whereas the small state school stresses national attributes and the situation-role model personality variables, the dependence-compliance/dependency approach is almost wholly concerned with economic questions, concepts, and categories. The concept of *dependence* which is central to this school should not be confused with dependency theory as developed in Latin America. Rather, it has much closer ties to the notion of interdependence and indeed may be construed as a *response* to dependency theory.

Dependence refers quite simply to *external reliance.* In this formulation, no country is totally dependent; rather, the global political economy is characterized by interdependence. Hence, even the strongest states with well-developed and diversified economies rely on other states, including underdeveloped ones, for raw materials, oil, and markets. Unlike dependency theory, therefore, which purports that peripheral economies are structurally dependent on the metropole, the dependence thesis is that the global political economy is defined through *mutual dependence.*[78] However, interdependence defined as mutual dependence does not necessarily imply *evenly balanced* mutual dependence or mutual benefits. For "it is asymmetries in dependence that are most likely to provide sources of influence for actors in their dealings with one another."[79]

It is this situation of asymmetrical interdependence that forms the fulcrum of the dependence-compliance approach. Neil R. Richardson, the chief exponent of this approach, argues that the interdependence framework allows for the examination of "the opportunities that actors may have to alter the behavior of their partners. . . . Such *political* opportunities arise only if the interdependence is asymmetrical."[80] Following this line of argument, the compliance theory suggests that the greater the economic resources a nation has, the greater is its influence capability over a nation with lesser resources.[81] Economic resources are seen as instruments of reward and/or punishment used to condition or change the foreign policy behavior of states. Therefore, those states—ostensibly underdeveloped ones—which have high levels of external reliance will behave deferentially, that is their foreign policy behavior will show high levels of compliance. Further, due to high sensitivity and vulnerability interdependence, these states would not be able to absorb the costs of adjustment which may result from non-compliant behavior. Hence, "political compliance becomes an unwritten condition of economic transactions between unequals."[82]

While behavioral compliance may be the result of dependence, its intellectual roots are to be found in bargaining and exchange theory. Compliance should not be confused with compellence. In the latter, a subordinate actor is coerced by the dominant one to change or maintain its behavior; in this case the subordinate state is left with virtually no option. Compliance, however, involves a process of bargaining through negotiations in order to effect an exchange. "Bargaining is the process whereby a 'solution' is reached between two or more actors with partially conflicting aims. A solution is simply the way in which they divide up the benefits."[83] The situation of dependence or asymmetric interdependence does not compromise this process. At a substantive level "the foreign policy behavior of dependencies is viewed as partial payment in exchange for the maintenance of benefits they derive from their economic ties to the dominant country."[84] Theoretically, the process of bargaining is one of sequential exchange.

Foreign aid is the key area of dependence according to compliance theorists. Tied aid usually results in great costs to the recipient while simultaneously furthering the economic interest of the donor state. The nature of tied aid is such that the recipient state is forced to import from the donor. Apart from doing so at prices often higher than world market prices, the recipient state is also allowing itself to be penetrated by foreign products which may redefine the national demand profile or "typical basket of consumer goods." This may reinforce the dependence syndrome and in the long-term exert pressures on the balance of payments. Put differently, the economic vulnerability of poor states facilitates successful export promotion by dominant states via foreign aid. "Thus, foreign aid promotes the exports of donor countries by creating captive demand from recipients as a condition of the loans."

Bruce Moon rejects the essential proposition of dependence-compliance (bargaining) theory that dependent states follow in the footsteps of the United States in important foreign policy questions (as expressed in UN voting patterns) in exchange for foreign aid. Instead of the interlocking process of reward and punishment between the United States and the Third World, he proposes a dependent-consensus (or constrained-consensus) model. "The dependent-consensus model suggests that cross-sectional correlations between aid and UN voting are *largely spurious*, and it replaces the unified model with separate explanations for the behavior of the dominant and dependent nation."[85]

The point of departure for the constrained-consensus model is that the Third World is so deeply penetrated by the economic interests of the developed nations in that: (a) the economic interests of dependent states become mutually bounded up with that of the dominant states; and (b) elites in dependent states become socialized in the world view of the dominant states, such that, they accept the perspectives and policies of the dominant nation. For both these reasons, Third World elites generally push their respective states' foreign policies in a direction consistent with that of the dominant states.

The foreign policy behavior of dependent states is conditioned by a "long-term" and "indirect path" of influence. Accordingly, the dependency model ". . . regards the decision-making process as imbedded in a social/political structure which is itself distorted by the dependency relationship."[86] This social/political and economic structure generates consensus-producing forces through various networks and ties that bind ". . . the dependent nations to the global system in general and to the dominant nation in particular."[87] Moon identifies four interrelated mechanisms through which such ties operate to influence the foreign policy of dependent states. They are as follows:

(1) "[T]hese ties become an important element in the objective environment faced by the nation; consequently, all policy must be evaluated, at least in part, on the basis of its impact on their continuance."

(2) [T]hey shape the perceptions and attitudes of the citizens of the dependent state, thereby helping define the basic contours of the policy debate.

(3) [T]hey operate even more directly on elites who are supported by them and whose economic interest in their maintenance magnifies their impact on the perceptions and theories that shape policy preferences."

(4) [T]hese same ties tend to encourage the domination of the decision-making process by those elites most strongly linked to ongoing transactions.[88]

Three interrelated arguments are made in explaining the formation and reproduction of these ties, namely—(a) that there is a "transnationalized kernel" of the bourgeoisie which forms an alliance with the state and, which because of its economic interests and ideological disposition supports a pro-American foreign policy; (b) that elites and the mass citizenry alike are inculcated with North American values, perceptions, theories and interpretations of the international system through educational and media penetration; and (c) that the pro-western, and specifically pro-American policies of dependent states are necessary for the survival of these states.[89]

Moon's version of a dependency-theory approach to foreign policy analysis of the Third World is hampered by several major drawbacks. First, he assumes that the bourgeoisie in less developed states will invariably see their economic and political interests consistent with that of the international bourgeoisie and, as a result, "behave" accordingly. In the same vein and at a more concrete level, Third World elites are likely to cooperate with multi-national/transnational corporations since the overall objective of both expatriate and national capitalists are the same, namely, to broaden the scope and intensify the rate and magnitude of exploitation. Implicit in this argument is that this cooperation is further facilitated by the general congruence of the type of social order acceptable to both "branches" of capitalists. Is this not another form of generalization, which while generally useful, ignores specificity?

Thus while the above propositions are generally correct, Moon ignores the fact that classes, including capitalist classes, *develop historically* (not only logically) and that this has specific consequences for their attitude and behavior. In the case of the Third World it was not unusual for the capitalist classes to see foreign capital as "imperialist penetration" and consequently to oppose it. In societies that became highly mobilized in the struggle for independence, leading capitalists actually sided with nationalist and even socialist governments. This certainly happened in Jamaica where fourteen of twenty-two of the country's leading capitalists favored the unilateral imposition of a bauxite levy. This was a not only a frontal attack against the interests of North American multinational companies; it was planned by two of Jamaica's biggest and most influential capitalists.[90] Nationalism thus asserted itself over the abstract market.

Biddle and Stephens, who attempt a reconstructed dependency approach, are correct in pointing out that "the emergence of governments highly critical of the U.S., core transnational corporations (TNCs), and the international capitalist system is not simply a deviation but rather is a direct product of the negative and contradictory aspects of dependent development itself."

This perspective on the foreign policy of Third World countries does indeed go beyond the constrained-consensus model. The inadvertent consequence of the dependence determinism, especially as articulated in Moon's foreign policy framework, is that the Third World is constructed as a having no room for taking independent action. As Biddle and Stephens argue, with very few exceptions, ". . . few authors [in the dependency tradition] allow room for the action of subordinate classes in substantially influencing events in their interests."[91] In the same vein, the pre-eminent scholar on Caribbean foreign policy, Jacqueline Braveboy-Wagner, is also absolutely correct when she states that:

> A very small state will still be highly vulnerable to systemic influence and will still have certain aspects of its policy determined by its "dependent" linkages, but it is still capable of adopting strategies to project an individual presence abroad and even to develop penetrative linkages of its own.[92]

In their reconstruction of a dependency approach to the foreign policy of the Third World, Biddle and Stephens are much more sensitive to the nuanced relationships these states have with center states and metropolitan capital. Consistent with the alternative approach developed in the next chapter, they put considerable emphasis on the flexibility of poor countries to act in their own interest.

The problem with the reconstructed dependency approach is that it collapses political identity into class identity. Identity, of course, is a critical component in the normative capacity of any theory which has a emancipatory trajectory. Dependency theory falls in this category. Its pitfall is that it mechanically fleshes out the political from the social as if the two had some axiomatic correspondence. The political is indeed integrally related to the social but it is also ideologically produced. Citizenship and class belonging are only two elements in the fashioning of subjectivity. The identity of political subjects, that is to say, the bases from which the agents of historymaking operate, is always itself made through a multiplicity of conditioning situations. Understood this way, dependency theory of whatever version needs a reconstructed theory of ideology. Further, while dependency explanations are generally more historical and less positivist compared to the other approaches, they do tend to grope for law-like generalizations.

The need for a more historically grounded approach to foreign policy is badly needed. Such an approach need not abandon theory, but more importantly, it need not attempt to become the stepchild of the natural sciences. The next two chapters attempt to find such a path. A good place to start is with the method of historical structure which attempts to go beyond generalizations based upon entire classes of states, and is rather more historical in character.

# 3

---

# A Social Forces Approach to Foreign Policy

## Historical Structure as a Framework

A critical approach to foreign policy, and more broadly a critical perspective of international relations (as a critique of problem-solving theories) may be advanced through a "framework of action" which, at its most abstract level, ". . . is a picture of a particular configuration of forces."[1] This framework of action or "historical structure" is constituted by a configuration of three historical potentialities, namely, material capabilities, ideas, and institutions.[2] Material capability is an elastic concept sufficiently flexible to include both tangible and intangible sources of power. Thus, military power; economic strength (in the form of technology, natural resources, and financial power); as well as organizational capability; are included. Ideas are historical in nature, and may be divided into two broad components. First, intersubjective ideas are derived from past practices which over long periods of time serve to constitute the norms governing global politics; territorial sovereignty and diplomatic conduct are good examples of this. These norms are fairly stable. Secondly, there are ideas which are more specific to a particular world order, social formation, or a historical conjuncture. Ideas really are the abstracted forms of interpretations underpinned by different social forces; that is, they are not free-floating. Unlike the normative consensus which characterizes intersubjective ideas, conjuncturally specific ideas are in a constant process of contestation. Finally, institutions refer to the domestication of material capabilities and ideas into identifiable patterns of daily life. In turn, institutions also play an important role in producing ideas and the objective conditions for the production of material capabilities.

Although these three categories of forces interact in a structure, none is privileged as a point of departure. Rather, the stress is on their reciprocal influences and the specificity of their combinations in specific historical contexts. This open ended and holistic approach remains historical materialist because instead of confining the materialist dimension to production, all the categories are *material*. Further, production itself must be understood in materialist rather than narrower economic terms. This approach to historical materialism, articulated through a problematic of social forces, represents a significant methodological break with economic reductionist arguments and, in particular, with the tradition of historical economism.

The framework of action as developed by Robert W. Cox is a conceptual device through which seemingly disparate phenomena might be efficiently ordered and rendered intelligible for analysis.[3] The operationalization of the framework in concrete historical terms takes place at three interlocking (but methodologically distinct) levels, namely, at the levels of production, forms of state, and world order.[4] At the first level, particular emphasis is placed on the organization of production and the social forces generated through the reproduction of the attendant social processes. Secondly, the method of historical structure is applied to forms of the state "as derived from a study of state/society complexes." The problem-solving concept of state as a thing/institution standing above society is jettisoned in this instance. Thirdly, at the level of world order the analysis is focused on "... the particular configuration of forces which successively define the problematic of war or peace for the ensemble of states."[5]

The three levels are interrelated in such a way, that changes at one level have consequences for the other two to the degree that corresponding changes might occur. According to Robert W. Cox, "[c]hanges in the organization of production generate new social forces which, in turn, bring about changes in the structure of states; and the generalization of changes in the structure of states alters the problematic of world order."[6]

This conceptualization of the relationship among world order, forms of state, and domestic social forces is perhaps one of the most significant historical materialist critiques of the neo-realist perspective on international relations. It stands in diametric opposition to Waltz's sophisticated, but reified structuralist notion, that the dynamics of the interstate system have absolute autonomy. World order does not stand in high heaven above domestic social formations, and outside of history as it does for Waltz; nor are societies impervious to world order pressures.[7] On the contrary, not only do world order, forms of state, and domestic social forces interact as a structural totality, but each is produced through historically conscious action. This general framework is built around a system of critical concepts, which are now examined.

## Hegemony

Like most concepts developed by Gramsci, hegemony is dialectical in nature since, by its very definition, it is constituted through historically specific balances of coercion and consensus. In its negative sense, hegemony designates a system of social control, and specifically the control of the subaltern classes and groups, without the preponderant use of force/coercion.

Drawing on this "leadership," the representations of capitalist social relations are diffused in such a way that, to a degree, the subaltern classes participate in their own domination by accepting "the imagined communities"constructed. In other words, the subaltern classes give consent to their own political and economic subordination by living the "passing present" without calling into question the extant social (or world) order. Thus, according to Joseph Femia, hegemony refers to "a psychological state, involving some kind of acceptance—not necessarily explicit—of the sociopolitical order or of certain vital aspects of that order."[8]

Hegemony is not a purely superstructural concept; rather, it involves the dialectical relationship between substructure and superstructure. In contradistinction to the economic reductionism of the Third International which simply extrapolated culture, politics, and ideology as necessary and logically determined effects of the "laws of motion" (of capital and the commodity economic principle), Antonio Gramsci was keen on specifying the organic relationship among these categories and, more broadly, between production and ideology. The concept "organic intellectual" establishes the connection between the two foregoing "ensembles" in the context of hegemony. According to Gramsci, each social class produces its own intellectuals who concomitantly construct an appropriate world view of that class. The task of organic intellectuals is to socialize the view of their own class so as to make this view the dominant and prevailing one. If and when a social class succeeds in having its world view accepted by other social classes, this class is said to be hegemonic. Hegemonic practices, however, are never purely class practices, since as a matter of historical experience, social classes themselves are overdetermined. Elements of race, ethnicity, and gender are often imbricated in the very configuration of the social structure of accumulation. Further, since hegemony goes beyond mere class dominance to broader issues of culture, these elements often perform significant roles in the historically specific processes of articulation required for stable reproduction.

The strategic purpose of hegemony is to preempt the possibility of any fundamental challenge to a particular social order or the social system in general. The concept hegemony embodies ". . . a hypothesis that within a stable social order, there must be a substratum of agreement so powerful that it can counteract the division of disruptive forces arising from conflicting interests."[9] This substratum of agreement is achieved by the production, articulation, and socialization of a system of values, norms, and beliefs, which in its totality constitutes an intellectual regime pertinent to the *stable* reproduction of daily life. This regime of "knowledges" defines the parameters of common sense, and supplies the appropriate/authoritative criteria of evaluation of the social order, as well as the basis for the rejection of competing and alternative interpretations which may threaten the extant order. Hegemony, therefore, is a moment in a war of position insofar as it organizes resistance to any fundamental transformation of the production structure and attendant social relations. The overarching strategy is to rationalize contradictions by transforming structural antagonisms into simple differences. Whereas the former might call into question the social order *in its entirety,* and thus generate a "revolutionary" movement, the latter is well disposed to reconciliation (collective bargaining being a good example) within the boundaries of the existing order. Through various interpellative strategies, hegemonic practices translate the core assumptions of the social system, as a whole, into desirable properties as they are "presenced" in *specific cultural systems of meaning.*

The concept of hegemony may be used at the level of global politics to pinpoint the ways in which relations of exploitation and of subordination become inscribed in specific "world orders." Hegemony must be distinguished from the notion of "dominance."[10] Dominance is an essentially realist/neo-realist concept which places considerable stress on overt power, often meaning only military power. The emphasis on dominance reduces the problematic of power to relations of force, and implicitly, to relations among nation states. Even if economic power is included, as in the case of hegemonic stability theory, the analysis of international relations does not go beyond "power over."[11] Two further points are in order here.

First, by privileging overt power through dominance, realist and neo-realist perspectives essentially treat world order as a *fixed universal* grounded in a fixed logic/relation of power.[12] Substantively, this means small, weak, and/or poor states, are incapable of transformative action in any given international order, and accordingly, must accept their situation as permanent. Secondly, if indeed small states do not matter, as expressed in Kenneth Waltz's aphorism referred to earlier, then the only important problems for international relations are those concerned with the distribution of power among the Great Powers. It is further assumed that the international system resolves the problem of capability by moving toward a balance of power and, for that reason, the analysis of the conditions for the emergence of this balance become the prized subject of study. Failing that, the most dominant power will exercise leadership in the system with the strategic objective of managing stability. As such, generalized weakness of most states on the one hand, and the dominance of a particular state on the other, is seen as apposite to stability. Stability itself is offered up as the most salient value of the international system.

The application of the concept of hegemony introduces substantially different problems to global politics. Military and economic power, far from being privileged as the only determinant instances of world order, may be situated in a much wider and more complex global system. Considerable emphasis must be placed on the making of the intersubjective contexts in which and through which "international relations" are conducted, and authoritatively explained. Hegemony, therefore, goes beyond dominance and refers to "a structure of values and understandings about the nature of order that permeates a whole system of states and non-state entities. In a hegemonic order these values and understandings are relatively stable and unquestioned."[13]

The ideas which are constitutive of a particular world order are not the product of abstract thought or free-floating signifiers; rather they are produced through concrete history, and in real material circumstances. This history is not restricted to the history of states to which neo-realist problem-solving theory imputes an absolute autonomy. To speak of "hegemonic leadership" as if it is the result of autonomous state action (as hegemonic stability theory does) actually reifies the social bases of the state and mechanically relegates "the hegemon" to the status of "an actor" interested in securing or maintaining stability. In this scenario, "hegemony" is presented as something that is necessary in order to avoid chaos, and hence, a desirable condition for the world. The neo-liberal theory of hegemony is largely *regulatory* in character, since it sees the management of various international regimes as the terrain on which hegemonic leadership is exercised. This version of hegemony incorporates politics in its analysis only to the extent that international rules, norms, and decision-making procedures (enforced by the "hegemon") would discipline "free-riders" and punish other forms of recalcitrant behavior by other *states*. The more obscure political logic of this version of hegemony, however, is that states (and the people who live in states) ought to defer to the "hegemon," since it is the latter that guarantees stability; democratic freedoms; and ultimately, progress. Further, since neo-realism and neo-liberalism present hegemony as a state-to-state affair which is largely about rule enforcement, a certain instrumentalism attends the concept/ practice, resulting in obfuscation of the social bases of hegemony.[14]

The new historical materialist application of the concept hegemony to global politics rejects the state as the only "container" of "hegemonic leadership"; the asocial bases of hegemonic practices; and the notion that stability is the key (and desirable) outcome of the "hegemon's actions." On the contrary, hegemonic practices must be seen as more diffuse; firmly grounded in the social; and as the modality through which exploitation and subordination on a global scale are stabilized, albeit, with a modicum of institutional legitimacy. The real issue then is not abstract stability, but what is stabilized, by whom, by whose authority, and in whose interest. Put differently, hegemony is conceptualized as a concurrent set of domestic and global practices underpinned by conjuncturally specific configurations of domestic and global social forces. This configuration is not a given, but is made through the *conscious activity* of the world's dominant classes who telescope the long term interests of what might be called *world social capital*. In this sense, global hegemony is not a result of the most dominant state benevolently "stepping in" to offer its leadership in a time of international instability. Moreover, hegemony cannot be reduced to the "hegemon's" enforcement of international rules and other regime requirements. Such a conceptualization of hegemony gives the impression that the "hegemon" is a neutral global law enforcement officer who makes sure that all states follow norms and rules which have been agreed to by all, or by that elusive entity called the "international community." On the contrary, "[h]egemony derives from the ways of doing and thinking of the dominant social strata of the dominant state or states insofar as these ways of doing and thinking have acquired the acquiescence of the dominant social strata of other states."[15]

We may, therefore, establish a structural connection between the interests of dominant classes and groups in the dominant states, and the ways in which the combined power of these two define the broad parameters of world order. Implicit in this formulation of global hegemony is the idea that the world's dominant classes exercise influence far beyond the reaches of their economic control. This is achieved by global intellectual leadership, a phenomenon which Antonio Gramsci himself described as follows:

> Every relationship of "hegemony" is necessarily an educational relationship and occurs not only within a nation, between the various forces of which the nation is composed, but in the international and world-wide field, between complexes of national and continental civilizations.[16]

This understanding of global hegemony gives a lot less weight to rule enforcement, and state interest per se, and a lot more to the structural power of capital and its various ideological and cultural manifestations.

### Three Moments of Hegemony

Three forms of hegemonies may be delineated—these being, "integral," "decadent" and "minimal" hegemony. Integral hegemony is a "paradigm case" or an "ideal type" in which ". . . mass affiliation would approach unqualified commitment. The society would exhibit a substantial degree of 'moral and intellectual unity.' "[17] While there may be contradictions in the society, the social order as whole is seen as non-contradictory. Contradictions that do surface are seen as mechanical aberrations which, in any event, could be explained *within* the social and ethical order.[18] Again, this situation approximates what Robert Cox calls a "fit" among ideas, material capabilities, and institutions.

Decadent hegemony obtains in those social formations where ". . . widespread, cultural and political integration is fragile."[19] This type of hegemony is appropriate to modern capitalist societies, where, despite a dominant world view, there are powerful alternative ideologies. In this case the fit among ideas, institutions, and material capabilities becomes fluid, if not incoherent. The system's productive capacity is no longer able to meet the social demands, and social discontent is translated into political protest. Importantly, significant fractures begin to occur within the ideological structure and alternative perspectives gain some ground. This is a form of intellectual resistance and if developed as a cohesive discourse, could be the basis for counter-hegemony. Thus "the potential for social disintegration is ever-present: conflict lurks just beneath the surface. In spite of the numerous achievements of the system, the needs, inclinations, and mentality of the masses are not truly in harmony with the dominant ideas."[20]

Minimal hegemony is akin to *passive revolution* to the extent that the level of integration between the ruling classes and the masses is extremely low. Instead of integration, "this type of hegemony rests on the ideological unity of the economic, political and intellectual elites along with 'aversion to any intervention of the popular masses in state life.' "[21] The political strategy that underpins minimal hegemony is *trasformismo*, that is, the co-optation of the leadership of the popular masses into the state apparatus. Unlike "integral" and "decadent" hegemony which incorporate mass participation, "minimal" hegemony is exclusionary. Like hegemony, passive revolution can "happen" at the domestic as well as global levels of civil society.

## Passive Revolution

Passive revolution or revolution/restoration is a historically derived concept that Gramsci used to describe and analyze the nature and process of bourgeois transformations/revolutions that did not take the cataclysmic path of the French Revolution. Gramsci made a distinction between those societies which had experienced ". . . a social revolution and worked out fully its consequences in new modes of production and social relations," and those ". . . which had so to speak imported or thrust upon them aspects of a new order created abroad, without the old order having been displaced."[22] In the first instance, such as in England and France, the landed classes had lost their hegemonic position to the rising bourgeoisie. But if the objective conditions were propitious for such structural transformation in England and France, this was not the case in other European societies. Drawing from Marx's *The Critique of*

*Political Economy*, Gramsci posited "that no social formation disappears as long as the productive forces which have developed within it still find room for further forward movement."[23] In other words, the pre-capitalist production structure was capable of expansion and, concomitantly, the extant social forces in those societies were strong enough to resist a fundamental rupture with the old order. This is especially so in developing countries when pre-capitalist atavisms play a key role in the formation of historical structures. The result is often a crisis of legitimacy and an "exceptional" form of state.

In this situation where there is dual pressure for change (from the popular classes and capitalist forces, in conjunction with externally generated currents) but in which the old order is still strong, an organic crisis of the state develops. No social class is powerful enough to seize state power and consolidate itself as the hegemonic force in the society. The lack of "universal" legitimacy of any bloc of the ruling classes creates uncertainty, since the possibility of a mass-based social revolution is considerably enhanced. To forestall such an eventuality the ruling classes orchestrate comprehensive reforms from above, that is, passive revolution. As Anne Showstack Sassoon points out, in this context "passive" refers to . . .

> ". . . the nature of the attempt at 'revolution' or development of the productive forces through a degree of State intervention and the inclusion of new social groups under the hegemony of the political order without any expansion of the real political control by the mass of the population over politics."[24]

Ergo, if the world's political economy is seen as an integrated global state/civil society complex, it is possible to conceptualize metropolitan hegemonic influences, in conjunction with local ruling classes, as the modality of organizing passive revolution in a global civil society.

From the foregoing discussion the following elements of passive revolution may be specified: (a) external forces have played, and continue to play, an important role in capitalist modernization. National development takes place through a dialectical interplay between domestic and international social forces. Specifically, the advanced capitalist countries generate certain pressures, both economic and non-economic, which may trigger fundamental changes in "developing" countries; (b) the transition from pre-capitalist/proto-capitalist social formations does not necessarily take place through a cataclysmic rupture, but can be effected through reform; (c) there is an historical tendency for countries with proto-capitalist structures and social forces (which remain viable), and where the rising bourgeoisie is not hegemonic, for the transition to take the form of passive revolution. To put it another way, we can say that capitalist modernization takes the form of revolution/restoration in those societies that have powerful pre-capitalist sedimentations; (d) revolution/restoration is the form of capitalist development that occurs in countries where the bourgeoisie is not hegemonic, (in the integral sense); (e) because no class, and especially the bourgeoisie, is not hegemonic, the state plays a crucial role in capitalist modernization; (f) the state is constituted as a contradictory historic bloc based on domestic and foreign capital and proto-capitalist social forces; (h) mass participation, that is, the participation of the popular classes, is passive, and (i) in developing countries, the *form* of transformation (to capitalism), that is, whether revolutionary or "passive," is directly related to a balance of internal and external forces.

## The Concept of Forms of State

The concept of state can be handled best if it is recognized that there is: (1) an administrative, coercive, and legal apparatus; (2) an historic bloc that determines or at least conditions which functions the former should perform; and (3) a functional role for the state in relation to the economy, so determined. In this formulation it is possible to treat the state as: (a) continuous from one mode of production or historical structure to another, that is, an entity that remains the same but is merely adjusted to perform new functions with changing circumstances, or (b) discontinuous as a sequence of historic blocs as determined by differently combined social forces.[25]

### An Administrative / Coercive Apparatus

The work of Gramsci led many historical materialists to see that bourgeois rule reproduces itself not only through "violence" (by the state), but also through the consent of the dominated. Gramsci used the concept "hegemony" to analyze and elucidate the nature and *forms* of bourgeois domination. The trajectory of this analysis led to a wider view of the concept of state, and specifically the institutions which make up the state apparatus. Since, for Gramsci, domination in capitalist society is based on the socialization of the relations of subordination into acceptable common sense, he included a number of seemingly neutral institutions in the state apparatus.[26]

### Historic Bloc and the Functions of the State

Gramsci used the concept "historic bloc" to denote the class-based nature of the state. More specifically, historic bloc addresses the balance of class forces in a social formation, as well as the nature of "historic partnerships" which underpin and sustain state power.

The concept historic bloc can be understood at two distinct levels. First, a historic bloc obtains within a social class itself when there is a world view *(Weltanschauung)* that is strong enough to unify all the seemingly unconnected interests of a particular class into a coherent and unifying discourse. The second level of the historic bloc develops where the world view of a particular social class provides the basis for the incorporation of other social classes in the society.

Like hegemony, historic bloc is not a purely superstructural condition, but an intermeshing of substructure and superstructure. The key factor here is that as a class develops itself *in history*, it does so within and through concrete social relations of production and, simultaneously, through the fashioning of *otherness*. This formulation does not reduce historic bloc to class alliance. For the conception of historic bloc as class alliance "ignores the relationship of an historical to an intellectual and moral bloc."[27]

Not all historic blocs are hegemonic, although hegemonies do develop out of historic blocs. Many historic blocs are built on "minimal hegemony," although within a particular bloc one social force (or fraction of a class) may gradually develop a "decadent hegemony." By definition, therefore, all historic blocs are based on social forces underpinned by the complementary interests of the social classes, or fractions thereof, that make up the bloc. The conflicting interests of the dominant classes are reconciled in light of a more fundamental challenge from the subaltern classes. Thus, the making of the hegemonic historic bloc (as a cohesive unit) is directly related to the specter of resistance/revolution, and the "power bloc" always develops through historically grounded socio-economic ideocultural and political struggles. The key point here is that the convergence of interests of the dominant classes is not all that matters. What is equally significant is the particularity of their cohesion, and the form in which their identity of interests is expressed; for example, in some states this interest is expressed in military terms, while in others there may be a formal democratic political shell but substantively, the country may be governed through authoritarian practices.

In general, the concept historic bloc makes possible an alternative conceptualization of the state. The state can be seen as a historic bloc, that is, a bloc constituted by the dominant economic classes and by groups which share their "world view." In this context it is possible to see the state as an institution structurally imbricated in the social structure of accumulation, and consistent with the dominant social forces of a particular historical structure. The state is not a permanent thing/institution, but a sequence of historic blocs which takes certain historically concrete organizational and institutional forms. These organizational and institutional forms are, from time to time, transformed to express the constant metamorphosis of the social structure of accumulation, and the reconfiguration of different balances of social forces.

In the historical development of capitalism, certain social classes (mainly the landed aristocracy-oligarchy and the merchant capitalists) have been reduced from their "dominant" and/or hegemonic positions to "governing classes." New classes also rise in the new configuration of state power (such as the bourgeoisie), or struggle to be in that configuration (such as the working class). With this in mind, it is now possible to conceive of the state as a sequence of historic blocs which (as a terrain of political and ideological struggle) is "constantly" transformed and reconstituted on the basis of new (and sedimentations of old) social forces.

*The Functional Role of the State in Relation to the Economy*

If we interpret the economy in the wider sense as a production structure and attendant forms of social relations, we find that historical materialists generally agree that the state intervenes on behalf of capital. At the broadest level, this intervention has the strategic aim of securing the objective conditions for the implantation and/or reproduction of the juridical principle of *meum et tuum*. The German theorist E. Altvater, who works within the state derivationist school, has neatly summarized the intervention of the state for the purpose of reproducing the social relations of production and the continuous development of the material forces of production. According to Altvater, there are four broad areas of state intervention. These are as follows: (a) providing the general material conditions of production (what is generally known as infrastructure); (b) establishing and guaranteeing general legal relations, through which the relationships of legal subject in capitalist society are performed; (c) regulating the conflict between wage-labor and capital and, if necessary, the political repression of the working class, not only by means of law, but also by the police and army; and (d) safeguarding the existence and expansion of total national capital on the capitalist world market.

The state assumes these responsibilities in capitalist societies due to the impossibility of these functions being performed by individual fractions of capital. This conceptualization of the state's intervention in the economy seems, at first glance, consistent with liberal versions of state theory. There is, however, one major difference. Whereas historical materialists see state intervention as class motivated (in the interest of total social capital), liberal perspectives posit that such intervention is class neutral and thus in the interest of society as a whole. The differences are enormous; for example, whereas the former sees "foreign policy" (and particularly economic policy) as very much influenced by class interest, the latter speaks more of "national interest."

*Is the State Continuous or Discontinuous?*

A problem-solving approach to the state would suggest that the state is continuous, that is, an institution or set of institutions which adapts from one historical structure to another, or through different phases within a particular structure, *while remaining the same state*. Alternatively, and from the perspective of critical theory, the state is not a permanent thing/institution but a sequence of historic blocs which takes historically concrete organizational and institutional forms. State power, therefore, always rests on specific configurations of social forces and the entrenchment of these in various political spaces/institutions. The organizational/institutional forms are never fixed, but change over time depending on the balance of forces. For the sub-discipline of international theory, it is also important to add the influence of external pressures, since these do play a role in the making of specific forms of state.[28] When these shifts occur, different historic blocs are configured, thereby transforming the state; its institutional/material forms; and its relation to the economy.

## The Concept of Social Force

The concept of social force is important in the development of a new historical materialism. Social force is a deliberately open-ended concept intended to accommodate a multiplicity of structuring factors and antagonisms present in social formations and in the global political economy. Simply put, the concept is more inclusive than the concept social class, the latter having occupied a privileged position in more traditional forms of historical materialist problematics. The inclusion of social forces allows for the conceptualization of relations of power both at the state and of civil society levels, as well as in the domestic and transnational realms. While social forces are principally generated by the production structure and by the modes of social relations, they may also be over-determined by a whole host of elements critical to a historical structure, such as race, ethnicity, and gender. As such, civil society has to be seen as constituted through a multiplicity of social forces. These latter are not static; rather, it is their demands and constant struggle to occupy strategic spaces that condition the shifting balances of forces in the society. Society itself, for that matter, is not a pre-given. It is *made*.

The usefulness of the concept is that it remains materialist without being (economic) reductionist. While production involves economic processes in the narrow sense of economic, it is not restricted or reduced to the latter. Rather, production itself is part of a larger system of social relations, all of which are material in nature. Social forces are also materialist in nature without being economic *qua* economic. How is this possible? The answer is that in contradistinction to historical economism and other forms of mechanical Marxism, social forces, including class forces, may be understood as being generated *in* the process of production, not *by* that process.[29] Accordingly, social forces are historical rather than logical; materialist rather than economic; and exist as historically generated potentialities rather than as pre-given "empirical sets." Conceptualizing the political in a manner consistent with the plurality of social forces, is one of the most promising benefits that accompany the widening of the social, from social classes to social forces.

## Counter-Hegemony and Hegemony

The new historical materialism is not without its share of problems. Firstly, while there is rigorous analysis of the dialectics of hegemony, there is not sufficient incorporation of resistance and counter-hegemony in the *theorization* of hegemonic practices.[30] The necessity of consent (as the infrastructure of ideological/political management) tends to be derived largely through analyses of the interests of the dominant social forces, and the ways in which their interests become embedded in institutions. On the other hand, resistance and counter-hegemony are too often seen as *responses* to the embedded interests already formed, rather than theorized as dialectically defining the conditions which make hegemonic practices historically "necessary" in the first place. In keeping with a historicist epistemology, it might be more useful to understand hegemony, and counter-hegemony/resistance, as a simultaneous *double movement*, the consequence of which is the reciprocal configuration of each other. Put differently, the requirements and forms of hegemonic practices develop directly against the specific forms and modalities of counter-hegemonic pressure. As such, counter-hegemonic practice must be seen as a fluid and unstable *engagement*, rather than a settled *response* to hegemony.

Secondly, despite the methodological openness of the concept "social force," best developed by Cox, there is too much weight on the relations of production in the problematization of the political. It is not that politics are seen as having a logically necessary and unmediated correspondence with production per se, since for most historical materialist this is an historical question. Further, the problem it is not so much that economic or class-determined forces drive the political, since for the new historical materialism both of these categories are parts of a more encompassing concept, namely "material life." Rather, the difficulty with the treatment of the political is that there is not sufficient weight given to the *overdetermination* of political identity and, as a consequence, there is a tendency to undervalue the plurality of political spaces. It may be reasonably inferred that for the new historical materialism, and certainly for Cox, there is too much hope for a *unified and coherent* political project of counter-hegemony, instead of one based on the strategic articulation of social forces. More recently, William Robinson has articulated a position for a "variable alternative program" of counter-hegemony. This may very well be the best strategic option for the marginalized.[31] Counter-hegemony need not be a set of unified practices, nor need it be a strategy aimed at transformations which occur all at once. Counter-hegemony is more likely to be effective by proceeding from one trench to another. The point that needs to be considered seriously here, however, is that counter-hegemonic practices, in part, shape the hegemonic practices.

It is important to recognize that while the exercise of hegemony may be coherent (that is, the welding together of seemingly disparate economic, political, and cultural factors into a non-contradictory unity), it is differential in its consequences. This should not be surprising since the objective of a social hegemony is precisely to weaken whatever antagonisms may exist and subsequently subsume them under some general hegemonic points of reference, such as the national interest, order, stability, or progress. Seen this way, hegemonic practices implicitly acknowledge that there is indeed a plurality of political spaces. On the other hand, to insist that all forces of resistance/counter-hegemony merge into an equally non-contradictory unity amounts to the abandonment of their historical specificities and their *raison d' etre*. The difficulty of a unified subaltern political project is multiplied when it comes to who should decide what this project should look like in the identification and conceptualization of the problem(s); in the strategies and methods of political struggle; and in the articulation of an alternative vision.

Finally, while critical theory deals comprehensively with the *origins* and *consequences* of hegemonic practices, there is not sufficient focus on the disciplinary techniques through which authoritative "common sense" is produced. To some extent, this omission comes from the direct extrapolation of the ideological from the social, meaning that ideology is (structurally) located in the social structure of accumulation and emerges as a matter of objective interests.[32] This does *not* mean that there are *pre-determined* ideologies which correspond to pre-determined class interests. Critical theory generally rejects anything pre-given. The problem rather, is one of not fully establishing the articulatory practices through which objective interests are translated into ideological discourses of signification and representation.

## World Order Pressures

National sovereignty in theory, and substantially so in practice as well, affords considerable autonomy to states. Quite often, however, sovereignty leads to the misguided notion that a neat line can be drawn between what is internal and external. Sovereignty, of course, confers formal political legitimacy on states, and in the dominant discourses of I. R., states are taken as givens, and as the authoritative actors. Foreign policy is often conceptualized as the pursuit of the states' interests in the international arena. But as argued earlier, the concept of state so used is not helpful, since the real issue is the *form* that the state takes. Pressures emanating from the level of world order exert influence in shaping the form of state. World order is understood here to mean the combination of the interstate system and the world economy, which is another way of saying the global configuration of power and wealth.

Power and wealth as the essential elements of world order are critical in shaping international institutions and the norms, principles, and rules which become authoritative. Specific world orders, therefore, are concrete historical manifestations of material capabilities, ideas, and institutions. Historically specific world orders, such as existed from 1945 through (roughly) 1989, themselves must be situated in broader structures which have developed over time. It is important to make the distinction between world order as a level of analysis, (so to speak), and the more concrete historical structures. The former is more long term in its development, and changes within it are hardly decipherable. It maps the broad structural features of the global system. The rise and consolidation of states; the interstate system; and the development of capitalism are the essential products of this development. Thus:

> [S]ince the Treaty of Westphalia in 1648 the nation state has been adopted as the principal form of political organization. The secularization of the state, and the principle of national sovereignty which were sanctified by this Treaty was first accepted in Europe. In the 20th century the principle of self-determination, an associated concept of national sovereignty, would form the central articulating moment of decolonization.[33] Similarly, the development of capitalist forms of production in Europe entailed fundamental transformations in the economic, social and cultural bases of those societies. Moreover, the sustained expansion outside of Europe which ensued, especially in the form of colonialism, globalized these capitalist forms of production relations. The world economy thus became a global *longue durée* element, conditioning the international economic relations of states.[34]

The most important point here is that foreign policy is not simply a matter of the decision making process, narrowly defined. The very decisions which are taken, are themselves partly explainable by the global context in which a particular state is operating. Put differently, the structure of world order presents both opportunities and limits. It would be extremely difficult, for example, to talk about state survival outside of the structure of an interstate system. While there is a sense that the broadest features of world order are fixed, this is not the case with specific global historical structures. The reasons for this are obvious. The temporal moment is more within grasp, and the distribution of power and wealth in the system is easier to deconstruct. Importantly, the "hand" of human agency can be linked to benefits, reward, punishments, and exclusions. Accordingly, specific world orders are highly contestable.

Perspectives on world order are never simply figments of the imagination which are translated into a menu of choices. Rather, they are invariably underpinned and circumscribed, defined and delimited, by their social bases. In the post-war conjuncture, the internationalization of production, finance, and the state, along with the increasing interpenetration of markets, spawned certain transnational social forces. Chief among these was the formation of a transnational historic bloc made up of the leading fractions of internationally mobile capital and established workers from North America, Europe, and Japan. This historic bloc became the basis of a transnational hegemony by articulating a set of specific economic, political, and intellectual positions. In this context Stephen Gill explains that:

> ... [T]he postwar mix of social democracy, and class compromise in the "mixed economy" based upon Fordist accumulation ... and growing international trade were key ingredients in an *international historic bloc*. This incorporated a range of class interests which sustained not only the modernisation of the "mixed economies" of the West, but also the liberal international economic order. Subscribing to this perspective were not only moderates in conservative parties, but also liberals and social democrats, and the leaders of many elements of non-communist organised labour. There was a broad-based political consensus in the Atlantic states which in effect served to generate the ethico-political concepts of civilisation which cemented the bloc.[35]

In the post-World War II period, certain specific global social forces came into being, all of which would figure significantly in the making of Jamaican foreign policy. Firstly, the Western Allies of the War, under the leadership of the United States, would fashion a global multilateral system geared toward the diffusion of market ideology and economic policies. This Bretton Woods system, as it came to be called, set up the conditions for considerable interference in the economies and societies of countries which were then becoming independent. This was a hegemonic set of institutions in that, it attempted to shape the world through a mixture of rewards and punishment. As we will see, Jamaican foreign policy was substantially affected by this mixture. The multilateral institutions in question were informed by a coherent picture of the world, and the practices which followed were not passive regarding desirable outcomes on the part of the global hegemonic bloc. It is possible to argue, therefore, that the global objective of the *system of regimes* has been to strategically manage popular upheaval from below in the periphery. Regimes have created the economic, political, and ideological space, therefore, for passive revolution in the Third World. Structural adjustment policies, one of the key *products* of the International Monetary Fund and its regional agencies, provide excellent examples of capitalist and market modernization, organized from above, and abroad, vis-à-vis developing states.[36] These multilateral institutions must be understood as the institutional forms of global market forces.

On the other side of the global equation, if indeed it might be framed like that, the rise of the Soviet Union would have a major impact on world politics. The rise of the USSR coincided with the quest by colonies for political independence. The timing of these two phenomena was not without consequences. On the one hand, the Soviets saw the opportunity of mobilizing those disenchanted with colonial exploitation, in a larger global effort to "fight imperialism." Many of the new states would take up the offer, and by the 1960s the combination of Soviet military power and Third World socialist clients would become a global force to be reckoned with.

But there was a also a broader and deeper force unleashed in this period. It had to do with cultural decolonization, a project consistent if not synonymous with strategic counter-hegemony. At the base of this project was the attempt to end economic marginalization wrought through the colonial structuring of the economies of poor states. But a more fundamental issue was at hand, namely, to recover the dignity of peoples which had been compromised for so long through colonization and continuing practices of apartheid. The brilliant distinction made by David Campbell between "Foreign Policy" (as the prosecution of interest, i.e., the conventional understanding) and "foreign policy" (as the production of the self/

identity) comes to mind here.[37] The Third World states had to engage in a double practice, the first being erasure of their colonized identities, and the second being reconstruction of national selves and peoplehoods. This second aspect of "foreign policy" would give rise to intense nationalism, often driven by a quest for racial justice. The active economies of racial oppression in Africa, and the silence of the states with the ability to intervene, served only to call into question the very notions of democratic freedoms propounded by the keepers of democracy. More than that, this recovery of the self was not arranged along the lines of Westphalian sovereignty. Third World nationalism was in fact transnationalized, and the common denominator was, *inter alia,* global anti-racism.

Hedley Bull understood the multiplicity of demands being made in this "Third World revolt against Western dominance." For him they were: (a) the struggle for "equal sovereignty" by those states which had secured their independence in the nineteenth century but "which enjoyed only a subordinate or inferior status"; (b) the anti-colonial struggle for national independence by Asian, African, and Caribbean states; (c) the struggle for "racial equality" beginning with Garveyism in the early twentieth century and rearticulated at the Bandung Conference in 1955; (d) the struggle for global economic justice beginning in the 1960s and most cogently expressed in the New International Economic Order movement; (e) the struggle by non-Western peoples for "cultural liberation." The objective of this struggle has been to "throw off the intellectual or cultural ascendency of the Western world so as to assert their own identity and autonomy in matters of spirit."[38]

The struggle by non-Western states was not restricted to "issue areas," but rather called into question the fundamental underpinnings of the world order as a whole. For this position to be properly developed, a more explicit theory of ideology is needed. Further, for us to understand the productive role of "foreign policy" (pace Campbell), it is imperative we go beyond the usual adaptation of models designed for western, industrialized countries.

### The Argument: A First Cut

At a general level, the foreign policy/behavior of developing states can be understood in terms of a dialectic of cooperation and resistance, vis-à-vis, world order (defined in terms of the dual pressures of the international states system, and the world economy), and the balance of domestic social forces. Cooperation as used here does not necessarily mean benign cooperation, that is to say, forms of relationships bereft of domination, subordination, and exploitation. On the contrary, the point is that the nature of the post-1945 U.S.-led world order has been one of hegemonic "leadership" with the strategic objective of realizing passive revolution on a world scale. Of course, this leadership was not "integral" and was met by various forms of resistance, and practices of disarticulation.

The historical, and simultaneously, the conceptual particularity of "developing states" is that the fundamental properties of the international states' system and world economy were defined and, to a considerable extent, are still maintained, by the developed industrial countries. To put it differently, the fundamental principles, norms, rules, and decision-making procedures of successive world orders since European outward expansion have been made by states other than the Third World.[39] It is on similar grounds that Robert Jackson argues that Third World states are actually quasi-states that have only "negative sovereignty."[40]

World order pressures are constituted through a combination of three conceptually distinct but historically interacting categories. Firstly, the international states' system defines certain specific requirements and responsibilities which all states are obliged to meet if they are to maintain their status as independent and sovereign entities. Of these, all states must protect their "core values," among which the territorial, political/cultural, and economic sovereignty are fundamental. In this sense, the historical tendency of the states system has been to discipline states into adopting policies which would ensure their survival *within* the extant system. Internally, this translates into the management of national cohesion through various political, ideological, and even coercive practices, and into investments in military preparedness which can absorb a significant portion of national resources. Externally, states may adopt policies which range from declared neutrality, alliances or defense treaties, imperialism, destabilization of hostile foreign governments, or war. Substantial resources are also put into diplomatic activities, especially through the auspices of international organizations.

Secondly, the world economy also exerts pressures on the state. In a narrow and restricted sense, "any state first and fundamentally extracts resources from society and deploys these to create and support coercive and administrative organizations."[41] The extent to which specific states are able to do this depends in large measure on their position in the world economy.

Thirdly, world order pressures also generate transnational social forces which "overflow state boundaries." This is different from those approaches which assume the state as the dominant actor, and which make a rigid separation between domestic and international sources of behavior. In contradistinction to the latter, it is important to insist on an analysis of civil society and transnational social forces. Thus, "the world can be represented as a pattern of interacting social forces in which states play an intermediate though autonomous role between the global structure of social forces and local configurations of social forces within particular countries."[42]

Domestic social forces condition foreign policy/behavior in two ways. First, the entrenched forces in a social formation define the broad "limits of the possible," that is to say, the structural parameters in which the state in question can adopt and implement policies in pursuit of what comes to be recognized as the authoritative national interests. While the logic of the states' system and global economy play critical roles in shaping systemic non-negotiables (such as state survival), the specificity of national interest is strongly influenced by the configuration of state power. Further, while social classes and groups do offer "inputs" into what gets accepted as the national interest, the latter is also the product of ideological and discursive conscription. In recognition of the discursive negotiability of the national interest, classes and groups which are economically weak and electorally marginalized may yet play a critical role in the making of what is important to the nation. Although their channels of input are outside the formal mechanisms of government, economically weak classes, in fact, can and do significantly influence foreign policy. This is one of the challenges to the new historical materialism as applied to international relations.

Finally, foreign policy is a critical factor in the making and consolidation of nation-statehood. David Campbell's brilliant work on this subject in some sense leaves little to be said.[43] At the same time, it must be noted that while the logic of interpellative practices between United States and Third World foreign policy and nation making might be similar, the historical contents are so different, that a view from below is warranted. This is particularly so for those countries which have only recently emerged from colonialism. Formal sovereignty is only formal recognition of statehood which, apart from strict legality, (including diplomatic acceptance), leaves *the state* as an "empty set." In point of fact, there is no necessary ontological essence, *modus ponens*, which writes the topography of nation and state. The syntactic particularity of nation and state are forged through the politics of mobilization, much of it forged in the consolidation of independence. In this regard, foreign policy in the Third World is used as an instrument not only of national constitution, but also of sovereignty, and any explanation of it must recognize this distinctiveness. Foreign policy, therefore, may be seen as a practice which is aimed at producing a non-contradictory discursive totality, aimed simultaneously at the juridical and political sovereignty, and a national self. A proper understanding of these developments requires an examination of ideological practices.

# 4

---

# Ideology, Culture, and National Interest

## The National Interest versus Ideology

In general, problem-solving explanations of foreign policy assume the external behavior of states are a function of their respective national interests, and that these interests are based on the reality of the nation and the international states' system. The fixation on national interest in explanations of foreign policy is, of course, not limited to Third World approaches; it is a problem with problem-solving international theory as a whole.[1] This fixation on the national interest as a *pre-given reality* is perhaps best reflected in the dismissal of ideology as superfluous to state behavior.[2] The only usefulness problem-solving explanations assigns to ideology is that it is used to *justify* the policy and behavior of a state.[3] In other words, the nation-state is assumed to have *objective interests* based on equally objective realities and, once these are recognized, ideology is called upon to provide moral cover, (in the form of justifications and rationalizations), for the smooth prosecution of these interests.[4] Thus, no less a figure than Hans Morgenthau states: "I call an ideology, regardless of the motive or the state of mind of its propounder, any system of thought which rationalizes or justifies a particular social position."[5] Outside of these narrow functions, ideology is simply dismissed as distortion of the truth, or in Clifford Geertz's words, "ideology has itself become thoroughly ideologized."[6] Critical theory fundamentally rejects these assumptions.

### The "Constitutivity" of Ideology and the Production of "Reality"

In contradistinction to problem-solving theory, what we know as the national interest is really a *way of life*, and it is the defense or transformation of this which informs state behavior. This way of

59

life, or for short, *culture*, is not solely or mechanically defined by national attributes, such as the economic and political systems and territorial sovereignty, as is usually accepted. These latter are merely unarticulated macro-structural variables (or "raw materials") which go into the production of the nation. Territory, economy, and state/ polity are combined with other components, such as ethnic and linguistic traditions, religious beliefs, philosophic discourses, and other properties of daily life into conceptions of national identity, which when formed, presents itself as the nation. The point is that the nation as a historically specific construct (in time and space), is a contestable representation born out of the *perspectives* of competing social forces engaged in ideological, social, and political struggle. The challenge of critical theory then is to unravel the formation/making of the nation as a stable reality, (and its associated national interests), as a singular and reconciled general equivalence of divergent perspectives. This brings us back to the epistemological and ontological questions of knowledge, power, and reality, discussed in the last chapter.

*Levels of Reality*

There is a first level of reality (hereafter "Reality I") which exists as the day-to-day empirical properties of life. We can quite easily ascertain that there is a physical world which has identifiable topographic features—rivers, mountains, deserts, land space, and so on. We may just as easily identify physical objects made by people—bread, guns, computers, books, bombs, aircraft carriers, and the list can go on and on. Finally, we may introduce a third category of physical reality, namely, people. What we cannot do as easily, however, is to assume that there is some obvious reality in the three corresponding categories called, *states, commodities,* and *subjects.* These latter are *historical realities* (hereafter "Reality II"), produced in specific space and time, under specific social, political, technological, and cultural circumstances, and underwritten by specific configurations of power. Moreover, the *meaning* of these realities is never fully formed, completely stable, or entirely closed off. Rather, they are constantly subjected to "interruptions"; negotiation; struggles; and/or recombination, all of which constitute the politics and social bases of their reproduction and/or transformation. This can be so, however, only if we accept that individual historical realities are always produced in the context of discursive formations. This is precisely where the "new historical material-ism" needs further development.

The discursive articulation of seemingly disparate components into a coherent and common-sense system constitutes "Reality III." The latter is the transformation of Reality II (which has made conceptual sense of Reality I), into the language and assumptions of day-to-day life, that is, the essential coordinates of ontological systems. An obvious problem here is the criteria of delineation between Reality II and Reality III, since both seem to be outcomes of theoretical practices. The framework of historical structure is extremely useful in resolving this dilemma since it speaks directly to the problem of subject-object unity in particular space and time. Thus according to Cox:

> Historical structures express the unity of the subjective and the objective. A nation, a class, a religion are not real physical objects, yet they give real form to the human situation. They are ideas shared in the subjectivity of innumerable individuals who are real physical beings. In being so shared, these ideas constitute the social world of these same individuals. They attain objectivity in the structures that circumscribe human action. These structures are as much a part of the material existence of people as the food they eat and the clothes they wear.[7]

Seen this way, Reality III is an elaborate system/apparatus for the *domestication* of Reality II. People do not *experience* the territory in which they live as states; the things which they consume as commodities; and themselves or others as subjects, for after all, these are conceptual categories. For these categories to be meaningful, as they are at the level of everyday life, they must be translated into experiential categories and sutured through a comprehensive sign system which establishes relatively stable referents of past, present, and future. This is precisely what Louis Althusser means when he says that "there is no practice except by and in an ideology."[8]

The principal theoretical claim here is that ideological practices are constitutive of reality, with the assumption that reality exists only in, and as a system, of cultural meaning. While Reality I may exist physically as matter, the sense that is made of it is always socially written through practices which confer identity, and which defines the matrix of its representation. In this context then, we can affirm that reality is nothing more, or less, than the constant flux of social forces which become translated into perspectives and ultimately into cultural thought/practices.

In even broader terms, culture may be seen as a public trafficking in significant symbols which, in total, act as a control mechanism in our daily lives. Understood in this way, culture is an essential condition for our existence as humans, and not just ornaments of social existence.[9] Cultural practices, defined as a way of life, are appropriated by organic intellectuals and reproduced in discursive formations as ". . . the authoritative concepts that render [them] meaningful, the suasive images of which [they] can be sensibly grasped."[10] The discursive apparatuses which produce everyday, common-sense reality, is precisely what is meant by ideological practice here. Geertz underlines the cultural production of reality when he states the following:

> [C]ultural patterns—religious, philosophical, aesthetic, scientific, ideological—are "programs"; they provide a template or blueprint for the organization of social and psychological processes, much as genetic systems provide such a template for the organization of organic processes.[11]

While some theoretical distance from *economic* reductionism is warranted, ideological practices cannot be divorced from the *material* bases of social formations. The specific problem with historical economism is the tendency to privilege the "economic instance" in particular, and the level of production in general, as the constitutive "originiary" from which ideology springs up. Further, reductionist analyses claim that social classes have ideologies which correspond to their location in the production structure, without fully considering the impact of other factors which mediate and/or overdetermine the making of "world views." In reductionism, the concept "social class" is a master trope (containing social position and identity) which functions as a "general equivalent" and principle of theoretical unity in the points of departure, claims, and general propositions. It is out of the theoretical edifice constructed around this static notion of class, that class struggle emerges as the central articulating principle of politics, an effect which seriously limits the field of counter-hegemonic strategies.

More specific to the relationship between social classes and ideology, Ernesto Laclau has properly objected to the tendency of reductionism to attach necessary ideological dispositions to social classes.[12] Laclau notes that it is necessary:

> [T]o accept that "ideological elements" taken in isolation have no necessary class connotation, and that this connotation is only the result of the articulation of those elements in a concrete ideological discourse. This means that the precondition for analyzing the class nature of an ideology is to conduct the inquiry through that which constitutes the distinctive unity of an ideological discourse.[13]

Ideology as such cannot be *reduced* to class position, if by class one means the relationship of an individual to the means of production. While class position may generate a number of broad elements of *particular* ideological definition, it cannot be the basis of total interpellation, since as a matter of lived experience, the constitution of identities is veritably overdetermined.

Further, while some Marxist approaches can account for the structural conditions from which ideology emerges, and can demonstrate the relations of subordination embodied in ideological practice, they say very little about the *specific disciplinary procedures* through which ideology is actually produced. As noted earlier, this is partly the shortcoming with Cox's sophisticated historical materialism. For while it provides a comprehensive explanation of the *origins* and *effects* of the *contents* of ideology, it says little about *how* these contents are formed. This explanation requires reformulation since it is principally concerned with the motivation and institutional terrain through which bourgeois hegemony is "organized." That is to say, it limits itself to the medium of hegemonic socialization, rather than explaining the *mechanics* through which the raw materials of knowledges are specifically configured into authoritative knowledges; perspectives; strategies of interpretation; and, more "globally," the symbolic and referential nexus of both self-constitution and otherness.

As argued thus far, one of the conspicuous limitations of Marxian treatments of ideology, and more specifically, hegemony, is its incomplete account of the mechanics of formation which inscribe ideology and hegemony into culture. This theoretical absence may be bridged by use of the concepts *articulation* and *discourse* which have gained considerable prominence in post-Marxist and post-structuralist theaters. For purposes of the argument developed here, these concepts are used in the way in which they have been defined by Ernesto Laclau and Chantal Mouffe in their *Hegemony and Socialist Strategy*. They write:

> [W]e will call articulation any practice establishing a relation among elements such that their identity is modified as a result of the articulatory practice. The structured totality resulting from the articulatory practice, we will call discourse.[14]

In this theoretical ensemble, they also make a conceptual distinction between *elements* and *moments*. While elements are unarticulated, moments are actually connected within a discursive formation.[15] Methodologically, this is somewhat similar to the respective meaning attributed to Generality I (on one hand) and Generalities II and III (on the other) by Althusser.[16] The theoretical significance of this problematic is that it allows you to demonstrate the process through which "innocent objects" are transformed into constitutive properties of culturally specific realities. Of course, it is the configuration of moments within a discursive ensemble, and the articulation of these discursive ensembles that produces a stable conception of (ideological) reality, or put differently, hegemony.

A discourse analysis of the formation of reality is carried out in the *terms* of the fundamental ideas which govern the passage of an object from its shadowy and amorphous existence to the point where it is *recognized* and, therefore, becomes a fact/reality of social existence. This passage is in fact the articulation, that is to say, the bringing into relation, of the object with other objects. These are essentially relations which differentiate the object from other objects, and it is in terms of these relations of differentiation, that the object comes to assume *its* seemingly independent-objective identity among other objects. It is important to recognize that it is in its journey from non-fact to fact (or from thing to social reality), that the object is textualized. Reality can therefore be read as a form of textual practice, and as Edward Said puts it, ". . . texts can create not only knowledge but also the very reality they appear to describe."[17]

It should be clear by now that ideology is not a reactive practice which simply justifies/rationalizes the national interest extrapolated out of a pre-given core reality of the nation-state. Rather, as has been demonstrated, ideologies are constitutive of reality insofar as they define (and are being defined by) the field of articulatory practices and concomitant discursive formations. Just as important, while the raw materials of daily life are open to infinite discursive configurations, and while the political frontier is open and discontinuous, it does not mean that all meaning/reality is free-floating.[18] Thus, following Mannheim's distinction between the two approaches to reliable knowledge, meaning/reality may be understood in terms of relationism, not relativism.[19]

We are now in a position to reformulate the problem of hegemony and then specify more precisely the concept counter-hegemony. Having done that, the next step will be to demonstrate the theoretical grounds on which the interstate system and the global political economy (that is, world order) can be understood as a dialectic of hegemony and counter-hegemony, as articulated in foreign policy/behavior.

## Hegemony, Counter-Hegemony, and World Order

Methodologically, it is difficult to separate hegemony and counter-hegemony since, as historical practices, they are dialectically rather than sequentially configured. In fact, it is impossible to locate (in history) the practice of hegemony outside of resistance or counter-hegemony. If hegemony is organized through the production, circulation, and institutionalization of coherent narratives about a social order, then these narratives are, by definition, historically *required* for the reproduction of domination and subordination. For if historically there was *total consensus* (i.e., integral hegemony) about the social order nationally, and world order globally, there would be no need for the practices of "coercive orthodoxy." "Integral hegemony" is an impossible historical condition; there is always resistance to the conditions of the social order and its fundamental (ontological) assumptions. The historicity of counter-hegemony, however, is not active merely as a *response* to hegemony. Similarly, hegemonic practice is not first, fully formed, and *then* deployed. Hegemonic practices are, in fact, forms of defenses by the dominant classes (such as the fortification of the social order through the extended state) against the transformative actions from the marginalized. Is not the refusal by the hegemonic bloc to accept social change a form of resistance, backed up by state (official) power? Are not successful social revolutions really the triumph of the marginalized over the resistance of the hegemonic classes to preserve the social order? Hegemony and resistance/counter-hegemony, therefore, do not develop logically as anterior and posterior effects. Without resistance or practices of counter-hegemony from the marginalized, there is nothing for the dominant classes to hegemonize. Hegemony and resistance/counter-hegemony may be separated for the purpose of analysis, but as lived history and historical dialectics, they define each other. Contrary assumptions would tacitly render both practices as closed entities which are simply brought in frontal opposition through some ineluctable logic of (class?) antagonism. The latter would have no other consequence than, (a) to reduce human agency into two gigantic essentializations (i.e., those who have power versus those who want it), and (b) to collapse history into a teleological unfolding of the said binary opposition. Against this, hegemony and resistance/counter-hegemony must be understood as dialectically producing the historical conditions (in a state of flux) for the formation and exercise of the other, and in the process of so doing, simultaneously make the "passing present" we experience as historical reality. The systematic institutionalization of this history over broad expanses of time produces structures. In this historiography of "absolute historicism," no privileged position as the maker of history is assigned to the embodied agents of hegemonic practice (Western states and dominant classes), or to the voices of subalternity (Third World states and the marginalized).

If, as realists claim, there is a constant struggle for power, and if historically some states have always had more power than others, it is equally true that resistance also constitutes a basic fact of global politics. This is especially so in those cases where power (that is, power over) has been translated into *systemic* subordination and domination. While this is not difficult to demonstrate with respect to organized physical, and sometimes economic coercion, (i.e., war or economic sanctions, respectively), the same cannot be said for hegemonic domination.[20]

## Implications for Foreign Policy Analysis

The reconstructed concept of hegemony based on the relationality of material and discursive production of perspectives *and*, the place of resistance/counter-hegemony in this production, makes it possible to analyze the foreign policy of Third World states in a much more comprehensive manner. The following problems warrant further attention.

First, in addition to an analysis of the social and economic origins of the expansion of metropolitan capitalism we should now be able to pose questions in terms of a problematic of "global civil society." The latter does not exist simply because capitalism has been generalized into a world system. A global civil society exists only to the extent that social forces which were once peculiarly national in character and space, have now become transnationalized. Moreover, it is precisely the articulation of social forces across different national spaces that has made possible the production of transnational discourses and the formation of transnational identities. For the global hegemonic bloc, this translates into the world view of, *inter alia*, the World Bank, International Monetary Fund, and the Trilateral Commission; this was the making of a global (trans-Atlantic) historic bloc. The main objective from these quarters was to induce passive revolution on a world scale.

Transnational social forces with origins in Third World also generated specific discourses about the Third World, and of the Third World. Invariably these were discourses of liberation *from* "metropolitan-capitalist" exploitation, and cultural subordination. A plethora of organizations also arose to further the cause of the marginalized Third World, and the leadership of these states were keen on producing a generalized counter-discourse to the extant world order.[21] This took the form of a sustained assault on the ontological assumptions privileged by the metropolitan states. In the language of regime analysis, the goal was to move from "relational power" to "meta power."[22] In this sense, the non-aligned movement, and the requisite foreign policies (such as the call for a New International Economic Order) of member states, was the ideological strategy in a global war of position built on a "transnational imagined community."[23] The strategic objective of this attempt was to produce a *different* global perspective, that is to say, a counter-hegemonic discursive totality. Robert Cox puts it this way:

> Lesser powers do . . . alter the milieu of interstate relations. They have a collective interest in erecting limits on great power activity; and they encourage norms of international behavior that are anti-colonial and anti-interventionist, and which favor redistribution of global resources. Even as victim, the small state highlights a shift from hegemony to dominance, undermining moral certainties, underlining arbitrariness and departure from rule—consider the undermining of hegemonic beliefs in the cases involving Vietnam, Afghanistan, Grenada, Nicaragua, El Salvador, and Panama.[24]

Jamaica may very well have been added here given the indefatigable efforts of this country (from 1972 to 1980) in transforming the template of the post-war world order.

A second dimension of the expanded concept of hegemony, and one that is consistent with the new historical materialism, is that it is now possible to see the foreign policies of Third World states as integral to the making of world order. The key point here is that world orders are made and their making is not simply at the dictates of the Great Powers. Traditional approaches to Third World foreign policy, driven as they are by the assumptions of realism, commit precisely the error of seeing the international system as an expression of the wishes of Great Powers. This latter position, apart from suffering from the philosophical quagmire of obliterating any possibility of meaningful redemptive action on the part of Third World, runs into the quandary of reifying power.

The resistance *and* counter-hegemonic practices *inscribed* in the foreign policies of (some) Third World states in the period under consideration, therefore, were key to the specific form and institutional materiality of world order as it emerged. "Hegemony," as Ralph Miliband points out, "is not something that can ever be taken to be finally and irreversibly won: on the contrary, it is something that needs to be constantly nurtured, defended and reformulated."[25] As such, Third World foreign policy was not merely an appendage of some larger transhistorical demiurge (with its concrete manifestation in the behavior of Great Powers). In the perspective advanced here, the articulation of social forces emanating in the Third World, in conjunction with the actions of Third World states (especially at a collective level), defined the conditions under which the international system was configured and reproduced. At the broadest possible level, that is, at the level of civilizations, foreign policies must be understood as a means through which global power was negotiated, contested, and distributed, and, in understanding hegemonic world orders, as a *method* through which the dialectic of hegemony-counter-hegemony can be interpreted. More specifically, and consistent with the absolute historicism adopted here, the task at hand is to read the foreign policies of Third World states as a decisive force in the making of world order.

## Leadership and a Re-Statement of the Argument

Contrary to problem-solving approaches (and theories) of international relations, it is argued here that foreign policy is one form of a ceaseless global war of position, albeit one regularly broken by physical violence, and other forms of coercion. This does not mean that hegemony and coercion are opposed instances, for as Gramsci, Cox, Gill, Augelli and Murphy, Perry Anderson, and others have so forcefully argued, the threat of coercion is a critical moment in the effectiveness of consensus. What is important for us here is that if resistance/counter-hegemony is seen as dialectically constitutive of the conditions of hegemonic practices on a global scale, then *counter-leadership* must be a key object of investigation. Consistent with the new historical materialism, and also following Akhil Gupta, it is proposed here that a theory of Third World counter-leadership must recognize "the changing global configuration of postcoloniality and late capitalism have resulted in the repartitioning and reinscription of space."[26] Instead of national communities, identities, and interests (proper to the Westphalian system), ". . . we need to pay attention to the structures of feeling that bind people to geographical units larger or smaller than nations or that crosscut national boundaries."[27] Leadership, therefore, has to be wrenched out of the individual and national spaces, and recast on a global scale where broader historical forces have operated in shaping world order. The leadership of the hegemonic global bloc has already been systematically incorporated into the analysis of the global political economy, and especially so in the problematization of global hegemony. What is being proposed here is the completion of the global hegemonic equation by a study of the "Trans-Atlantic ruling classes" historical *other*.

In this case, an "isothermal" conception of counter-hegemonic leadership will focus on the lateral connections that bind social forces across national boundaries, as well as the attempt by states (from the Third World) to produce a common front against the ontological and operational bases of hegemonic global regimes. If as Craig Murphy argues, "regimes reflect a more or less shared ideological consensus among those who consciously contribute to them,"[28] then the concerted effort at disarticulating them has been the product of an ideological counter-consensus. While the approach adopted here is not conducive to an etiology of global leadership, it does pay particular attention to the deep socio-economic and cultural structures which inform global politics. Yet, the considerable stress placed on social forces at the level of global civil society does not mean national particularities must be abandoned. On the contrary, careful attention must be paid to the deep structures of national social formations.

As we proceed to Jamaica, it will become increasingly clear that the resistance and counter-hegemony of the People's National Party was very much rooted in some pervasive cultural and ideological forces in civil society. Moreover, it is precisely these forces and their concrete political expression in the form of social movements, combined with pressures from the extant world order, that impelled Jamaican leadership far beyond its material capabilities. Further, the balance of these forces have, per force, conditioned the vicissitudes of Jamaican foreign policy from "astute deference" (under the JLP) to counter-hegemonic leadership on the global front (under the PNP). It is for these reasons also that the two following chapters undertake a thorough examination of the deep structures and social forces of Jamaica.

# 5

---

## The Making of Modern Jamaica and the Emergence of Exceptionalism

### Social Forces in the Struggle Over Hegemony

The two foregoing chapters suggested that foreign policy is essentially conditioned by a configuration of domestic social forces, world order pressures, and the form of state. Now it is necessary to identify, describe, and conceptualize those domestic social forces which informed the making of Jamaican foreign policy. In so doing, the triangular framework of ideas, institutions, and material capabilities will be used as a heuristic device.

While the analysis of social forces might have close resemblance to what is usually known as *inputs* to foreign policy, the concern here is less instrumental in nature. Without doubt, social forces do often translate themselves into organized entities which make demands on the state through the politics of aggregation and the influence of pressure groups. But "instrumentalism" all too often reifies proximate circumstances into causal variables, thereby obfuscating the structural and conjunctural forces operating in the social formation. In contradistinction, the primary concern here is to establish the "limits of the possible," that is, the broad parameters which are defined by social forces and structural conditions. Only when this is done can proximate circumstances be rendered historically intelligible.

The principal domestic social forces relevant to the making of Jamaican foreign policy during the decades of the 1960s and 1970s were social classes, organized labor, racial consciousness, and derivatively, the politics of identity, nationalism, anti-imperialism, students, intellectuals, the established Church, and the media. As we proceed, it will become obvious that there is considerable reciprocity among these forces in terms of their structural determination and institutional expression, as well as in their interests. As such the analysis of Rastafarianism, the "rude boys" or "Rudies," the unemployed, "unprotected workers," Black Power groups, Young Socialist League (YSL), and the Abeng group will reveal a conspicuous *overdetermination* of race, class, color, cultural nationalism, and anti-imperialism. In fact, as we shall see presently, the very social structure of Jamaica is, in the words of Stuart Hall, "massively overdetermined" by race, color, and class. On the external front, the social forces which figured prominently in the making of Jamaican foreign policy were multinational capital, multilateral institutions, transnational cultural forces, Third World "solidarism," hegemonic discourses originating in the North Atlantic countries, and more generally, the forces of imperialist intervention.

## Plantation Economy and Society: The Making of the *Longue Durée*

In his classic work *Persistent Poverty*, George Beckford distinguishes among plantation system, economy, and society. To begin, he draws on W. O. Jones' definition of a plantation, namely:

> A plantation is an economic unit producing agricultural commodities (field crops or horticultural products, but not livestock) for sale and employing a relatively large number of unskilled laborers whose activities are closely supervised. Plantations usually employ a year round labor crew of some size, and they usually specialize in the production of only one or two marketable products. They differ from other kinds of farms in the way in which the factors of production, primarily management and labor, are combined.[1]

In the case of slavery, the plantation as an economic unit clearly combined management and labor in extreme polarities. The only task of labor was to follow direct orders given by those who controlled the plantation apparatus. The *plantation system* according to Beckford, refers ". . . to the totality of institutional arrangements surrounding the production and marketing of plantation crops."[2] Two general categories of relations define the *systemic* specificity of the plantation system. Beckford describes these as internal and external relations.

Internally, the plantation is a *system* because of its total control of "... all aspects of the lives of people within its territory."[3] For our purposes here, the important point to underline is the way in which a white planter class and, if we add the political functionaries of Crown, a white ruling class, took upon itself the task of defining the basic assumptions, values, norms, objectives, and in fact, the very rationality of early Jamaican society. In the words of Philip Curtin, "Jamaica as a society was not only molded by the plantation economy, it was created by it."[4] At the external level, the systemic component is defined by the country's links to the international capitalist system. More specifically, "the external dimension derives from two characteristics of plantation production—its export orientation and foreign ownership...."[5] Later in this chapter, it will be shown how these two dimensions have not only survived, but became critical to the articulation of counter-discourses (by nationalist and anti-imperialist protest groups), as well as the material bases occasioning specific foreign policy positions. In this particular instance, Andre Gunder Frank's notion of "continuity in change" as a fundamental feature of dependent economies, is remarkably poignant.

Generally, there are two types of plantation economies. First, some economies are characterized by plantations which are poorly integrated with the rest of the economy. The level of horizontal integration is very low resulting in minimal domestic economic benefits. The plantation, therefore, exists as a self-sufficient enterprise and has all the features of what are known as "enclave economies." In the case of Jamaica, this was hardly the case, although sugar was and has been characterized by vertical integration. Yet, when we come to the post-1945 period, the concept of enclave economy might prove useful in analyzing the bauxite/alumina and tourist industries.

The second type of plantation economy is the ideal type in which the entire national economy is fully integrated with plantation enterprises. If we use Beckford's criteria for the identification of plantation economies, we will find that in virtually every category Jamaica not only qualifies, but also falls in the fully integrated type, at least up to the World War II. Among these criteria are:

[P]lantation share of national economic aggregates, such as total output, capital, land area in cultivation, income, and employment; plantation contribution to government revenues,

and the country's foreign exchange earnings; evidence of
effects of the plantation on social and political structure
and organization; and evidence of . . . a general plantation
psychology.[6]

*Plantation society*, according to Beckford, refers to the totality
of the plantation (as a social institution), the plantation system,
*and* the plantation economy. This detour on the multiple and complex nature of the plantation was necessary for us to broach the
problem of social structure from both a synchronic and diachronic
perspective, where the former refers to the *longue durée* elements
(pace Fernand Braudel), and the latter, to the process of formation
and change in these structures. What is more, this slave plantation
society left an indelible imprint on the economic, political, cultural,
and social topography of the country.

The slave mode of production was dominated by a small number of European (predominantly British, after 1655) planters and
Crown officials at the apex of the social, economic, and political
pyramid. At the bottom was the mass of black slaves brought
from Africa via the slave trade to work on sugar plantations. Free
whites made up an intermediary group.[7] Also belonging to this
middle group, though not politically empowered, was an increasing "colored" (or brown) population. The latter group emerged
largely as a consequence of the shortage of white women. It was
not unusual, therefore, for the white planters to have black slave
mistresses, invariably under the rubric of live-in domestics. The
misigenated offsprings, of course, were lighter in color and by
virtue of this fact alone were automatically elevated up the social
ladder. Sociologically, status was also conferred upon them because they were spared the harshest kinds of field work. Under
the circumstances, it was quite the norm for black slave women
to aspire to become the mistress of a white planter or overseer.
This was almost an insurance policy that their children would not
suffer a fate similar to their own, or that of other people who were
"genuinely black."

A number of factors developed and consolidated during the
preemancipation period would prove to be *longue durée*, that is,
structural components of Jamaican society. And surely, while some
of these have been transformed and/or recombined, they still mark
the broad outlines of ideas, institutions, and material capacities.

## Postwar Transformations

Although the dependent character of the Jamaican economy persisted in the postwar period, there were some fundamental changes which substantively transformed the structure of the political economy. Up to the Second World War, the British government consistently blocked the call of Jamaican nationalists for industrialization of the economy. But in the wake of the 1938 rebellion on the island, and political protest throughout the Caribbean, the Moyne Commission recommended, *inter alia*, economic diversification which would lead to growth. It was hoped that this would alleviate unemployment and the political unrest associated with it. This coincided with the "import substitution" and the "industrialization by invitation" model advocated by the Nobel laureate economist, Arthur Lewis.

According to Lewis, the limited size of domestic markets meant that industrial development could only be feasible if production was targeted for exports. Secondly, given the shortage of domestic capital it was necessary to open the economy to foreign capital.[8] This thesis was supported by the nationalist movement. The heavy interpenetration of different factions of capital, merged as they are through family ties, reduced political friction. Further, this was entirely consistent with American foreign economic policy which sought the destruction of the British sterling area.[9]

Thus, the industrialization of the Jamaican economy was made possible by a fit among a number of seemingly disparate domestic and global forces. To reiterate, this particular form of industrialization satisfied: (a) the nationalist movement which was steeped in "progress and stability"; (b) domestic capital which was heavily interlocked, and which saw the opportunity for furthering its economic interests, especially in commerce and services which would be the inevitable backwash from rapid industrialization; (c) the British government, which saw industrialization as a strategy of political cooption of the nationalist movement and simultaneously the containment of popular pressure from below (especially in wake of the 1938 Caribbean labor rebellions on account of widespread unemployment); and (d) the United States, which was effectively replacing Britain as the dominant global power, and which saw free trade and foreign investment as keys to the emerging world order.[10]

In 1951, a Ten Year Plan which emphasized the development of the manufacturing sector was adopted. In keeping with this, the

Jamaica Industrial Development Corporation was founded in the same year by the JLP government. The PNP followed this up in 1956 with two key pieces of legislation—the Industrial Incentives Law and the Export Industry Encouragement Law. Jamaica was now on its way from coffee, bananas, and "king sugar" to furniture, metal products, chemicals, food processing, garments, footwear, and most of all, bauxite and alumina, the latter spearheaded by Canadian and American multinational investments.[11] Between 1950 and 1962 the economy expanded at an astounding average rate of 7.5 percent. This was especially the case in the first few years when the growth rate was in excess of 10 percent, with a gradual (but still high) tapering off from 1958. Gross Domestic Product (at constant prices), for example, grew at 11.3 percent in 1954; 10.0 percent in 1955; 10.3 percent in 1956; and a fantastic 14.5 percent in 1957. And, while there was a massive dip in 1958 to a meager 1.4 percent, there was a relatively buoyant turn around in 1959 and 1960, with 5.7 percent and 6.5 percent respectively. Moreover, when the figures are disaggregated into contribution by sectors, there is strong evidence of economic modernization, and a pattern of relative decline in agriculture.

## The Consequences of Rapid Industrialization

A number of consequences were to follow from this structural transformation of the political economy, some of which would form the social bases for the emergence of Democratic Socialism in 1972 and, more specifically, directly condition the foreign policy of the country. A brief examination of some of these will suffice for now.

To begin with, while there was a remarkable rise in the standard of living defined in terms of a much higher per capita GNP (from 15.1 pounds sterling in 1938 to 136.7 by 1962), there was also an appreciable concentration of wealth in the society. Thus, while the share of "Earnings of Employees" as a percentage of factor income earned in the creation of the GNP dropped a few points (from 50.4 to 48.1) between 1953 and 1961, there was a 160 percent rise in the share of "Earnings of Resident Corporations."[12] The JLP government acknowledged this in the 1963–1968 Development Plan, stating that ". . . available evidence shows that there are serious imbalances in income distribution in Jamaica which require urgent attention."[13]

The concentration of corporate wealth was matched by an in-creasing concentration of land and, concomitantly, by massive dis-possession of small farmers and tenant holders. To begin with, land tenure in Jamaica has historically been skewed, with the largest and best land held by a few wealthy concerns, while the smaller and less arable land is distributed thinly among peasants and smaller farmers. During the industrial expansion, we find the total number of farms dropping (from 189,906 in 1954 to 158, 941 in 1961) while the average acreage was on the increase. The amal-gamation of farms holdings was accompanied by centralization of ownership. Government statistics showed that:

> In 1954, 18.6 percent of all farms were part-owned, part-rented, and by 1961 this proportion had been reduced to 11.4 percent..., [and],... in farms of under twenty-five acres, the proportion of holdings part-owned, part-rented, had fallen from 43.7 percent to 24.9 percent between 1954 and 1961.[14]

This concentration of land holding and ownership in an economy where 37 percent of the population depends on agriculture for its livelihood (or if defined more broadly as "primary industry"—48.9 percent) resulted in massive rural to urban migration. Between 1943 and 1960, the population of Kingston increased by 86 percent, de-spite the heavy migration to Britain during the 1950s.[15] Given the low rate of employment absorption in the industrial sector due to capital intensive accumulation, unemployment became a serious problem. By 1960 unemployment was already 13 percent but, what is more, the rate for Kingston was 19 percent, and St. Andrew 16 percent; the figure for other parishes (i.e., mostly rural) was closer to 11 percent.[16] This would eventually unleash some powerful social forces which future governments would have to reckon with, not the least being the PNP between 1972 and 1980. In 1963, the conserva-tive JLP government was already admitting that "unemployment is clearly the major social and economic problem in Jamaica,"[17] un-aware that this was just a portent of a major "political time bomb" waiting to explode. As a matter of fact, the marginalized began to emerge as a real fetter on the pace and depth of modernization.

Another consequence of the immediate postwar transformation was the gradual shift of the Jamaican economy from Britain to the United States. While Jamaica would remain a British colony until

August 1962, there is clear indication in the 1950s of a gradual
shift from the colonial power to Canada and the USA. This was,
*inter alia*, expressed in a changing of trade and investment patterns. Thus,

> Whereas in 1953, 55% of imports originated in the sterling
> area, in 1962 the figure had dropped to 39%. The percent-
> age of imports coming from the dollar area increased from
> 33% in 1953 to 42% in 1962. On the other hand, the per-
> centage of exports going to the sterling area decreased from
> 62% to 30% while exports to the dollar area increased from
> 31% to 58%.[18]

Politically, Jamaica also began to identify more and more with the
United States. While this was in part due to official U.S. support
for decolonization, it also had to do with a more pervasive Ameri-
canization of Jamaican society, especially among the upper strata
of the society. During the 1960s this process would continue, albeit
with a distinctive new political dimension, namely, the influence of,
and identification with, the civil rights movement.

**The Modern Social Structure**

The social structure of Jamaican society is characterized by
what Anthony Payne calls a "polarized and discordant class system," and equally, by a sharp division of labor based on race and
color. The relationship between race and class is symbiotic and
structural rather than contingent, deriving as it does from the
institutions of slavery and plantation society.

Recall that in the preemancipation period, a relatively small
number of Europeans were at the top of the social and political
pyramid, while at the bottom were the mass of blacks brought from
Africa as slaves to work on sugar plantations; free whites made up
an intermediary group. After emancipation in 1838, large portions
of the black (ex-slave) labor force left the plantations, creating a
labor shortage. The planters responded by importing East Indian
indentured labor as they did for the rest of the Caribbean (especially in Guyana and Trinidad).[19] The East Indians joined the ex-
slaves at the bottom of the social rung in Jamaica and have basically
remained there, excepting for the much later addition of the "Bombay

merchants" and professionals who now form part of the upper middle class.

Also forming part of the middle groups are the Syrians, Lebanese, Chinese, and Jews, who along with the recently arrived "Bombay Indians," dominate the tertiary sector. While some members of these groups are engaged directly in production, for the most part they are principally merchants and occupy an important position in imports/exports. The Chinese, in particular, have disproportionate representation in retailing, while a good deal of recently arrived Indians are in the medical profession. Along with these groups are the older middle group of coloreds who have consistently migrated up the social ladder, populating a significant section of the civil service; they are also heavily presenced in management. Finally, we may add to the middle groups, educated blacks who also hold key positions in government, the civil service, management, the professions, and, increasingly after World War II, into small business.

## Class, Race, Color, and Hegemony

If indeed the 1938 labor rebellion inaugurated "modern Jamaica"[20] as is generally acknowledged, it certainly did not mark a clean break with some of the most pervasive and deeply rooted cultural and political circumstances of the country. Rex Nettleford's observation about the Caribbean, ". . . that the more things change the more they have remained the same," is particularly germane to Jamaica in the areas of social values and culture.[21] In this section, an attempt is made to demonstrate the way in which the modernizing thrust of dependent capitalist development fermented with some of the more "authoritarian" and "elitist" elements rooted in the society to produce a hegemonic social formation.[22] Methodologically, this calls for careful attention to the continuity, transformation, and recombination of elements constituting the historical structure. What follows will set the stage for further analysis of the dialectic of domination and hegemony on one hand, and resistance and counter-hegemony on the other. This discussion will also examine the overdetermination of race and class, and will point to some of the marginalized sources of discontent.

The relationship among class, race, and color in the Caribbean in general, and Jamaica in particular, received one of its earliest and most systematic treatments by the distinguished sociologist

M. G. Smith. Drawing on the work of the economist J. S. Furnivall, who had written extensively on the colonies of the Far East, Smith purported that Caribbean societies were cultural concatenations constituted through distinct cultural *sections*, with distinctive institutions, world views, and to some extent, political practices. These separate cultural enclaves were held together by a political system which was first imposed by the colonial power, and subsequently maintained by the dominant section.[23] For Smith, therefore, Caribbean societies were inscribed through *cultural pluralism*. With specific reference to Jamaica, he examined a whole range of institutions—kinship and marriage; religious forms; education and occupation; economic institutions; property; marketing; law; government; language; recreational patterns; material culture; and value systems. His analysis led him to specify three general cultural sections, namely, "white," "brown," and "black," with the first of these at the apex of the stratification system, and blacks at the bottom. At first glance this categorization seems to posit a division based solely on race. In anticipation of such criticism, Smith provided the following caveat:

> Although it is difficult to state the precise significance of racial difference in a few words, it can be said categorically that *race and its symbol, color, do play a very important part in structuring relations between individuals within Jamaica....*[24]

He was equally careful on the question of color. The latter, he argues, does not have a *logically necessary* sociological import, and must be understood in terms of its structural determination in the society. As he put it:

> The structural dimension consists in those factors and aspects of social process, and the relations between them, that give the society its distinctive form as an arrangement of units and processes. Thus the structural dimension is an abstract analytic category reflecting the distributions and types of power, authority and knowledge, and wealth, which together define and constitute the social framework. When we speak of structural color, we imply an allocation of these variables among—differentiated groups which obtains presently and reflects historical conditions.[25]

Notwithstanding charges of cultural determinism and the analytic "repression" of social classes, both of which have considerable merits, Smith actually was able to arrest the force of race and color in the making of the class structure, and the structural position of European values within the society. It is important to recognize this, given that the process of class formation during import substitution industrialization reproduced and further consolidated the racial and color elements critical to previous historical structures defined in terms of ideas, institutions, and material conditions.

Recall that the division of labor in the plantation/slave mode of production was strictly defined by race, and that in the postemancipation period, race and color were *generative principles* in the determination of the social structure, and of the discourses and practices of status which obtained.[26] The continuity of these generative principles in the postwar period and the cultural pluralism of Smith is well captured in the *Report on the Conference on Social Development* which states that:

> ... if we take an inventory of the present Jamaican population, classifying each individual by economic status, by color and by any other information we could obtain about his attitude and pattern of life, we should find that these items of our classification were not distributed at random but that at one end of the income scale we found people who were poor, propertyless, black, in unskilled occupations, distrustful of police, living in common law unions and attending churches of local origin, while at the other end of the income scale would be people who were rich, white, in managerial or professional jobs, firm supporters of the police, legally married, and adherents of "respectable" churches.[27]

Despite this conspicuous *correlation* among race, color, class, and culture, and the social conflicts which emanate from their multiple contradictions, there is considerable dispute about the causal lines of connection. An overview of the contending claims and propositions is in order here.

Carl Stone, using what accounts to a relative deprivation model, argues that while Jamaica does have a distinctive class system due to the legacy of colonialism, social conflict is more akin to class, rather than race antagonism. For Stone, the society is stratified on the basis of material possession; it is the unequal distribution of economic wealth that generates conflict. He calls into question Smith's proposition that conflict is a function of the inability of the social system to "culturally assimilate" blacks.[28] To his thinking, the problem is defined by the failure of the *political system* to distribute goods and services to the dispossessed masses who are also black. The notion that it is the political system's failure is used in quite a specialized sense by Stone, since he sees Jamaican society as heavily dominated by clientelism. Given the lack of input and influence in the political system by the marginalized African-descended masses, they are thus excluded from the chief distribution mechanisms, namely, the two main political parties. In an argument that resembles that of the Marxist Ken Post, however, he points out that the expression of material dispossession is racial in character, that is to say, economic oppression takes on the form of racial antagonism. He explains:

> Perceptions of race conflict are rooted in the unequal distribution of material affluence between the racial groups. Affluent racial minorities such as whites and Chinese are consequently perceived by the black dispossessed in terms of having antagonistic interests, viz., those strata. The findings support the view that attitudes towards these privileged racial minorities are more akin to class perceptions than to racial orientations based on a preoccupation with racial prejudice and discrimination.[29]

A far more radical departure from Smith, and for that matter, from most of the scholarship on Jamaica, is that of the South African scholar, Adam Kuper, who argues that the relationship among race, color, and class is a thing of the past.[30] In direct a attack on the theoretical apparatus of cultural pluralism, Kuper insists that there are no clear cultural differences among Smith's "cultural sections," "whatever the differences in style and opportunity."[31] And, if race and color exercise an influence on class, status, and political power at all, it is very subtle, ambiguous and fading. He substantiates his argument by pointing to the rise of black civil servants and, in particular, black political leaders.

The question of color is not a trivial one in Jamaica, for as suggested earlier, it does have an impact on all manner of social relationships. In fact, a detailed ethnographic study in the mid

1950s found definite relationships among race, class, and color, where the latter would often mediate the first two categories. From his study of 322 adults at Runaway Bay, Council Taylor found that respondents could identify twenty-two colors/shades, "white" being the most prestigious and "hugly black" (*sic*) the least. It is worthy of note that "hugly black" and its two other runner up categories "black" and "Negro" refer not only to color qua color, but to "kinky hair," broad nose, and thick lips.[32]

Given this penetration of race and color in Jamaican society, it is highly suspect, therefore, for Kuper to so whimsically dismiss their relevance as things of the past. In fact, he succumbs to a kind of legal reification, since his point of departure is that "the law" does not discriminate on the basis of race and color. Of course, this is also the official position of successive Jamaican governments, not the least of them, the JLP administrations between 1962 and 1972.

Notwithstanding these differences, Smith, Stone, and Kuper seem to have a great deal in common in respect to class, race, and color. Thus, while all three see the basic structure of the society formed in slavery with the heavy preponderance of race and color on class, in the modern period all three seem to play down the constitutive function of class, especially when it comes to relations of subordination.

Stone is openly critical of Marxists, and this, with sharpened leverage against those who attempt to derive class domination out of production relations. For him, Marxist class analysis is too economic determinist; it is on this basis also that he boldly dismisses any notion of a Jamaican ruling class as "meaningless."[33] In his "distributionist model," no social class (or more appropriately no sector) has exclusive access, *as a class/sector*, to political and economic power. As noted earlier, for Stone, inequality is more a function of ineffective distribution written into the system of clientelism. His "proof" that it is not class domination that characterizes the social order is found in the absence of the "upper class" in the state machinery. This position is evidently informed by a restricted concept of state which reduces the latter to the apparatus of government. Alternatively, a wider conception of state which includes the considerations of the relative autonomy and "ideological apparatuses" of the state in capitalist societies, as outlined in chapters two and three, would suggest that there is nothing peculiar about the institutional expression of the form of state in Jamaica and the place of those who own and control private property in it.

Smith is similarly apprehensive about class and, in fact, "about the very existence of classes themselves," as Charles Mills points out.[34] In the pluralist *problematic* it appears as if "cultural sections" constitute fully *self-contained* "economies" which are not only separate and distinct, but also mutually exclusive. Given the comprehensive range of institutions considered by Smith it would appear that each "section" is a self-contained and self-sufficient space. The nature of the linkage in this problematic is one of *co-existence*, a proposition which amounts to saying that since blacks, browns, and whites live in their own worlds, it is impossible for relations of exploitation and subordination to exist among them.

The issue here is that the cultural pluralist problematic obfuscates, in fact denies, the generative consequences of social classes and simply grafts it on to the explanation only *after* the sanctity of culture has been theoretically secured. This privileging of culture as the *determinant instance* disallows recognition of what Stuart Hall calls "the absolutely distinctive feature of Caribbean society," namely, that "its stratification systems and the relations between social groups are massively overdetermined."[35] Noting that it is this "overdetermined complexity" that needs to be analyzed, Hall proceeds to flesh out one the most important theoretical pitfalls of the pluralist thesis. He writes:

> It does not help . . . to depress some factors of this matrix, e.g., race/color, class, in favor of others, e.g., culture, and then, analytically, to subsume the former into the latter, since it is precisely the generative specificity of each, plus, the overdetermined complexity of the whole, which is the problem.[36]

Clearly, Smith's problem here is one of assuming that elements of the structure are relationally contiguous but do not exist as a *structural combinatory*.[37] That is to say, each element or section, develops independently as an institutional materiality and, only after each is formed into a *closed entity*, is it brought into some kind of relation with the other elements or sections. As in the case of Stone, the dominant relation is *formal* in nature, insofar, as it is the political system which articulates the disparate groups into society. Yet it is the specificity of this political system, and the society it maintains, that really needs to be understood in greater detail.

## The Hegemonic Bloc and the Ideology of Exceptionalism on the Eve of the 1970s

The discussion of the power and power relations in Jamaica, thus far, has been of a general and theoretical nature. At this point it may be useful to provide more objective and empirical information on the society on the eve of the 1970s. Particular attention will be given to the composition of the "business class," the established church, and the media, given the importance of these three "forces" in the reproduction of power in the country. Having done that, we will be in a better position to proceed with the operationalization of hegemonic practices as lived experience.

### The Established Church

The established church has a long history in Jamaica, dating back to the days of slavery. Throughout this history it has been characterized by two features. First, the priesthood has always been dominated by foreigners and, up to 1962, the Church of England served as the legal and authoritative referent of religious "knowledge." The second characteristic of the church is that the priesthood has exercised considerable influence in virtually all aspects of Jamaican life.[38] Careful examination of one comprehensive source (*Who's Who, Jamaica—1969*), which might also be read as a *registry* of the upper classes, shows in staggering fashion that the foreign orientation of the church had barely changed in the years following independence. Subsequent analysis will demonstrate the role played by the church in the cultural war of position during the postwar period.

*Who's Who, Jamaica—1969* profiles seventy one Ordained Ministers of the Christian Church; no faith of non-European origins is included despite the fact that there are several other forms of religious practices. Of the seventy one Ministers, thirty seven were of the Catholic Church. Thus Catholic priests made up more than half of the established priesthood (recorded in *Who's Who*).

First, more than half of the Ministers (all the denominations combined) *were born outside* Jamaica; twenty-eight were born in the United States, and eleven in the United Kingdom. Of those born in Jamaica most had studied in Britain or the U.S., and some were of ethnic backgrounds consistent with the "brown-man" power elite in Jamaica. This is significant in a country where ethnic background

and color are key signs of worth, and especially so when the established Ministers of the Church are not only resistant to social and
cultural change, but are seen as carriers of Anglo-Christian hegemony.

Secondly, the problem of foreignness becomes more acute once
it is recognized that of the thirty-seven Catholic Ministers in the
"registry of power" only nine were Jamaican born. Of the twenty-
eight born overseas, twenty seven were born in the U.S., and of
these, all excepting two, were born in the state of Massachusetts.
This was extra-ordinary for a country that is overwhelmingly non-
Catholic. The registry showed the same situation (of foreignness)
for the other denominations. Ten of the twenty two non-Catholic
Ministers were born in the United Kingdom. One Catholic Minister
came from Northern Ireland.

The entries under the category of Ministers of the Church gives
a good indication of the status of "high European churches" in
Jamaica. Clearly, the "official churches" are presented as the keepers of religious morality, while indigenous religions are very much,
if not completely, ignored. "High European Christianity" is part of
the ruling ideology as is evidenced in its popularity with the political leadership. Thus Rex Nettleford writes:

> Political leaders have repeatedly declared Jamaica to be a
> "Christian country." Political creeds are given Christian
> sources of origin or inspiration when they are to be promul-
> gated and "sold" to the general mass of people. Europe here
> again reigns.[39]

Religious practices which have an African heritage, such as
Kumina, Pocomania, and Rastafarianism, are marginalized through
silence or outright attacks. This marginalization has been inten-
tional, since the "Afro-centric" religions became a basis for possible
cultural/political mobilization against a semi-authoritarian state
during the decade of the 1960s. Outside of the political question,
the established Christian churches in Jamaica have a long history
of "supremacist" tendencies, vis-à-vis other forms of religious practices. Taken as a whole, these churches must be understood as part
of the hegemonic historic bloc.

### The Economic Ruling Class

As discussed earlier, there is a very high correlation between
race and class in Jamaica. This race/class relationship is politically
and culturally intensified on account of the fact that a large section

of the Jamaican ruling class is actually foreign. Analysis of the
*Who's Who* (1969) provides strong evidence of this.

Of the seven hundred and sixty entries under the categories—
Company Director, Managing Director, Director, Proprietor, Busi-
nessman, Business Executive, Planter/Farmer, Industrialist,
Financier, and Chairman, two hundred and twenty-six (that is,
one-third) were born outside Jamaica. Of these expatriate "businessmen," one hundred and seventy-eight were born in Europe or
North America—with the U.S. and U.K. as the largest sources.
Eight were born in the Middle East, four in India, with one each
from the Philippines, Mauritius, and Nigeria. The remainder were
from the Caribbean. Some of the most powerful families of the
ruling class, such as the Alexanders, Ashenheims, Mahfoods, Chin
Sees, Bovells, Bicknells, Brahams, Brandons, Brandts, Changs,
Harts, Fletchers, Chens, Chin-Loys, Chin Yees, de Lissers, Henriques, Issacs, Issas, Lais, Levys, Marzoucas and of course the
Matalons, are clearly of foreign, non-black backgrounds. Judging
from photographs in the registry of power (i.e., *Who's Who,
Jamaica—1969*), it would be rather difficult to know that Jamaica
is a predominantly "black country."

The fact that a large section of the ruling class is foreign by
birth is of considerable significance in Jamaican politics, and as
will be demonstrated later, has in fact impacted on Jamaican foreign policy. Thus, surveys by W. Bell and J. Gibson have found that
the majority of the "economic elites" see themselves as "Europeans"
or "Euro-Americans."[40] The consequence of this has been threefold.
First, the fact that economic elites have great access to the state
apparatus gives them considerable influence in the making of public policy, foreign policy included. Secondly, the cultural values of
the foreign elite, in conjunction with the acceptance of these values
by the local elite, and coupled with the influence of the recognized
churches, and foreign media (especially American TV), became a
major force in defining what Jamaica "is" and "is not." These social
forces have invariably seen Jamaica as a Western, Christian, and
anti-communist country, which offers opportunity to all irrespective of race, class, or color; Obika Gray has referred to this representation of Jamaica as the ideology of "exceptionalism." The third
partial consequence of "foreignness," and concomitantly the ideology of exceptionalism, is that it spawned considerable resentment
and became the basis for a sustained cultural war of position
by the marginalized. Later on, it will be shown the ways in
which "foreign policy" was influenced by aspects of this cultural
contestation.

The elite should not be seen as a monolithic since, even within
this class, questions of race, color, and origin do bear upon perceptions, attitudes, and behavior. Data collected over a sixteen year
period by different researchers (but using the same methods) provide useful information in this regard. The project was begun by
Charles C. Moskos Jr., who did surveys in 1958 and 1961–62, and
was subsequently taken up by Wendell Bell and J. William Gibson
Jr. in 1974. It is interesting to note here that the research project
began by selecting respondents listed in *Who's Who, Jamaica*. In
general, the early surveys found the elite to be extremely pro-
western in its attitude to international affairs, strongly attached to
economic liberalism, quite authoritarian in political culture, and
very much "Anglo-European" in terms of cultural identity.

In the same year that Jamaica got its sovereignty from the
U.K., twenty-one percent of the elite respondents strongly objected
to an independent Jamaica and another twenty-nine percent were
"reluctant."[41] This negative attitude toward independence (that is,
national sovereignty) was consistent with the elite's political/cul-
tural perceptions of the marginalized as expressed in their responses
to political identification. Thus, twenty-six percent felt that voters
are "incompetent and that democracy is not suitable;" an equal
number (Cynical Parliamentarians) said that democracy is suitable
but voters are "incompetent," and nine percent felt that while voters are competent, democracy is not suitable (for Jamaica and
Jamaicans). On the other hand "Full Democrats"—those who believe voters are competent and democracy suitable, stood at thirty-
nine percent. The staggering thing about these attitudes and
perceptions is that, as late as 1974, there was practically no change.
Whereas the 1961–1962 survey found a paltry thirty-nine percent
of "Full Democrats," in 1974 that figure was forty percent. To
emphasize the point, therefore, two years into the first administration of Michael Manley, sixty percent of the Jamaican elite were
self-confessed "Authoritarians" of one sort or the other. It is
significant to note that the same survey revealed sixty three percent of the elite defined their "cultural identity" as "Anglo-European,"
while the other thirty seven percent considered themselves "West
Indians/Jamaicans."

The political and cultural orientation of the elite corresponded
with its attitude to Jamaica's international relations. On the eve of
independence, the Moskos survey found that seventy-one percent
of the elite preferred alignment with "Western nations," with only
twenty-six percent favoring association with "neutralist countries."
The cultural dimension of this orientation was very much under-

scored by the reasons given by one respondent who stated that: "We have three hundred years of association with Western culture. On the whole it has served us well. Little of our inheritance is bad."[42] The 1974 survey showed a marked redefinition of alignment preferences among the elite. Whereas in 1961–1962 "Western nations" were preferred by seventy-one percent of the elite, by 1974 that figure dropped to thirty-six percent. In part this may have resulted from the addition of two categories in the choice of preferences, namely, "Jamaican self-interest" and "the Third World." Careful examination of the data would also suggest, however, that despite the significant reduction in the preference for "Western nations," there was strong continuity in what may be called "Anglo-European" orientation. A solid indicator of this orientation is that preference for the West still recorded the highest score. The elite thus rated "Jamaican self-interest" *lower* than "Western nations" in their international priority! Of equal significance, the 1974 survey also led to the determination that, "despite the general trend, changes were greater for some subgroups than for others, the largest shifts away from the West occurring among older, more highly educated, brown and black, and relatively less wealthy elites."[43]

In general, the "ethnic minority elites" still favored Western nations. The reasons for this continuity are complex. For the moment, however, it is important to recognize that one reason for "elite dependency" on the West has to do with the question of the security of elite ethnic minorities, vis-à-vis the demographically dominant "black masses." This "minority" had traditionally looked to the British government for protection (in the preindependence period), and then increasingly, to the United States of America in the post-1962 period. The problem here is that the concept "minority" in the case of Jamaica is one of (historical and institutional) power and privilege, rather than exploitation and exclusion normally associated with minorities.

It is precisely this economic privilege, and its political and cultural defense by the elite, that partly defined the antagonisms and the sustained war of position which were becoming evident by the early 1960s. In this "war," the elites found a ready and willing ally in the media.

## The Media

The media (both domestic and international) constitute a significant social force and must be understood in the context of the larger cultural and socio-economic struggles under consideration.

To begin with, the local media are owned and controlled within the "twenty-one families." Two of the major newspapers, the *Star* and *Daily Gleaner* (the latter being the oldest, largest, and most reputable daily), are owned by the Gleaner Co., ". . . which is controlled by established wealthy institutions and groups of the society." The third news paper, *Jamaica Daily News* is owned by a company in which the US-based ITT has thirty percent of the shares, and one radio station is "70% owned by Rediffusion Ltd. of the U.K."[45] Apart from the question of ownership, the international media, mainly, *Time Magazine* and *Newsweek* (both U.S. based), also played significant roles which are consistent with American global hegemonic practices. It should be noted that the publicly owned Jamaica Broadcasting Corporation was used by the Manley government in the 1970s to advance the cause of Democratic Socialism which was declared in 1974.

The *Daily Gleaner* is a bastion of conservative ideology and represents the interests of the dominant classes in Jamaica. The paper has always been the most influential news source in the country and it is generally held that "if it was in the *Gleaner*, it was true."[46] E. H. Stephens and J. D. Stephens observe:

> . . . [T]he paper, which was owned by a conservative segment of the capitalist class and, by and large, represented their views, was an extremely potent political instrument as well as an important element in the apparatus of capitalist ideological domination of the middle and upper-middle classes.[47]

Members of the established church, the planter families, and the bourgeoisie made regular contributions to the *Gleaner*.[48] The thrust of these were to attack Democratic Socialism, black cultural nationalism, and the PNP's foreign policy. A typical *Gleaner* editorial read:

> The fact remains that Jamaica has always been very firmly on the side of the West. Any sudden departure from this, whether it be good or bad, has to upset some people. And those who are most easily upset are those who have investments and money to invest.[49]

Apart from the general conservative disposition informing the *Gleaner*'s editorials and columns, the newspaper took a deliberate position of debasing the legitimacy of the Manley government. The level and nature of this activity were such that leading officials of the PNP, including the Prime Minister, publicly charged the newspaper with being part of an effort to destabilize the democratically elected governments. Manley himself likened the tactics of the *Gleaner* to the Chilean newspaper *El Mercurio*, which was implicated in the 1973 overthrow of the socialist government of Salvador Allende.[50] At the end of it all, it was felt by many that the *Gleaner* played a major role in removing Manley from office. As Jack Johnson-Hill noted, "The diabolical campaign of vilification waged against Manley by class interests in the *Daily Gleaner*, Jamaica's leading newspaper, was perhaps the most decisive (but least recognized) contributing factor to Seaga's victory."[51]

The international media was an important element of the hegemonic coalition. Leading American news sources, including *Time, Newsweek, Miami Herald*, and *U.S. News and World Report* carried out a systematic campaign against the PNP governments during the 1970s. These sources consistently sought to link Manley to Cuba and Castro, communism, dictatorship, and anti-Americanism. Opposition leader Edward Seaga was touted as the one able to save Jamaica from these dangers. The conservative and pro-American Seaga was portrayed as "Harvard educated," adept at economics, and committed to freedom and democracy.[52]

The multinational media exercised its bias not only by commission, but also through omission. According to Johnson-Hill, "...the most incriminating omission of all is the absence of any allusion to race" in a society where race and color are of such importance.[53] As this author points out, "the critical problem of the 'dependency syndrome,' where darker Jamaicans tend to look to lighter leaders of any nationality for 'deliverance,' is simply never broached."[54] This was a significant omission by the media at a time when race, culture, and national identity were major sources of discontent in the country. In part, the exclusion of the racial dimension may have been deliberate and strategic, given the opening up of the PNP to the subject, and the fact that Manley was able to secure the support of the marginalized "sufferers."

## Exceptionalism: The Ideology of the Hegemonic Bloc

As noted in the last chapter, ideology has a constitutive function insofar as it articulates seemingly disparate social, cultural, and economic "instances" into coherent discourses through which identities are formed. Bearing this in mind, as well as Cox's argument that ideologies are historically specific to the social forces which articulate them at a given conjuncture, the argument will now proceed by describing and situating the ideology of the ruling classes in Jamaica. This ideology, which Gray calls "exceptionalism" (or "consensualism"), must be understood dialectically, that is, in its relation to the counter-hegemonic ideologies and practices present during the 1960s in Jamaica.

As Gray points out, the 1960s saw the emergence of social forces in Jamaica which called into question the very ontological foundations of Jamaican society. The challenge developed as a response to the massive dispossession and marginalization of black Jamaicans by a minority ethnic ruling class, in conjunction with the interests of foreign capital. The counter-hegemonic disarticulation was of such depth that the very legitimacy of the Jamaican state was at stake. This challenge from below began at a time when the ruling classes (and groups) were attempting to consolidate their hegemonic leadership. As Gray notes:

> Exceptionalism therefore was both a counter-ideology meant to stem challenges to class inequalities posed by expanding race consciousness, and a means to secure the moral-ideological framework for the country's development strategy.[55]

In essence, exceptionalism was a deliberate and systematic strategy for: (a) mobilizing those social forces which had the most to gain from a defense of the existing system of social relations in the country. This in part meant a "suspension" of whatever antagonisms existed among the ruling groups (for example, between foreign and domestic capital, or between minority ethnic elites and black elites), in the larger "plot" of securing the more general interest of capital as a whole, and (b) delegitimizing and disorganizing the counter-hegemonic social forces through a balanced strategy of consensus and *trasformismo* on the one hand, and coercion on the other.

An even wider view of exceptionalism suggests that it was primarily aimed at securing the political and ideological conditions through which passive revolution may be organized. Given the ruling classes' emphasis on foreign capital for national development, Jamaica could not afford to be seen as a country deeply divided by class and racio-cultural conflict. In the eyes of the bourgeoisie, Jamaica was making rapid progress toward the status of a "middle level country" (a description mentioned every year in its annual address to the United Nations General Assembly), and thus, could not allow any disruption. Accordingly, the ruling classes presented Jamaica ". . . as possessing an exceptional consensual culture which earned it an international reputation for political stability and interracial harmony."[56] This of course is only half the picture, since the sanctity of a hegemonic ideology requires a concurrent debasement of competing ideologies.

In response to those social forces pressing the claims for cultural (black) empowerment and socialism, the Jamaican Labor Party (in office through the decade of the 1960s), as the most organized "agent" of exceptionalism, averred that racial discontent was a thing of the past and, while people may come from different classes, all Jamaicans have equal opportunities. The proof of these claims was that Jamaica is "democratic." Thus, even if there are remnants of racial and class inequalities, exceptionalism counsels that Jamaicans must *continue* to work their problems out *peacefully*. Witness, for example the admonitions of Jamaica's first Prime Minister, Sir Alexander Bustamante:

> In the early days of Jamaica's social and economic revolution, there were two principles that were most important to me. The first was that capital and labor should learn to work together—capital had to learn to respect and be fair to labor. Labor had to learn, in spite of any past advantages taken of workers, that destroying capital would destroy one's hopes of development and thereby destroy labor itself. The second principle was, that people of all races, must learn to live together, work together and respect one another. To me acceptance of both of these principles was not only fundamental but vital to Jamaica's future, if we were to gain a reputation for stability.[57]

Not to be outdone, Norman Washington Manley (Jamaica's second Prime Minister), who insisted during the 1960s that "race is a thing of the past," noted:

> Jamaica's whole future depends upon our reputation for political stability and for sensible government. We live in a competitive world. There is not much capital free to move. Everybody is fighting to get money brought into their country so that you may procure the capital goods which is the

foundation of development. Those countries get help that have reputation for stability, for people will come here and spend their money and develop things because they feel secure.[58]

Clearly, the two Prime Ministers were exponents of representing the interests of minority ethnic elites and capital, in that, although they recognized the growing ranks of the marginalized, their emphasis was on stability. A "war of position" as complex as exceptionalism, however, could not be sufficiently secured by the words of political leaders. In order for a hegemonic *weltanschauung* to be established and reproduced, the state, as principal organizer of this hegemony, needs to secure the resources of all social forces committed to the project of hegemonization. This is so because hegemony becomes embedded through the slow and unrecognizable repetitions of daily life, not through coercive imposition. In the case of Jamaica, this required the constant circulation of the "trafficking symbols" of exceptionalism in all areas of life—work, school, church, media, art forms, national identity, and "foreign affairs," among others. The Jamaican ruling classes needed such a total "quarantine" because the challenge to the JLP government, and more broadly, to the conditions of marginalization, was pervasive. The following chapter maps out this challenge to exceptionalism, a challenge which in the end, led to Democratic Socialism at home, and a democratic socialist foreign policy abroad.

# 6

---

## Counter-Hegemonic Forces

### The Poor in the Making of History

Let us continue with the analysis of those social forces important to the making of modern Jamaican society and to the country's foreign policy. Considerable emphasis is placed on the role of civil society, and especially the poor and the powerless, in explaining external behavior. Although the poor are economically marginalized, when organized in social movements they are entirely capable of mounting a counter-hegemonic challenge to the established order of things. Such a challenge, which shall be called *strategic counter-hegemony*, is critical to the form of state. To fully understand the role of the marginalized in the historical specificity of the form of state, however, the *forms of social protest* must be established. This requires a return to the dialectics of race, culture, and economy, as well as to the dynamics of state/civil society relations. As we press on with the analysis, the confrontations of the local and global will also emerge more clearly. Labor is as good as any group to begin with.

### *The Material Versus the Economic and the Limits of Laborism*

Fernand Braudel's distinction between economic and material life is useful here in specifying more precisely the differences between the unions and established parties on the one hand, and non-traditional counter-hegemonic social forces on the other. In general, the unions limited their struggle to questions of economic betterment—higher wages, improved benefits, and better working conditions. Moreover, the unions had a solid core of established workers whose interest and influence was uppermost in the minds of the union leaders. Most of the non-union groups wanted much broader changes than "economic" benefits. They wanted fundamental changes in the material circumstances of everyday life. While this would involve economic "betterment," the more substantive project was to change that which Braudel calls the "... repeated actions, empirical processes, old methods and solutions handed down...."[1] As we will soon see, a great deal of the resentments from the underprivileged social forces had a far more complex class morality than is usually associated with the "means of production" discourse which was widely accepted by the labor movement in Jamaica.

In general, the labor movement came up against its own limitations in addressing the plight of the poor. To begin with, the high levels of (structural) unemployment meant large sections of poor people were not part of any of the institutions within the realm of collective bargaining or parliamentary politics.[2] Simply put, the great mass of ghetto poor were not union members, nor were they recognized as a legitimate political constituency within the established political parties. The unions had enough of a challenge in allocating resources to union members who were also party members, and the parties themselves were too attached to the middle and upper classes—and foreign capital—to risk systematic incorporation of the urban poor. In fact, it is at this point that some of the economic and cultural interests actually fuse. Not only did the big parties distance themselves from the marginalized in the economic discourses, but they also treated them as dangerous and destabilizing. Later on, although M. Manley and the PNP made some significant steps toward including the marginalized, he ultimately failed because of the overall structure of power in the country and, in particular, within the party. The evacuation of this space left an opening for other groups to fill the void. This void in fact had been there for a long time, nurtured as it were by the hegemonic ideology of exceptionalism.

## The "Lumpenproletariat" and the "Rude Boys"

During the 1960s, it became increasingly evident that exceptionalism was failing to incorporate (or interpellate) the urban poor. Apart from the Rastafarians, who had already established a culture of resistance, two other groups began to articulate discourses of what might be called "subaltern anti-exceptionalism." One section of the marginalized, the lumpenproletariat, though not necessarily organized, emerged from the "hard core unemployed," and principally from the ghettos of West Kingston; the other was made up largely of youths (mostly male) from the ghettos. While both groups were influenced by Rastafarian ideology and black consciousness, they had some distinctive features about them.

The lumpen anti-exceptionalists did not have a coherent ideology as did the Rastas, and as such, did not quite form a social movement engaged in organized resistance to the hegemonic practices. Nonetheless, through the daily routine of lived experience, the "way of life" of this section of the urban poor amounted to a fundamental rejection of the values, norms, habits, manners, and more generally, the sensibility of the middle and upper classes. Obika Gray captures this neatly:

> ... the militant hard-core unemployed, who existed outside the confines of all the "normalizing" institutions of the society, developed a sub-culture of alienation. This outlook was at once anomic and ideologically antagonistic in its assault on the standards of civic virtue and the modes of bourgeois respectability being deployed by the political leadership and the upper class. To the latter's status of superiority, paternalism, and insistence on deference, the lumpenproletariat responded with an antagonistic nihilism. They defied political authority, rejected the dominant cultural sensibility, and affirmed ghetto culture and ideology as legitimate rivals to the dominant Anglophile. This celebration of ghetto morality exalted a combative refusal to be submissive, a spontaneous militant affirmation of blackness, a disposition to adopt menacing postures toward those perceived as "oppressors," and a readiness to challenge those found guilty of vaunting their class position and "high" skin color.[3]

A parallel phenomenon to the lumpen's self-exile (from the "brown-man way of life") was to be found in a more deliberate praxiological critique of consensualism through ghetto youth culture. While the youths had a great deal in common with the "lumpenproletariat," they were a lot more volatile, and perhaps even farther away from the exceptionalist world view. To begin with, and as Nettleford points out, "Black Jamaican ghetto-youths [even] object to being referred to as lumpen proletariat."[4] By their account they are "Rude Boys" or "Rudies."

To the established classes the Rudies were the product of "bad breeding." The men and women of "high etiquette" saw the Rudies as a bunch of hooligans living off criminal activity, and destroying the image of Jamaica; they often explained the youths' behavior in terms of the latter's obsession with blackness. Deeper explanations suggested that these "outlaws" (i.e., the youths) had failed to learn anything from the respectable institutions in the country. One such explanation came from an Anglican Bishop in 1964 stating:

> The real problem in Jamaica so far as hooliganism is concerned, is not just a question of a few hundred of youngsters here and there who disturb the public weal and are a nuisance to the community, but it is that people of all ages, particularly between the ages of 15 and 22 . . . come under no influence whatever either of Church or state.[5]

The Anglican Bishop's statement was quite accurate, although as Gray points out, he did not ["draw] out the political implications" of his explanation. In fact, the Bishop was insisting that Jamaican youths do precisely what they were rejecting, namely, accept brown-man moral, cultural, and political leadership.

The charges of criminal activity against the youths were well-founded, and indeed many parts of Kingston lived with a garrison mentality largely informed by fear of crime. Criminal activity had a considerable impact on the day to day lives of not only the established classes, but "ordinary" working class people as well. Perhaps the most profound impact of crime in terms of the daily life was that it regulated public space, this being particularly so for women. The visibility of crime, and its attendant emotional reaction was a significant factor in the registration of exceptionalism with the public. Crime is, after all, more easily identifiable than hunger, homelessness, and cultural oppression, and in this war of position, the *Daily Gleaner* was always at the ready to defend "law and order" and "respectful conduct." While the individual elements of middle and upper class values might indeed be honorable (to those classes), it was the implications of exceptionalism's policies and perspectives that created the cleavages in which "violence" developed. In this respect "violence" and "resistance" must be understood dialectically in two ways; first as elements of a single chain of responses, and secondly, as historically specific to the contradictions of rapid modernization in a society deeply divided by race, class, and culture. As Gray notes:

In inventing what might be called a culture of resistance, the youths selected those aspects of the moral codes most cherished by the middle and upper classes and inverted them. In matters of speech, dress, comportment, forms of salutation, and even the etiquette of courtship, the rebellious youths reversed the official codes. They deliberately went without socks; shirts were not tucked in; wash rags were substituted for handkerchiefs and left to hang out of their back pockets. Caps were worn askew atop an uncombed head, and other ways were found to assume an alternative costume. To the speech affections of the middle class, the youths responded with a variation of working class speech.[6]

The antagonisms just described, and the specificity of their articulation clearly pointed to a deep cleavage in Jamaica underpinned, as it were, by a multiplicity of factors. Race, class, and problems of culture were very much at the center of the fault lines of Jamaica during the 1960s, and the social forces relevant to the "battle for Jamaica" were aligning themselves. It was in this context that two new organizations entered the fray.

### The Unemployed Workers Council and YSL

The abandonment of the urban poor by the union-party cartels (that is, the NWU-PNP and the BITU-JLP configurations), left large numbers of people unrepresented in a political system (viz., parliamentary democracy) defended by exceptionalism. In March 1962, however, the "sufferers" found a voice in Ben Monroe, who formed the Unemployed Workers Council "among the shanty dwellers of West Kingston."[7] Monroe was a Marxist and part of the old PNP left which was purged by Norman Manley in 1952. According to Obika Gray, Monroe was very much influenced by the Communist classics and the UWC was deeply inspired by "Leninism—particularly its critique of imperialism and its antipathy toward reformist parties of the Left. . . ."[8] The UWC was also inspired by the Cuban Revolution, and Article 23 of the UN's Charter of Human Rights which alludes to the "Right to Work."

The UWC was very critical of the institution of political unionism and, on account of this, elicited the derision of the established organizations (JLP, PNP, BITU, and NWU). The politics of the

Council was in fact very much opposed to the established classes in Jamaican society. Thus, its positions included:

> . . . a commitment to socialism, affirmation of the right to work, criticism of the drift toward suppression of liberties, opposition to external control of the economy, and resistance to the two party practice of clientelism and victimization in employment.[9]

One element of "resistance," however, was absent, namely a cultural critique of the consensualism propounded by the hegemonic social forces. This omission was not accidental, and in fact was shared by the Young Socialist League (YSL) which was formed shortly after the UWC.

The YSL was formed in 1962 as an arm of the PNP with the intention of incorporating urban youths who had thus far remained outside of any organized participation in the country's politics. Support for the formation of the youth organization from the middle and upper class leadership of the PNP, however, was not automatic, as it was felt that the "young Turks" were too radical, and would cause divisions within the party mainstream. The fact of the matter, though, was that the youth members of the party were highly motivated and were beginning to establish strong connections to other youths outside the ranks of the PNP. Mindful of the party's recent defeat at the polls and calculating the electoral assets to be reaped, the PNP leadership acquiesced to the youth organization. Within months of the YSL's launching, however, the right wing of the PNP and even Norman Manley, the leader of the party, were having grave doubts about their decision.

The YSL had among its ranks a number of deeply committed socialists who were university educated. In addition, the youth organization also began to receive advice from a number of left-wing professors (such as N. Girvan, G. Beckford, and Bertell Ollman) attached to the Mona campus of the University of the West Indies. Among the YSL members were Trevor Munroe and Hugh Small. Munroe was reputed to be "gifted theoretician" and was versed in the Marxist classics, and Small would later become a lawyer. These men engaged in a process of recovering (via the YSL) the PNP 1940 declaration of socialism, a declaration which the party had abandoned in 1952. The conservative wing of the party was very worried about this recovery, not the least because the new socialism presented itself as relevant to the hitherto neglected urban sufferers, youths included. The YSL went one step further by forming an unofficial alliance with the UWC.

In conjunction with the UWC, the YSL launched a sustained campaign against "business unionism"; the union-party cartels; economic neo-colonialism; and imperialism. The two organizations, however, differed on the general strategy of changing Jamaica. In the minds of UWC activists (and especially Ben Munroe), the YSL's affiliation with the PNP was regressive given that the party was very bourgeois and "brown-man" in character. Accordingly, the UWC implored on the YSL to break away from the PNP, and bolstered its arguments by citing the refusal of the PNP leadership to allow the youth organization into its policy making council.

While the UWC was correct about the PNP's "regulation" of the YSL so long as the latter remained in the party, it in fact shared with the YSL a much graver problem. This problem was that both organizations defined their struggle largely in the language of the Workers' Struggle. The debates surrounding the YSL's potential break away from the PNP in fact highlighted the issue. In response to the UWC's call for disassociation from the PNP, Trevor Munroe of the YSL theorized that such a break would effectively mean losing the working class, since the party had control of the National Workers Union, and some smaller trade unions. The Unemployed Workers Council could not find a reply to this argument, and the issue was laid to rest. The fact of the matter is that the UWC itself saw the struggle for change in terms of working class agitation, narrowly defined. Given the overdetermined identity of the urban poor, as articulated in a multiplicity of counter-hegemonic practices, the UWC and YSL clearly suffered from some theoretical and strategic blind spots. As Gray observed:

> These blind spots included a tendency to reduce all social struggles to the class struggle; a bias in treating ideological struggle as a means to defend "class" but not "race," and a practice which implied that labor activism was sufficient to challenge the *moral* sway of the dominant classes.[10]

These limitations notwithstanding, the UWC and YSL did form an important part of the struggle against exceptionalism. More importantly, these organizations put key questions on the political agenda during the 1960s. These questions; the proposed manner of their resolution; and even some of the people involved; would later be "drafted" by Michael Manley in the 1970s.

## The Rastafarians

During the decades of the 1960s and 1970s the Rastafarians emerged as one of the most significant protest groups in Jamaican society. The ontological basis of their radical critique and resistance was of such a nature, that it called into question some of the fundamental assumptions of the society's culture and values, as well as the very orientation of national identity and direction. Although at one time seen as the principal danger to exceptionalism, by the late 1960s both government and opposition parties were caught busying themselves with winning Rastafarian support, or at least to effect some measure of political/cultural rapprochement. It was no accident, therefore, that by the 1972 general election campaign, Michael Manley found it necessary to parade publicly with notable Rastas like Bob Marley. By this time the Rastafarian movement had gone a far way in disarticulating the hegemonic discourses so carefully woven and expressed in such putative cultural/political symbols like: "Out of Many Come One," "Jamaican multi-racialism," racial harmony, and a whole apparatus of consensus producing texts. As we shall see presently, the Rastas were at the forefront of bringing into ideological crisis the contradictions of dependent capitalist development and its various legitimizing technologies, as well as generating some of the objective conditions for a sustained war of position. Further, the Rastafarian critique was one of the few that was successful, at least in part, in graduating from the politics of frontal opposition, to a praxis which contained counter-hegemonic possibilities.[11]

### The Influence of Garvey and the Recovery of Historical Memory

Whether the Rastas are cultist, millenarian, or conservative peasants who have been dispossessed, one thing is unmistakable: their visceral identification with Africa and the place of black consciousness in their structure of interpretation and critique. In light of this and the conditions of their historical origins in the 1930s, it is important to establish their connection with Marcus Garvey, whom they hold as a prophet. Garvey, of course, laid the foundation for black consciousness, not only in Jamaica, but in Central America, the United States, Britain, the Caribbean, and perhaps ironically, Africa itself.

Garvey's conception of black freedom burst out of the proximate conditions of Jamaican society, as well as the situation of blacks in Central America and the United States. In his judgment, the oppression of blacks was a global phenomenon and thus required a strategy which privileged racial liberation over traditional national aspirations. For Garvey, the two principal social forces responsible for black oppression were white culture with its celebration of whiteness (that is, literally skin color as well as a value system), and the global thrust of imperialism. It is important to recognize that imperialism for him was not conceptualized simply as capitalist penetration and conquest of foreign countries for economic gain. Rather, the fact that this imperialism was exercised by "white civilization" with enormous consequences for black people the world over was constitutive of the very definition of imperialist domination.[12]

When the Universal Negro Improvement Association (UNIA) and its publication *The Negro World* were launched, therefore, race was the principle of articulation for resistance by black people; national and/or class liberation, though important, were not deemed adequate. Thus Horace Campbell is entirely correct when he argues that:

> The importance of Garvey and Garveyism can be analyzed not only in the thrust of the UNIA in its form, but also in terms of the content of the real philosophical basis of the challenge which was essentially taken up by a movement of poor oppressed blacks.[13]

Domestically, the impact of Garvey on cultural consciousness has been enormous. The fervent religiosity, coupled with the massive dispossession of large sections of the population, has occasioned the production of some peculiar cultural forms, to which we soon turn. More immediate to our concern is the way in which Garvey lives on in the culture "of the oppressed," and the way in which his presence is still embodied in daily life. Garvey is often retrieved and deployed by the masses of poor black Jamaicans in their struggle for equality and social justice. According to Barry Chevannes, "myths about Garvey are part of the national consciousness of the Jamaican poor, dispossessed Blacks, once the object of enslavement, still the object of oppression. . . ."[14]

No doubt the longevity of Garvey has a great deal to do with the continuing relevance of his critique of black oppression which, in the context of post-war Jamaica, means the marginalization of a significant portion of the society in terms of economic well being, political power, and questions pertaining to cultural/racial identity. After all, Garvey's project had introduced a comprehensive *perspective* on black liberation, one that was so different from the all too familiar renditions of black people and their history which made them out to be the "white man's burden." His explanation of black people's position in society was not limited to the traditional canons of academic practice, such as objectivity, and value-free judgement, but provided a platform for cultural empowerment and, some would argue, even revolutionary "incitement." For black people in the early part of this century revolution meant, *inter alia*, bursting the chains of racial/cultural degradation which had tied them through the institutional and ideological apparatuses of slavery and colonialism. If these latter had engineered a reality which systematically emasculated anything positive in blackness, Garvey's intervention went some distance in unhinging the "philosophical unity" of their narratives. As Miller puts it:

> For Black people Garveyism challenged and contradicted the traditional characteristic negative perceptual set, conceptual mode and evaluation bias evident in the Self images of people in this society. It challenged and contradicted these patterns fundamentally, totally and unequivocally. In a very real sense *Garveyism tackled reality itself*—as far as Black people were concerned—since a person's perception of reality is the only reality he knows, no matter how distorted and inaccurate that perception may be. *Garveyism, therefore, provided a new reality, a new frame of reference within which Black people were encouraged to conceive of Self and evaluate Self worth.*[15]

The Rastas have internalized Garvey myths more than any other group in Jamaica, and on certain subjects have taken him almost literally. In some measure this played a part in the genesis of the movement. Thus, Garvey is reputed to have made the following prophecy: "Look to Africa, when a black king shall be crowned, for the day of deliverance is near." When in November 1930 Ras Tafari was crowned as the "Emperor Haile Sellassie, King of Kings, Lord of Lords, and the conquering Lion of the Tribe of Judah," there was occasion not only for celebration, but hope. Of course this did not in and of itself create Rastafarianism, for the intellectual preparation necessary for its emergence had been in the making for some time and continued with even more vigor after the

Emperor's coronation. Apart from Garvey there were a number of other organic intellectuals "preaching" the sin of racial domination on the one hand, and Africa as the fount of cultural liberation, on the other. Among these were Alexander Bedward,[16] Leonard P. Powell, Nathaniel Hibbert, and H. Archibald Dunkley. All of them preached the divinity of Ras Tafari and his role in the redemption of black people. Specifically, the emperor was thought to be invested with both biblical and historical authority to "overthrow white domination by racial war." He was deemed the head of the Niyabingi Order which defined the world between white oppressors and oppressed blacks, and which was dedicated to destroying this arrangement of power. According to Smith, Augier, and Nettleford's authoritative study on the rise of the Rasta movement,

> This violent notes (*sic*) had already been struck by Howell, and Niyabingi was defined in Jamaica as "Death to black and white oppressors." Some of those people who worshiped the Emperor and were locally known as "Ras Tafaris" or "Rastamen" came to describe themselves as "Niyamen" that is, members of Niabingi. The Niyabingi commitment to racial violence generalized the violence. . . .[17]

*Rasta Doctrine: A War of Position Against Anglo-Christian Hegemony*[18]

In the wake of persistent harassment by the state, press, and police, Mortimer Planno (a noted Rasta), approached the Chancellor of the University of West Indies at Mona and requested a study of Rastafarianism in Jamaica. The Chancellor agreed and asked three distinguished Caribbean scholars (M. G. Smith, Roy Augier, and Rex Nettleford) to undertake the study. The team began an intense survey among the Ras Tafari brethren of Kingston on July 4, 1960 with the aim of providing an ". . . account of the growth, doctrines, organization, aspirations, needs and conditions of the Ras Tafari movement in Jamaica, especially in Kingston, the capital."[19] Two critical findings emerged from the report which ought to concern us here, namely: (a) that the Rastas were a diverse group of people who were essentially welded together as a protest group, and (b) that the movement was rooted in unemployment and "unemployability."

In contradistinction to the popularly held view that the Rastas were a monolithic group of parasitic, uneducated rift-rafts, too lazy to work, and guided by a common philosophy of self negation, the team reported that the brethren were a "heterogeneous group." According to the report:

> Rastafarian hold in common only two beliefs: that Ras Tafari is the living God, and that salvation can come to black men only through repatriation to Africa. On all other matters the opinions of the brethren vary as widely as the opinions of the rest of the population. Some wear beards, others do not; and only a small minority wear the locks. Some are men of the highest moral fibre, while at the other extreme are men of crime and violence. Some smoke ganja; others abhor it. Some are excellent workmen, while others avoid work. In all matters except two, the divinity of Ras Tafari and the necessity of repatriation, Ras Tafarians are a random group.[20]

The heterogeneity of the Rastas was not an unimportant finding. For one thing, after the report was published, and indeed widely circulated and discussed, it became increasingly difficult for the hegemonic social forces in the society to wantonly compartmentalize the movement in an effort to isolate Rastas ideologically and politically.[21] But why was this necessary in the first place? Surely, if indeed the Rastas were merely an odd collection of society's outcasts living on the periphery by choice, there would be no need for the type of systematic strategy to "discipline" them. A closer examination of the movement's doctrine and beliefs will point to the necessity of such a response.

In a strict sense, the divinity of Ras Tafari comes from Proverbs 22, Isaiah 43 and John 16—"For I am in the Father and the Father is in me." Haile Sellassie is the "Living God, the Returned Messiah and the Representative of God the Father."[22] But as the team found out, the strict sense is only the narrow Biblical version of the divinity of the Emperor; far more ideological and politically radical versions exist. It is worth quoting at some length one such interpretation, since such a *symptomatic reading* reveals a number of ideological elements which call into question the hegemonic order of things. It goes as follows:

> The Bible contains the Word of God, but Scripture shows that half of this has not been written save in your hearts. King James I of Britain, a white man, translated the Bible,

distorting and confusing its message; but to those who, by virtue of Ras Tafari's divine power, have been given inspiration and prophetic insight, the false passages put in by the white man for his own purposes are easily detected. . . .[23]

A couple of points need to be clarified and explained in terms of the wider context of Rastafarianism. First, for Rastas, Babylon is a concept which denotes the entire white western world and its culture, as well as the status quo in every country, Jamaica included.[24] Ethiopia is exempted from this concept. The agents of Babylon are such people like the Queen Elizabeth I and II of England, King James, the Pope, and all other Heads of State, including the Prime Minister and Governor General of Jamaica. There are some notable exceptions, namely, Fidel Castro and the revolutionary Government of Cuba, and among some of the more racially moderate brethren, the former USSR. The latter two are held to be allies in the destruction of Babylon's oppression.

Secondly, there is no doubt that the more radical Rastas established a system of connection among some of the symbols of imperialism, colonial Christianity, and racial oppression. Further, it is not at all unusual for them to include blacks who support the status quo, be it in the form of the Jamaican government, various state apparatuses such as the police, or even more indirectly, in the form of culture. Some other beliefs of the brethren will serve to further highlight not only their world and its relation to class and racial oppression, but the extent to which, as a force in civil society, they were able to ruin the prestige of "brown-man" consensualism. Included in this profile of beliefs are those of the 1960s generation of Rasta culture known as Dreadlocks.

### Appearance

Although not true of all of them, Rastas do not believe in cutting their hair. There is indeed a biblical reason for this, but perhaps more important is the feeling that the type of grooming that is normally required is part of the cultural strategy of Babylon to discipline bodies into docile undifferentiated objects.

The critical question here for the brethren is resistance to European and European-inspired definitions of "neat appearance" and beauty. This has elicited the wrath of the mainstream population who have generally accepted European, and more recently (white) American, values and standards. It goes without saying as well that the power bloc was especially critical of the brethren given that the former are predominantly white or "pass-for white."

## Politics

While a few of the brethren have actively participated in electoral politics, especially with the "integration" of some more mainstream parts of the population in the movement, the general position is one of active disengagement from the official political process. In large measure the brethren's position is informed by a conviction that the electoral process as constituted is wholly inadequate, designed as it were out of the experience of European societies. In particular, the movement has been openly critical of the office of the Governor General, which they see as a neo-colonial institution. In a letter dated August 22, 1979, for example, the "Divine Order of the Nyabingi, Order of Melchzedec" demanded:

> The full abolition of the indefensible inconsistency and cultural incompatibility of the/Governor General: the representative of post-colonial British authority, from administration of the responsibilities and obligations of the children, and descendants of the Emancipated Slaves of African origin and Ethiopian nationality, and the people of the ALMIGHTYJAHRASTAFARI![25]

Although this "policy" was to continue and does so to date, an important modification was made during the 1972 election campaign when Rasta musicians took to the political platform with Michael Manley. Later on it will be shown how this was really a situation of the PNP being forced to acknowledge Rastafarianism as a decisive cultural force in the society, one that had made such inroads in the popular imagination that it could no longer be ignored.

The response of the Jamaican government and mainstream society to the Rastas' political position during the 1960s was a mixture of derision, charges of treason and destabilization, and outright repression. The movement was painted as a threat to duly constituted political authority in the country, and indeed, there were some grounds for these charges within the prevailing constitutional and political arrangements. Some of the less "racially inspired" brethren saw the Soviet Union and Cuba as political allies of the oppressed in Jamaica. In fact, in June 1960 after an attempted putsch by several Afro-Americans who had allied themselves with the brethren, the police discovered not only arms but a letter written to Fidel Castro. The letter read, in part:

> We wish to draw your attention to the conditions which confront us today *as poor, underprivileged people* which were brought here from Africa by the British slave traders over 400 years ago to serve as slaves. We now desire to return home in peace, to live under our own vine and fig tree, otherwise *a government like yours that give justice to the poor*. All our efforts to have a peaceful repatriation has proven a total failure . . . therefore we want to assure you Sir, and your government that Jamaica and the rest of the British West Indies will be turned over to you and your government . . . we are getting ready for an invasion on the Jamaican government therefore we need your help and personal service.[26]

These aspirations clearly ran against the grain of socialized common sense in Jamaica during the 1960s. After all, the Prime Minister had boldly proclaimed that Jamaica not only is aligned to the West, but *is* the West. There was thus an overdetermined ideological crisis here. For not only was the brethren working to disarticulate the discourse of Jamaican "multi-racialism" by positing Africa as the proper point of cultural reference, but they were also, if one will, taking a position on the Cold War on the side of the communists, even if inadvertently so. In both instances, the West's cultural heritage and political institutions were called into question.

### Religion and God: Africa versus Europe

Jamaicans are a profoundly religious people, but according to Rastafari critique, this is a fundamental part of the cultural oppression of black people in the country. Rastas, of course, are religious themselves. The problem is not one of religion *qua* religion, for both the brethren and the mainstream society cull religious wisdom from the Bible. The problem exists in terms of the cultural appropriation of the Holy Book. The brethren insists that the King James version of the Bible (which is most popular in Jamaica), is a culturally specific interpretation of revealed truth designed to further the mutual interest of western civilization, imperialism, and their local "agents" in Jamaica. For them, Jesus Christ was an *invention* by the Roman Catholic Church which declared him God.

Of this they have no objection, once that is, it is understood that Christ as God was a product of very specific historical and cultural circumstances.[27]

God is by definition a cultural invention and "the Creator is a myth which is present in most religions."[28] As one Rasta intellectual explained:

> ... man and God are one and the same and the concept of Creator has to be a culture bound concept. We are all made in the image of God therefore God has to look like us. When one looks in the mirror one has to see God looking back.[29]

Conscious of this, the brethren read the Bible quite selectively, concentrating only on those parts that speak to their oppression and are relevant to an "Afro-centric" interpretation.[30]

The critical point for us here is that the Rasta movement was, during the 1960s, openly critical of one of the major institutions of daily life in Jamaica. What gave their invective some legitimacy in this matter was their unremitting commitment to exposing the relationship between established religion on the one hand, and slavery and continuing cultural oppression on the other. For the established order, this was a crisis of values and identity which was beginning to have some impact on the prevailing world view.

*Education*

In the area of education the Rastafari have considerable reservation. Indicative of this is their transliteration of the word/concept education into what they think it really entails—"headecation," alluding as it does to "mental decay." The brethren is extremely suspicious of western education and its institutionalization in Jamaica. As in politics, religion, family, and personal appearance, they are convinced that education in Jamaica is essentially neo-colonial in terms of the "authoritative sources" of knowledge (i.e., European) and its pedagogy. Thus, for Rastas "education for children is dangerous, since the Babylonian schools enchain them mentally with false doctrines," a position remarkably similar to the thinking of Althusser and Gramsci.[31] According to Brodber, the hegemonic position of what she calls "mulatto-orientation," vis-à-vis an African orientation, has been "produced and ... successfully maintained" by educational practice in Jamaica. She puts it thus:

The unlettered lower class, depending on the oral tradition for its information, was kept in touch with its past of Africa and slavery and with its African identity. The other was exposed to English textbooks, curricula and examinations which taught about and distributed certificates for jobs based on an understanding of European ways.[32]

As a matter of concrete practice, therefore, Rastas either do not send their children to school, or if they do, send them to "... private schools run by teachers who are either adherents of this doctrine or sympathetic to it."[33]

### Work, Property, and Material Gain

As a general principle, the Rastafari sees capitalist wage employment as a continuation of slavery, not only in Jamaica, but throughout the world capitalist system. The fact that the Jamaican economy is heavily penetrated by imperialism in the form of foreign capital only adds to the intensity of this interpretation. The question of work, however, is very complicated where the brethren is concerned. In part, this is due to the fact that unemployment in Jamaica is very high, and as some have argued, the rise of the movement is directly correlated with structural unemployment. Arguably, therefore, there is a sense in which the failure of the capitalist system (meaning wage employment here) to provide jobs has resulted in the brethren's rejection of the system as a whole. According to this thesis, the articulation of racial consciousness with oppression, is merely the *form* that working class protest has taken. And perhaps there is some credibility in this insofar as, the same way in which not all Rastamen wear locks or beards, not all of them abstain from wage employment. Of course, quite a plausible argument could be made from the same material set of circumstances: that although many Rastas are engaged in wage labor, they nonetheless adhere to some of the fundamental beliefs of the movement. One interpretation this author cannot accept, however, is that put forward by the eminent scholar, Ken Post, who argues that Rastafarianism is "false consciousness."[34] False compared to what?

With respect to property and material gain, the brethren stand in diametric opposition to the dominant values of Jamaican society. Again, while many of the brethren do want property and seek material gain like most of the society, there is a general philosophical principle that the acquisition of property is one way of tying people of African origin to Babylon. Further, consumerism is seen as a peculiar western/capitalist cultural trait through which, identity, self-worth, and ultimately meaning, is constructed.

*Language and Music*

The treatment of language and music as structurally related categories is not accidental given the historical relationship between the two in the form of expression of the oppressed, namely, the oral tradition. Since the days of slavery, orality was the chief communicative strategy of resistance, this being especially the case in light of the suppression of the written word. Singing (and dancing) were permitted by slave masters who saw no threat to the social order through these supposedly innocent practices. For the oppressed, much of their own history and that of Africa have come via the oral tradition. In twentieth century Jamaica, we find the continuing fecundity of this tradition in the narratives of liberation propounded by the subaltern. We find a rather valorized oral economy of resistance on the one hand, and the suppression of the written word on the other by the state. This dialectical relationship between the oppressed and oppressor, and in our case between hegemony and counter-hegemony, must be understood in terms of the wider cultural explosion that took place in Jamaica during the 1960s, a period when the culture of Dread graduated from its former compartmentalized innerworld of the "sect/cult" to a major space in the popular imagination. Reggae and "I talk" began to occupy the strategic location of "trafficking symbols" in a concerted oral war of position.

The conscious intention of the Rasta is to subvert the cultural-ideological system of the neo-colonial dominated culture of Jamaica and to publicly establish social and political distance from Jamaican exceptionalism. Most Rastas speak semi-Creole, and their language is saturated by an "I" sound. Pollard explains that the "I" is not an accident, nor is it frivolous, or simply stylistic. "I" plays on the "eye," which appeals to historical vision and understanding. Selassie's name is always preceded by or ends with "I"—e.g., "Selassie I." In the Rasta philosophical system, Babylon has blinded black people—and for that matter all people—with massive narratives of untruth through the practice of "head-decation." Understanding, vision, and the bases of cultural/political struggle, therefore, get lost in the hegemonic language; "Selassie I" and the whole battery of "I" words/concepts are really aimed at building a vocabulary of resistance, one which cannot be easily penetrated by Babylon. Semaj also points out that the phrase "I and I" is meant to subvert the rampant individualism of Western society. "I" is followed by "I" in the formation "I and I" because according to Rastafarianism, the individual is impossible. All human communities are social and thus, by definition, self is always socially determined. The brethren sees self as collectively formed and expressed, deriving as it does from African kinship traditions. Semaj puts it thus: "Rastafari clearly can be identified on this dimension whereby self is more than I, myself and me. For Rastafari self is I and I representing a total collective."[35]

Rastas also replace a lot of standard English words, usually by placing "I" as the initial syllable. Further some words are inverted to "... bear the weight of their phonological implications—e.g., "downpress" for oppress."[36]

Some references have already been made to the way in which Dread culture began to spread during the 1960s and developed into a veritable paroxysm by the end of that decade. One of the reasons why this happened was the increasing stature of the Rasta-inspired (and performed) reggae music. Reggae music facilitated (a) the penetration of the British/European/American cultural hegemony so deeply entrenched in the society, especially among the middle and upper classes who are white or "near-white";[37] (b) the bringing into public focus a radical critique of the social order (which the Rastas, among other social movements, had been articulating for years), and (c) internationalizing the problem of oppressed black people, especially in Africa where some countries were still fighting for independence. The enormous popularity of reggae critique, not only in Jamaica and the Caribbean but further afield, was increasing testimony that the hegemonic discursive chain which had sutured dependent capitalist development, progress, racial harmony and its associate multiculturalism, and not the least—Western values and norms, were about to be dismantled. But for us to fully understand how one historic bloc came apart and was "replaced" by another, further investigation of the elements which would change the balance of forces is required.

## Cultural Nationalism and Anti-Imperialism

By the middle of the 1960s, Rasta ideology was beginning to become more diffuse and acceptable in sections of the population which had hitherto looked upon the brethren with circumspection. This had enormous consequences for the ideological war taking place over the meaning of Jamaica. The JLP government responded with a more determined offensive of exceptionalism. The ideological quarantine which had been placed around the island since the Cuban Revolution deepened as all left wing and black nationalist literature were banned. Passports of left wing activists were seized and travel to socialist countries restricted. Bertell Ollman (the Marxist university professor at the UWI and advisor to the YSL) was expelled from the country despite a major attempt by students, socialists, human rights groups, and sympathetic faculty members to "save him." Police brutality also increased, with Rastafarians and ghetto youths bearing the brunt of what often was illegal force. Through all of this the established classes began to worry a great deal, as it was becoming increasingly clear that exceptionalism might not be able to fully consolidate the cultural and class oppression in which modern Jamaica was made. Just about the time when it seemed that the battle lines were fully drawn, the counter-hegemonic front was infused with two additional and powerful social forces—the Black Power Movement and university intellectuals.

## *Walter Rodney and Black Power*

The management of consensualism in Jamaica had always depended on the discursive location of Jamaica within the world of the North Atlantic. The established classes and the JLP pointed to Britain and the U.S. as models of good governance and economic progress. Both countries were seen as shining examples of equal opportunity for all, despite the institutionalized exclusion of African Americans from mainstream America. There is a sense in which Britain and America, but particularly America, formed a kind of founding myth through which the consensualists in Jamaica had imagined themselves and the Jamaica they wanted. By the middle of the 1960s, however, it was becoming increasingly difficult to sustain this myth. In large measure, this had to do with the explosion of the civil rights movement in the United States. While the civil rights movement allowed working class (i.e., protected workers) Jamaicans to imagine the U.S. through human rights lenses, the Black Power movement in America drew a more visceral response from the race conscious sufferers of the ghettos. It was at this conjuncture that a young Guyanese historian (Walter Rodney), who was once an undergraduate student at Mona, returned to Jamaica (in January 1968) to take up a lectureship. Rodney became a major asset to the marginalized, and to the counter-hegemonic front.

Rodney became very involved with the marginalized in the ghettos by visiting these communities. He engaged in lengthy "reasoning sessions" with the Rastas, youths, and unemployed, and was able to secure the trust of these groups. He also began a lecture series on African history at the Mona campus which attracted not only students and faculty, but the urban poor as well.[38] In general, the theme that Rodney pursued in his lectures was a (re)production of African history in a manner relevant to national and cultural liberation in Jamaica.[39] In Obika Gray's reading, "Rodney boldly linked the cultural affirmation of blacks and their political liberation."[40] This project of liberation was posed at both the domestic and global levels.

At the global level, Rodney (much like Marcus Garvey earlier in the century) suggested that "there was a correlation between color and power in the contemporary world," with whites controlling and exploiting nonwhite people.[41] As such, racial oppression must be seen in a transnational context, and race itself as a transnational social force.[42] The implication of this argument was that the Black Power movement in the U.S., and the cultural resistance in Jamaica against the ethnic-minority elite, were part of the same struggle. In the case of the West Indies (Jamaica included), Black Power for Rodney meant "three closely related things: the break with imperialism which is historically racist; the assumption of power by the black masses in the islands; [and] the cultural reconstruction of the society in the image of the blacks."[43] The JLP government felt very threatened by Rodney and, not the least because he was able to fuse socialism and cultural nationalism, and also to bring university intellectuals and the urban poor together. Moreover, "Rodney's experience had shown many middle class youths that they need not be afraid to identify with Africa or the Rastas, and there was a new wave of identification with the movement among different sections of the society," including university intellectuals.[44] The latter in fact turned out to be a powerful social force by the late 1960s.

## The Intellectuals and Abeng

The rise of Black Power in the Caribbean and, particularly, Rodney's popularity in the movement, occasioned the intellectuals from the region to reexamine their involvement in political struggle. The New World Group which was formed earlier in the decade by Caribbean scholars became divided over the issue of political involvement. The head of the organization, Lloyd Best (a Trinidadian economist), insisted that the central preoccupation of intellectuals should be confrontations with "reason," with the aim of providing objective knowledge relevant to economic and social advancement. He specifically criticized Rodney's position on Black Power, arguing that blacks already have power and that there was no need for West Indian blacks to be led by the interests of "American Negroes." In part reflecting the regional debate over Black Power, the Trinidadian economist went so far as to publish a punishing attack in the *Daily Gleaner* against Black Power and the supposed misguided intellectuals who support this cause. In the meantime, the JLP government expelled Rodney from Jamaica, causing a major riot by students and the ghetto poor. A group of Jamaican academics and some members from the UWC and YSL responded by launching an "alternative" newspaper called *Abeng,* which was dedicated to ". . . [making] *racial* uplift and a defense of the black "sufferer" its main cause."[45]

Ideologically, the paper drew heavily from the orientations of Rastas and the lumpen-proletariat; there was also a concerted attempt to rediscover the "legend" of Marcus Garvey.[46] A special section called the *"Sufferer's Diary"* was devoted to unedited remonstrations from the poor. This populism was politically important, since it was on this terrain that several historically unarticulated antagonisms could be, and were, reconciled. Thus racial empowerment, socialism, anti-imperialist nationalism, cultural affirmation, "alternative religion" (including Islam and Rastafarianism), and academic criticism began to congeal in the face of a common enemy, namely, Jamaican exceptionalism and its "political agent," the JLP. The paper also attracted Dr. D. K. Duncan, who was a committed socialist, and Marcus Garvey Jr., the son of the late Pan Africanist.

The socialist and anti-imperialist content of *Abeng* was quite forceful. Foreign capital was severely criticized for exploiting Jamaicans and controlling the resources of the country. There were calls for nationalization of foreign concerns, and as senior a figure as George Beckford blamed the JLP for allowing "foreign white people . . . [to] own our basic resources."[47] Capitalism as a whole was attacked and there were suggestions for the restructuring of production relations along the lines of co-operatives. The control of large tracts of the best agricultural lands by a few local land owners and foreign companies was also criticized, and calls were made for urgent land reform.

## A Society of Deep Cleavages

Post-World War II Jamaica was clearly a society of deep divisions. The material and intellectual differences between the propertied and marginalized were in fact so complete that the "two Jamaicas" of the nineteenth century which Phillip Curtin described in detail, were still very much present. The middle and upper classes had invented a myth of Jamaica as an "exceptional" country (of peace, economic progress, racial harmony, and political democracy) through which they sought to protect a structure of socio-economic, political, and cultural privilege. But the interpellative capacity of this myth was weakened as the subaltern social forces developed counter-discourses (based on their material existence), which were aimed at delegitimizing this common sense from above. If indeed the task of counter-hegemonic activism is to "ruin the prestige of middle-class culture . . ." as Georges Sorel once suggested, it could reasonably be concluded that this class was very much on the defensive.[48] The sustained counter-hegemonic pressure from below, and the threat to the social order associated with this pressure, combined with the desire of the dominant classes to press on with capitalist modernization, left the JLP with very little room for maneuver. The major challenge was how to continue with the process of modernization without involving the masses, whose ideas of such forward movement were "revolutionary" in character. The answer was found in a strategy of change from above, that is, a strategy of passive revolution.

# 7

## Facilitating Passive Revolution

### The JLP's "Exceptionalist" Foreign Policy

The ways in which polarized social forces were engaged in a sustained "war of position" over national identity and questions of socio-economic equality in Jamaica during the 1960s has been established. On the one hand, the dominant social forces (made up of the JLP, established churches, foreign capital, media, and the local economic ruling classes) attempted to consolidate hegemonic leadership through the ideology of exceptionalism. On the other hand, those social forces opposed to the contents of exceptionalism (namely, youths, Rastafarians, socialists, academics, students, Black Power activists, and the urban poor as a whole) embarked on a project of strategic counter-hegemony, aimed at disestablishing what may be termed "common sense from above." Further, it was suggested that exceptionalism itself must be understood in the larger context of an attempt at passive revolution by the dominant social forces in conjunction with the interests and representatives of foreign capitalists. The relationship between exceptionalism and passive revolution is further developed through an examination of JLP foreign policy during the 1960s.

Vaughan Lewis, a noted scholar on the international relations of the Caribbean, suggests that during the 1960s JLP foreign policy was characterized by "relative passivity."[1] Lewis is correct only in the sense that the JLP did not diverge much from the North Atlantic Triangle in matters of trade, investment, aid, and cultural location. If "relative passivity" means little change, then Lewis' point is well taken. The history of this period, however, shows that the JLP did not *passively continue* its traditional external relations. On the contrary, the 1960s was a decade in which the JLP had to wage a continuous struggle to maintain Jamaica's external linkages. This struggle was of course warranted on account of the unprecedented challenges from within the country. While indeed the JLP did not venture much beyond "the well known," its foreign policy was in fact a *determined one* aimed at defending the interests of the ruling classes in Jamaica. It is also important to keep in mind that "foreign policy" and "domestic policy" are not separate entities, but instead are complementary aspects of the same "project."

A project of passive revolution, as discussed earlier, involves rapid change (usually called modernization), with a *concurrent demobilization* of the "popular classes." In the case of modern Jamaica, passive revolution required both a lateral expansion of capitalist production relations, and an intensification of the rate of surplus value extraction. These latter processes, however, could not have taken place without wider socio-cultural transformations through which labor becomes subsumed under capital. The substantive subsumption of labor also required what might be called "cultural deference" to capital, and the commodification of consciousness. Politically, since passive revolution sought popular demobilization, stability in Jamaica was of the first order of importance. Put differently, the Jamaican ruling classes, having accepted rapid capitalist modernization as the desired path (or more properly the ideology) of development, and bearing in mind the resistance from well mobilized social forces, found it necessary to *organize* this development from above. This involved guaranteeing stability at home, while inducing capital from abroad. In its foreign policy, therefore, the JLP extended the ideology of exceptionalism beyond Jamaica's borders.

## The JLP's Version of Jamaica's Uniqueness

Throughout the 1960s, the JLP government took pride in arguing that Jamaica was an atypical Third World country. Jamaica was represented as *different* from other developing countries by being free of racial or ethnic conflicts (which afflict other Third World countries); having a stable democracy, and a relatively well developed economic infrastructure, ready for industrial "take-off." One JLP representative to the UN stated Jamaica's uniqueness thus:

> These "middle level countries," as I shall call them, form a significant bloc. . . . It is from this group that the quickest successes of aid graduates will come. By and large they

have passed the halfway mark, yet they face a particular problem in that their needs always tend to be compared with the neediest, they are judged by the lowest common denominators in their wants. . . . It is commonplace in the "middle level" group of countries for them to experience a reduction of interest in their problems from quarters from which assistance might be expected.[2]

This unique category of the middle income Third World states, in which Jamaica imagined itself, demanded special recognition, and a distinctive approach from multilateral institutions. Instead of traditional foreign aid, the JLP government made it known that it was more interested in foreign investment and, even if aid is given, it should not be seen in the same way as assistance to other Third World states. In other words, Jamaica wanted net capital transfers without the stigma of being a foreign aid recipient. In delivering the island's first UN address, Mr. Hugh Shearer was careful to put the point thus: "I fail to see why the outflow of capital funds from one advanced country to another should be called investment, but the outflow of capital from an advanced country to a less developed one should be called economic aid."[3] Clearly, the JLP did not want Jamaica to be lumped with "those other poor countries" of Africa and Asia, for Jamaica was *exceptional,* and must be treated differently. The latter may be termed JLP "international exceptionalism."

Another representation of Jamaican difference was that the process of decolonization in the country was not marred by the types of conflicts and violence which occurred with other independence movements. This was an important point at the height of the Cold War, especially with the advent of the Cuban Revolution; the strength of the socialist People's Progressive Party in Guyana (which had won three consecutive democratic elections); and the experiments in the Dominican Republic and Guatemala, not to mention socialist, nationalist, and communist movements throughout the Third World. The proof of Jamaican stability and internal harmony was supposedly to be found in the fact that Jamaica was the first country in the Caribbean to receive independence from the United Kingdom. The credibility of Jamaican stability was also to be found in the anti-communist credentials of the JLP, and not the least in its leader, Sir Alexander Bustamante.

Bustamante was a strong supporter of the West, and a sworn enemy of communism. In a Parliamentary debate three months after independence, the Prime Minister stated his views in the most categorical terms. Said Bustamante:

> I would rather suffer death than live under the communist flag. That is why I declare in the United States, England and here that I am for the West and I am for the United States of America. . . .
>
> I have plenty of empty cells for communists to lock them up . . . That is my policy, to lock-up communists. Communism is evil. It is deceptions . . . (*sic*) I am for the West. I am against communism.[4]

The picture of stability and "good behavior" which the JLP was painting was not difficult to decipher. To begin with, the JLP and the dominant classes *opposed independence* from Britain, and since independence, not much had really changed. If these were indeed strong "exceptionalist credentials" based on the history of the country and the orientation of its current leaders, more proof was to be found in the record of Jamaica's external behavior.

Thus, at the United Nations Jamaica consistently voted with the West on Cold War issues. Generally, it departed from the western camp only in respect of resolutions pertaining to national independence of colonies and in support of African liberation. And even in regards to the latter, Jamaican voting in the General Assembly could not really be considered radical since many western countries voted in favor of self-determination or often abstained on controversial roll calls. The JLP's "follow the West attitude" was indeed underlined by Kingston's advice (to its Permanent Representative at the UN) to vote like Canada whenever uncertain.

There were other strong indications of the JLP's affection for the West. First, the day after independence, the Jamaican government, fully cognizant of Cuba's effort to have the Americans withdraw from Guantanamo Bay, invited the United States to open a military base on the island. There is no doubt that such an invitation during the height of the Cold War (especially from a newly independent country without a pressing external threat to its national security) was a clear statement of the acceptance of American leadership. The request was politely turned down by the United States.

Secondly, the British government continued to "guarantee Jamaica's security" and the JLP could boast that the Chief of Military Intelligence of the country's armed forces was a British national. Virtually all Jamaican officers were trained in Britain and the United States, and Jamaican diplomats were so "Western" in their manners and values that they were referred to as "Afro-Saxons" in UN diplomatic circles. The JLP government, which was in office for the entire period, displayed considerable deference to its erstwhile colonial "master," Great Britain, to the United States, and even Canada.[5]

Thirdly, if diplomatic representation is a good indicator of foreign policy priorities, the JLP government clearly had a preference for western states. Fully accredited diplomatic missions only existed in London, Washington, Ottawa, and the United Nations. A consulate was also opened in New York on account of the large numbers of Jamaicans living there, and that city's importance in mobilizing capital. An invitation by the Soviet Union to open diplomatic relations was rejected, but toward the end of the decade a consulate was opened in Ethiopia in answer to popular demands in Jamaica.[6]

## Multilateral Policy

Upon receiving independence, the JLP quickly established the country's presence in multilateral organizations. As would be reasonably expected of a small country, Jamaica placed much faith in the United Nations system.[7] But be that as it may, the country's diplomatic activity at this level clearly indicated general acceptance of the prevailing ontological assumptions of the existing world order. The challenge for Jamaica as the JLP saw it, was essentially one of maneuvering *within* the established regimes of global liberalism. The American version of multilateralism which emerged after World War II, and codified in Bretton Woods, was entirely consistent with the world view of the JLP. With the government's acceptance of American-inspired ideas and institutions, the quest for economic resources was to be prosecuted without causing any major rupture, vis-à-vis multinational corporations, international financial institutions, or bilateral relations with northern developed countries.

In this context, Jamaica's maiden speech to the United Nations General Assembly (17th session) was a veritable exercise of passive acceptance of an American-led world economy, albeit with an appeal for minor adjustments. Hugh Shearer, who delivered the address, merely drew the attention of the world body to the discrepancies in the terms of trade between developed and developing countries, applauded resolution 1710 (XVI) which inaugurated the first United Nations Development Decade, appealed for expansion in the resources of the International Development Association, and expressed regret that the UN's Capital Development Fund was not receiving universal support.

The acceptance of Bretton Woods was in fact consistent with the ideology of the dominant forces in Jamaica, and that JLP foreign policy during the 1960s was a means of establishing linkages with the dominant classes in the North Atlantic. Through these linkages with similar external social forces, the government hoped to thwart challenges to the domestic social order and consolidate its own position of dominance. The Jamaican government, per se, therefore was acting as a conduit for international capital and simultaneously in the strategic interest of *total social capital*. Cox explains the logic of this domestic/international partnership thus:

> The historic blocs underpinning *particular states become connected through the mutual interests and ideological perspectives of social classes in different countries*, and global classes begin to form. An incipient world society grows up around the interstate system, *and states themselves become internationalized in that their mechanisms and policies become adjusted to the rhythms of the world order.*[8]

JLP foreign policy clearly reflected an attempt to construct such linkages. The international dimension of exceptionalism was intended to separate out Jamaica as a country which was a strong defender of the existing world order. At the internal level, policies were specifically put in place to facilitate foreign capital and capitalist modernization. Yet, the perspective of the hegemonic bloc notwithstanding, the JLP could not completely ignore popular pressure from the marginalized. As such, while international exceptionalism was meant to create the objective conditions for passive revolution, it did not do so in a vacuum. The JLP's Minister of Finance, Edward Seaga, summarized the complex management of passive revolution thus:

> A cardinal feature of Government's investment program has been to complete the range of institutions required to provide the varied and specialized investment facilities required for a sophisticated modern financial environment. . . . But

the possibility of repatriation nevertheless hangs as a sword over the head of the economy, hence a sane and balanced policy must encourage foreign loan capital over equity investment; accept new foreign equity investment where desirable and avoid where unnecessary; begin the gradual process of greater local ownership by acquiring partnership interest in existing foreign-owned enterprises.[9]

It is of some significance that the Minister made this statement in 1971, by which time the counter-hegemonic social forces were so strong that the JLP had little choice but to acknowledge their existence as a fetter on rampant modernization. In fact, as early as 1963 the JLP's official *Five Year Independence Plan—1963–1968* admitted that "the Jamaican situation is a classic demonstration of the race between development and discontent."[10]

In this struggle between development and discontent, the hegemonic forces led by the JLP clearly chose the former as its focus. Moreover, the government elected to pursue a particular form of development, namely, modernization through foreign capital. This choice was clearly evidenced in the *Five Year Independence Plan.* The Plan set out a number of mechanisms and policies for foreign capital. The Industrial Incentives Law and the Exported Industry (Encouragement) Law (first passed in 1956 under the PNP) were not only continued, but embellished. Some new "laws" were also added. The combination of incentives and rewards for foreign companies included:

(a) "income tax allowances, including relief from income tax on their entire capital expenditure on depreciable assets, including extensions and additions made during the first 8 years of operations";

(b) "complete relief from income tax for the first 10 years of operation," or the right to elect a similar package depending on the companies' needs. The original tax relief period was 7 years;

(c) duty free imports on industrial inputs and complete relief from "tonnage tax";

(d) generous depreciation schedules and allowances including the option to write down at "the original cost of the assets"; and

(e) granting of "tax exemptions, for the 5-year period 1964–1969, on that portion of a manufacturer's profits which bears the same proportion to his total profits. . . ."[11]

These incentives to foreign capital were further enhanced through programs such as the Factory Construction and Textile Industry Laws.

In addition to the fiscal incentives provided to foreign capital, the JLP also formed a number of coordinating boards under the Ministry of Trade, Industry, and Tourism. These included the Industrial Development Corporation with separate branches for "Promotion" and "Factory Construction," a Tourist Board, Industrial Training Scheme, and a Small Businesses Loan Board. The capitalization of the entire program was 5,612,000 pounds sterling. A good indication of where the JLP placed its emphasis may be found in the relative distribution of the funding in the different categories. Of the 5.6 million pounds slated for "development," only 200,000 were allotted for Small Businesses, and a paltry twenty-five thousand for the Training Scheme.[12] This Plan was made at a time when the governments own figures showed that 26 percent of the labor force in the age group 20–29 were unemployed, while a staggering 39 percent of youths in the fifteen to nineteen age category, could not find work.[13] By comparison, the amount allotted for Industrial promotion (in effect for the attraction of foreign investment) was 1,100,000 pounds sterling.

The problem here is not simply one of numbers, but one of perspective and direction. A development plan is not merely a technical document based on some recondite economic rationality. While the Five Year Independence Plan does contain rationality, it is a question of whose rationality, and ultimately whose interests and perspectives. The generous offers to foreign capital contained the simultaneous exclusion of the Jamaican poor, especially on account of the low numbers of jobs created by capital intensive investments. Ultimately, this is not even a question of biased development strategy, but one of economic and political power. In Jamaica, of course, economic and political power is also a problem of ethno-cultural power, the structural power of foreigners through capital included. The calculus of power attending the process of passive revolution in this period is neatly summarized by Carl Stone who wrote:

The period [1956–1967] . . . gave rise to a vibrant, new and increasingly wealthy and influential entrepreneurial class.

*The political directorate treated the interests of the new entrepreneurs as equal to the interests of the economy as a whole* as the country's economic future seemed hinged on their continued expansion. They had easy access to the corridors of power and their policy advice was sought after by the relatively inexperienced political directorate.[14]

While foreign economic policy was an important component in the management of passive revolution, it was indeed only part of a larger whole. As noted earlier, class oppression in Jamaica gave rise to forms of resistance which were complex and overdetermined. In particular, the moral leadership, or the class morality of the hegemonic bloc, was not fundamentally challenged by the "labor aristocracy" since many members of the working class (those with full-time secured jobs) actually shared important elements of the ideology of exceptionalism. The most determined resistance came from the urban poor, and from other social forces marginalized by the vision of the ruling ideology. Yet, it cannot be said that cultural resistance is outside of class antagonism. On the contrary, the articulation of cultural nationalism and Black Power were, in fact, also forms of class resistance. The JLP was well aware of the strength of the combined anti-hegemonic social forces and, in part, attempted to at least acknowledge this through aspects of its foreign policy. It is in this context that the JLP's Human Rights and African policies must be understood.

## Human Rights and African Liberation

With regards to human rights, it was Jamaica that actually sponsored the resolution for the United Nations International Year of Human Rights. Speaking to this issue at the XVII Session, Prime Minister Shearer stated that: "It is apparent that one of the great unsolved problems of this age is the translation into actual practice of the democratic ideal of fundamental concern for individual rights and for the basic freedoms which man has been endowed by the creator."[15] Jamaica's commitment to human rights, and especially the International Year of Human Rights was so strong, that an informed commentator was led to acknowledge that Jamaica "has done more to promote this event than any other member of the United Nations."[16]

The support of the liberation of southern Africa and specifically the destruction of apartheid were also key aspects of JLP foreign policy. Jamaica is on record as the very first country to cease trade with South Africa, and in 1965 a government paper, approved by the House of Representatives, outlined a policy, vis-à-vis Rhodesia which was indicative of government policy toward the liberation of Southern Africa as a whole. In part the Paper stated:

> Jamaica will support any action taken by the United Kingdom, including the use of force to remove the illegal government in Rhodesia. The cabinet also decided that Jamaica will cease to trade with Rhodesia . . . passports issued by Mr. Smith's government will not be recognized.[17]

There is no doubt that the JLP took a determined policy, vis-à-vis the liberation of southern Africa. The extent to which this reflected the government's commitment to democratic governance, however, is at best shadowy. For while Jamaica was winning much praise on the international scene for its human rights commitment, the story was quite the opposite in Jamaica itself.

The limelight that Jamaica was enjoying at the United Nations on account of its Human Rights initiative was not necessarily duplicated at home. In fact, at the domestic level the JLP was on the defensive on human rights issues. Through the 1960s, the government sought out radical groups and either excluded them from "national development" or punished them through techniques that certainly breached the basic democratic rights of citizens. The government targeted the Rastafarians who constantly challenged the fundamental assumptions of Jamaica as a modern state, and left wing intellectuals who were critical of imperialism, neo-colonialism, and capitalism in Jamaica and the Third World. The JLP responded with debarment of non-resident intellectuals attached to the Mona campus of the University of West Indies, seizure of passports for residents who traveled to Cuba, and a spate of high-handed police actions. George Eaton captures these human rights transgressions succinctly:

> The increasing number of cases in which the J.L.P. administration found it necessary to resort seizure of passports in the post-independence period, gave rise first to suspicion and then the conviction that state power was being used to stifle criticism and opposition and effectively to infringe on the rights of citizens in the name of state security. The banning of certain literature, and later the playing of certain protest

records over the radio stations, only served to enhance the image of the J.L.P. as an authoritarian government.[18]

Clearly, important components of Jamaican foreign policy in this period were in direct contradiction to the government's domestic policies. How can some of these contradictions be explained?

The fact of the matter is that the balance of social forces in Jamaica was such that the JLP government was "driven" into action on the subject of African liberation. To begin with, the revival of Garveyism among the urban poor, and especially through the Abeng Group (recall that Marcus Garvey Jr. was writing for *Abeng*), actually recovered into current memory the legacy of anti-racist struggles earlier in the century. The Pan-African movement, of which Garvey was the symbolic leader, had put Jamaica in the forefront of black liberation well before constitutional decolonization. With the increasing distributive currency of Rasta ideology in large sections of the population, the JLP was outflanked. While exceptionalism could speak of racial harmony at home, the situation in southern Africa was indeed difficult to defend. As Horace Campbell puts it:

> The combined efforts of the Rastafarian and their leaders helped to place Jamaica in the anti-imperialist camp, so that by the time the South Africans invaded Angola in 1975, the Rasta movement and Jamaica consistently opposed the system of apartheid. Further, groups like Burning Spear, Bob Marley and the Wailers presented a variant of reggae music which centralized the question.[19]

The JLP's human rights policy on Africa, therefore, was more an extension of the claims of counter-hegemonic social forces emanating from Jamaican civil society. While the state does have relative autonomy in the formulation of international policy, clearly, in this case, government was principally restricted to determining the form such policy should take. In this instance, race as an ideologized force in the balance of state-civil society relations, propelled the issue of African liberation beyond the discursive parameters of consensualism. In assessing the relationship between the politics of cultural criticism (as expressed in the popular form of reggae) and state behavior, Campbell observes that:

> these artists, who were spearheading the development of a popular culture, were uncompromising in their identification

with Africa, such that in 1969 both the ruling party and the opposition leader made pilgrimages to Africa and Ethiopia in an effort *to keep abreast of this new pace.*[20]

In fact, the cultural pressure from below had been building up long before 1969, and in a desperate attempt to "appease" "Africa consciousness" Jamaicans, the JLP brought Haile Selassie on an official state visit to Jamaica in 1966. That visit was de facto acknowledgment of the cultural, cum political presence, of Africa in Jamaica. More than that, it was evidence that the "West" could no longer serve as the authoritative referential nexus of Jamaican identity.

Let us be clear as to what really happened here. In light of the government's deference to the West (expressed in its pro-Western policies), its vested interest in attracting foreign capital, and being mindful of the popular pressure to take a stand on African freedom at a time when counter-hegemonic social forces were gathering increasing internal support, human rights was sufficiently *neutral* and *universal* as a policy to meet the contradictory demands. Accordingly, the JLP sponsored the UN Resolution on Human Rights which was general enough not to offend the Western powers, especially since the same Resolution may be used against socialist, nationalist, and communist states. In other words, the JLP did not want to implicate the West for being silent on the problem of southern Africa, for it no doubt recognized that this silence was very much on account of the radical forces active in the African liberation movements.

At the same time, it had to respond to domestic mobilization around African freedom; Rastas for example, informed the JLP that they were ready to go to Africa to fight. To ignore the issue would have opened up the possibility of exploding the internal racial/cultural problems which the government had spent so much effort to neutralize. Having adopted the pursuit of international human rights as a declared government policy, the JLP then proceeded to deal with the African issue in that context. Seen this way, the JLP's human rights and African policies were different "sides of the same coin," balanced as it were between hegemonic global social forces and counter-hegemonic forces at home.

## A Fractured Hegemony and PNP Recuperation

The sustained and combined attack by the several anti-status quo social forces began to take effect on the dominant classes and the Jamaican Labor Party. As the decade of the 1960s wore on, the JLP increasingly began to rely on coercion in defense of the social order. Two incidents highlight this resort to state violence, as well as the increased politicization of hitherto unmobilized popular social forces.

The first incident, the anti-Chinese riots, occurred in late August/early September 1965. According to most accounts, a black woman was struck by a Chinese store owner (in his store) in the wake of an argument. This incident between two individuals quickly circulated in West Kingston and elicited a forceful response from the ghetto unemployed and youths. A four to five day riot ensued, with Chinese-owned property heavily looted and/or destroyed. Ordinarily, of course, a relatively minor incident between two individuals would not result in such a response from so many people. There is little doubt that the riot was in fact a response to the perception of generalized abuse of poor, marginalized, black people by ethnic elites. The riot was also further testimony to the increasing politicization of black consciousness in the daily lived experience of a significant section of the population. Put differently, the incident, and the riot, pointed to the *imbrication of race and class in the social order* as a whole, and the efforts to change this order.

If the Chinese riot of 1965 was "cultural" in inspiration, the Rodney riots of October 1968 were explicitly political. The riots developed in the wake of the debarment of the Marxist historian and Black Power activist Walter Rodney upon his return to Jamaica from a Writers' Conference in Montreal. Upon hearing the news of Rodney's *persona nongrata* status, students and professors from Mona decided to engage in a protest march from the campus to the city center. Despite an initial confrontation by the police and "goons from BITU" (the latter being a JLP controlled union), the march proceeded. Through the march the students and professors were joined by large numbers of the ghetto sufferers. Closer to the city, the protesters saw a machine gun on a bridge overhanging the road used. Confusion broke out, but while the students and academics scattered, the urban poor (especially youths) attacked [North American and British businesses "in spontaneous fashion"].[21] Stephens and Stephens sum up the what happened thus:

> Youth gangs and other participants attacked, burnt and smashed all kinds of property, including foreign-owned enterprises as well as white- or minority-owned Jamaican businesses, cars, buses, etc. Chanting of slogans like "black

power" accompanied these acts of violence and caused much fear, speculation and accusations concerning plans and plots of revolutionary violence. . . . [This violence] had the effect of profoundly threatening the Jamaican propertied classes and large sectors of the middle class, by revealing the explosive potential underlying the apparently smooth and consolidated surface of the Jamaican political system.[22]

A quick look at the establishments targeted and destroyed leaves little doubt that the riot, although without a "central command," was in fact not arbitrary. Terry Lacey provides the following list: [North American Life, Mexicana Airline, Canadian Imperial Bank of Commerce, Barclays Bank, Bank of London and Montreal, Royal Bank of Canada, Pan-American Airways, the Jamaican Public Service Company, Jamaica Omnibus Service, Shell, and Esso. According to Lacey, the "mob" also targeted establishments owned by white minority business families including: Uncle's Inn, China Radio and TV, Marzoucas Stores, C.D. Alexander & Co., Jamaica Mutual, Lions' Supermarket, and the offices of the Jamaica Chamber of Commerce].[23] The targets seem to have been deliberately picked.

At the same time that the JLP was beginning to lose its grip on Jamaica's supposed exceptionalist qualities, the PNP began to undergo some changes which, in the end, would result in the JLP's electoral defeat and a major reversal of both domestic and foreign policies. One of the most significant changes within the PNP was the stepping down of Norman Manley as leader of the PNP, and his replacement by his son, Michael Manley, in February 1969.

# 8

## From "Exceptionalism" to Democratic Socialism

### A Requiem for Exceptionalism

After the long decade (1962–1972) of "development from above" on the one hand, and resistance from popular social forces on the other, Jamaica was a country of deep cleavages. Cynicism about official politics (or politics as usual), ran across class lines. The middle classes were fed up with JLP corruption and mismanagement, and the upper classes were increasingly coming to the conviction that in order to maintain their dominance (since consensualist hegemony was in decline), some reforms would have to be made. In fact, the reforms were to be part of a process of re-hegemonization. As for the marginalized, there was a glimpse of hope when Michael Manley replaced his father, and immediately set about to incorporate into his political machine, those hitherto "disenfranchised." From about 1969 when the younger Manley assumed leadership of the PNP, to the general elections of 1972, the viscosity of exceptionalism began to break down. The material conditions for this decomposition was to be found in the marked rise in unemployment (from 12 percent in 1962, to 23 percent in 1972), a 30 percent decline in real income for the bottom 30 percent of the population, and a decline in overall economic growth.[1] Further, the resentments which these conditions generated made it more difficult to maintain notions such as multi-racialism, harmony, and progress. In the end, all the JLP was left with, was a putative defense of tradition and stability. This defense crumbled in 1972.

### The 1972 General Elections

The PNP did not come to office with a mandate for socialist transformation in 1972. The campaign was more "issue oriented" and, although there was much rhetoric about change and transformation, no *ideological break* with previous elections was registered. The PNP attacked the JLP's record on the economy, crime, corruption, victimization (especially with regards to jobs and housing), and abuse of the government-owned Jamaica Broadcasting Corporation. To the extent that socialism was mentioned at all, it was done in the name of "Christianity" and "Love," with Michael waving the Rod of Correction.[2]

It was quite clear that Michael Manley's strategy was to keep the class coalition the PNP had been building since 1969. His particular challenge was how to incorporate the blue collar and unemployed, without driving away the middle classes and bourgeoisie. A further challenge lay in keeping the support of the "cultural critics" without alienating the established church; both "groups" had significant moral/cultural influence in the country. These were precisely the challenges which Michael was justly known to meet with distinction, as the following excerpt of an election speech shows:

> I want it to be known that if it is God's will that I should face this awesome responsibility I would want to consult the Church for Guidance, to involve the small farmers in the creation of decisions that guide their fate, to get the help of teachers in the planning of a genuine educational revolution; the help and advice of doctors in any plan for social justice so far as medicine is concerned; I would want the Jamaica Manufacturers Association, the Chamber of Commerce, the trade unions, the genius of the University and all of the people actively involved in the decision making processes. Without them the future cannot be built nor can it be built without the youth groups and organizations. . . . we will face the election, when it comes in the faith that the New Jerusalem is ours to build and we will say with St. John in the Revelations: "And I saw a new heaven and a new earth; for the first heaven and the first earth were passed away. . . ." Comrades, let us now put our hands to that Holy task.[3]

The references to the Old Testament were backed up by reggae songs (such as "Beat Down Babylon," "Small Axe," and "Must Get a Beating") which ". . . expressed the outrage of many poor people toward the "oppressors," loosely identified as the JLP and associated groups such as 'capitalists.' "[4] The established church was also pleased with Manley on account of his talk of moral redemption, and his objection to a national lottery which the JLP wanted to start.[5] The JLP ran a less than energetic campaign focused on its record of achievements, fighting crime, and maintaining stability to facilitate economic development. In the end, Manley's ability to hold several constituencies together despite their antagonisms proved to be too much for the JLP. Perhaps more than anything else, Michael Manley presented Jamaicans with hope and vision after a decade in which the legitimacy of the state had been severely eroded.

The JLP was soundly defeated, with the PNP winning by the largest margin since (full suffrage) general elections were first held in 1944. The results showed that the PNP drew votes from all classes in the society, including the most influential capitalists, and blue collar workers. The victory would have been even more decisive had youths below age twenty-three been allowed to vote. Nonetheless, the PNP won 56 percent of the popular vote, and thirty-seven of the fifty-three seats in the House of Representatives. The multiclass coalition victory was very much reflected in the celebrations— big businessmen drank whiskey, while "the masses" smoked "herb."[6] Even the *Daily Gleaner*, traditionally in favor of the JLP, and put off in this election by Manley's courtship of the marginalized of the urban areas, praised Michael for running a "magnificent campaign." At this point it seemed as if everyone, save the JLP, was happy with the PNP. This would soon change.

## The Populist Interlude

During 1972 and 1973 the PNP introduced so many, and such diverse pieces of socially progressive legislation, that it is difficult to attach a label. More important than the label though, is the fact that the new government began addressing a significant number of issues which were decidedly in the interests of poorer Jamaicans. There was also a noticeable shift in the government foreign policy. Rather than haggle over whether this was a populist interlude, a precursor to Democratic Socialism, or a more benign form of what was referred to as passive revolution regarding the JLP in the 1960s, it is more useful to understand the policies of the new government in terms of the balance of social forces, bearing in mind that such a balance was fluid and still in the making.

The first thing to note is that leading members of the government were drawn from the ranks of the traditional dominant classes, a situation which would partly continue into the second government beginning in 1976.[7] In addition to the business families in the government, some noted PNP "moderates" such as W. O. Issacs, F. Glasspole, A. Issacs, and Rose Leon were also in the first Cabinet.[8] The only Cabinet Minister from the left was Anthony Spaulding, who became Minister of Housing, a position widely associated with mobilizing votes. The composition of the Cabinet and parastatals, however, did not seem to inhibit the introduction of popular programs. Consider the following initiatives in 1972 and 1973 respectively: 1972—Special Employment Program, Skill Training Program, Worker's Bank, JAMAL (Literacy Program), community health aides, Operation Grow, Land Lease, Youth Training, and a Public Housing Program; 1973—introduction of food subsidies, free education at secondary and university levels, equal pay for women legislation, increase in property taxes, and Jamaica Nutrition Holdings.[9] While space does not allow a detailed description and analysis of each individual program, there is little doubt that on the whole, government policy was very much reflective of the multi-class nature of the PNP. It is also important to recognize none of the initiatives really threatened *the economic position* of the dominant classes.[10]

The exceptionalist social forces which had rallied around the authoritarian state in the 1960s, were relatively calm in the first two years of the new PNP government. This happened for two reasons. First, well respected members of the capitalist class enjoyed high profiles in the Cabinet, and were generally trusted to be competent "night-watchmen" for the interest of "Jamaica" as defined by the dominant classes. The positions these people held in the PNP government were seen as desirable since, by the estimation of "the exceptionalists" themselves, some reforms were needed to diffuse the potentially revolutionary situation which had begun to surface in the last years of the 1960s. Moreover, the PNP had abandoned socialism since 1952, and the new leader of the PNP did not, up to this point, give any indication of resurrecting that "philosophy." There were concerns expressed, however, over the government's increasing intervention in the economy. These interventions were in fact prompted by deteriorating economic conditions.

*Democratic Socialism Arrives*

By 1974, the PNP had moved considerably to the left, and consistently criticized capitalism as social system, and imperialism as a function of the former. The leftward shift was perhaps best signaled by the assumption of the office of General Secretary of the PNP by Dr. D.K. Duncan, a former member of the YSL, and a well-known, committed socialist. Signals of the PNP's movement to the left however, were not necessary for Manley announced the new path in parliament, as well as at a rally in Kingston where some 75,000 people attended. In a statement to the House of Representatives on November 20, 1974, aimed at clarifying the party's future direction, Manley delivered what can safely be described as a *tour de force* against capitalism. Witness the following:

> ... Mr. Speaker, ... when we of this Government and in the People's National Party speak of Capitalism we are not speaking of any person or individual. We are not speaking of a businessman or any particular entrepreneur. *We are speaking of a total system.* ...
>
> In a Capitalist society, a Capitalist Government makes decisions primarily in the interest of Capital, the assumption being that once the owners of Capital are treated with due deference, the social order will take care of itself. Historically, this theory has proven to be totally fallacious and the consequences for humanity most disastrous.[11]

The Prime Minister proceeded to establish a discursive connection among capitalism, colonialism, and slavery. He was also careful to point out that capitalism as a philosophy, is "morally bankrupt" and, therefore, rejected by the PNP. In a moment of bold ideological assertion, the illustrious leader went on to proclaim that "the age of capitalist exploitation is dead." This last pronouncement notwithstanding, Manley noted that Democratic Socialism does reserve an important role for the private sector. The Jamaican brand of socialism was to be based on a "mixed economy."

In the same statement to the House of Representatives, Mr. Manley alluded to some of the basic assumptions of socialism. It is of considerable importance that Democratic Socialism be understood as a complex ideological, political, and cultural configuration. To begin with, the critique of capitalism and the effort to define an alternative (ideological) "world view" was deemed to be of strategic importance to the party. Manley himself considered the construction of a comprehensive perspective/framework outside of "capitalist philosophy" critical to the successful transformation of Jamaica.[12]

In the production of this alternative vision, however, the PNP was very mindful of the country's strong religious and anti-socialist tradition; its proximity to the U.S.; and not the least, the veritable paroxysm of "African consciousness" which were consolidating significant sites in a cultural war of position. "Democratic Socialism" was in many ways an effort to weld these disparate forces into a coherent ideological unity. The Prime Minister's own reflections bear strong testimony to this and it is worth quoting him at length:

> As to the name, we considered three possibilities. Christian socialist was rejected on the grounds that it might sound like a political ploy. We decided not to use the word socialist alone because it seemed to invite too much speculation. Quite apart from communism, there were a number of African socialist states organized on a one-party basis. Then again, the local communists were at the time in semi-hiding under the term "scientific-socialist." Since we were neither communist nor seeking to establish a one-party state, it seemed to invite unnecessary risk to use the term socialist without qualification. In the end we settled on democratic socialist.[13]

Although Democratic Socialism was declared in 1974, it is important to note that the official party document recognizing this was not agreed upon and adopted until 1978. This was no accident. The fact is that there were deep divisions over ideology within the party itself, and the delay in producing the *Principles and Objectives of the People's National Party* was a direct consequence of internal struggles. Quite reminiscent of the 1940s, the party was divided between left and right over the most fundamental issues of policy and direction. Michael Manley himself admits to these deep divisions noting that, despite every effort since 1972, the party could not resolve some basic questions of ideology. In his recollection, the most controversial problems had to do with the following:

> What was the position in relation to classes? Was there a class alliance? If there was a class alliance, whose class interest should be first served if there was a conflict? In a mixed economy, should the public or the private sector play the leading role? Some were arguing that a class alliance is a contradiction in terms since Jamaica is part of the capitalist system and a capitalist class exists to exploit the working class.[14]

## A Democratic Socialist Foreign Policy

As suggested before, domestic and foreign policy should not be seen as exclusive fields of activities. The two spheres are not only reciprocally connected, but are geared toward the same objectives defined by the government in office, and reflect the balance of social forces in the society.[15] Ideology is crucial in establishing the links between the two by specifying a coherent framework of thought; a guide to action; and the criteria for evaluation of performance. The examination so far of ideology at the domestic level is only a matter of organizational and analytical convenience, not one of theoretical privilege.

The PNP's *Principles and Objectives* devotes an entire chapter to "International Policy." It described the foreign policy of Jamaica prior to 1972 as a "servile relationship with imperialism," noting that this was "consistent with the capitalist orientation of the past."[16] In establishing its difference from this past the document affirms the following:

> ... the objectives and nature of the Democratic Socialist process in our country form the basis of our International Policy. *Therefore, the form and substance of our relationship with other countries are significantly determined by the objectives and nature of their political process.*[17]

Two significant clues about the motivation of Jamaican foreign policy may be extrapolated from the foregoing statement. First, the PNP government publicly and officially declared that its foreign policy is guided by ideology, and specifically, that of Democratic Socialism. The implications of this are not to be underestimated. For if socialism means a challenge to a capitalist social order at home, then quite reasonably, the same applies at the international level. That is to say, a democratic socialist-inspired foreign policy necessarily means an attempt to transform the world order through an alliance with like-minded states and transnational social forces. In principle, the moral foundations of the transformed world order would itself be grounded on assumptions of non-exploitation, justice, and equality.

Secondly, and as a extension of the first proposition, the statement of policy is clear about the factors which determine Jamaican policy, vis-à-vis other states, namely, "the objectives and nature of *their* political process." In contradistinction to the abstruse diplomatic rhetoric proper to Westphalian protocol, the Jamaican government was candid about the politics of its own foreign policy.

The constitutive weight of ideology in Jamaican foreign policy could be further extrapolated from a speech made by Prime Minister Manley to the Parliament in May 1974. First, the Prime Minister challenged one of the key assumptions of political realism by insisting that "size and power are formidable things . . . but the world has no combination of size and power that can permanently arrest the force of ideas."[18] Mr. Manley went on to depict the extant world order as a terrain of struggle between forces that are determined to secure justice and equality through structural transformation, and those that are bent on maintaining the status quo.[19] He pointed out that Jamaican foreign policy is aimed at marshaling progressive global forces and states in *collective action* against the entrenched "international regimes" which have kept the Third World in a near permanent state of destitution. Jamaica's role, and policy, in this struggle is akin to the leadership of a radical trade union movement fighting for economic, political and social rights. In the Prime Minister's view, Third World states are similar to workers, while the North/West occupies the position of employers. In this regard, Jamaica must play the role of an *organic intellectual* of the oppressed of the world. Substantively, this means challenging the ontological foundations of the world order from the perspective of socialist morality. It is with this in mind that Manley told Parliament the following:

> Just as we say that the citizens of each nation are part of an ethical system that rests upon the notion of equality, so do we assert the principle of equality as between the different national families that make up the world community. I beg, Mr. Speaker, that we do not waste our time by suggesting that morals are irrelevant. *The whole of the world's crisis flows from the fact that so much political and institutional leadership of the world rejects the relevance of moral and ethical ideas.*[20]

And again,

> Our simple task is to play our part in the uniting of those nations into a kind of world trade union for the poor that can articulate the conditions of justice and back up the speech with power.[21]

The chapter on "International Policy" goes on to itemize "the fundamental elements of Party Policy." It is interesting that the first item concerns anti-imperialism and not the United Nations which is the second. Other "elements" include regional and international cooperation. Support for the National Liberation Movement, condemnation of all fascist and racist regimes, full support for the creation of a New International Economic Order; assistance to other underdeveloped countries; and establishing and maintaining relationships with capitalist and socialist countries. There is considerable evidence in this section of the *Principles and Objectives* that the vision of PNP foreign policy was toward restructuring the world economic order, an assertion of the principle of self-determination, and questions of fundamental political rights for marginalized peoples.

### Unilateral Policy: Fighting the Bauxite MNCs

The PNP's policy of restructuring Jamaica's relationship with the world economy was forcefully expressed in its policy, vis-à-vis North American bauxite multinationals operating in the country. After months of unsuccessful negotiations with the MNCs, Prime Minister Manley in a statement to the parliament announced the unilateral imposition of the Bauxite Production Levy Act, retroactive to January 1, 1974. The Act resulted in an immediate seven fold increase in revenues from the industry and set the basis for further structural changes, such as acquisition of surface rights and joint ventures. The Companies (Kaiser, ALCOA, Reynolds, and Alcan) responded with legal actions and eventually with a range of economic "instruments." The Jamaican government expended a good deal of diplomatic effort in averting confrontation with the United States over this issue. Prime Minister Trudeau of Canada committed not to intervene on condition Alcan was treated fairly. On account of the significance of bauxite/alumina for the Jamaican economy, and the issues raised in the PNP action, it is important to go a bit deeper into the government's bauxite policy.

By the time Michael Manley came to office, bauxite and alumina had already become the mainstay of the Jamaican economy; this position of importance, however, was gradual and suffused with foreign domination. As late as 1951, there was no entry for bauxite and alumina in the government's official statistics on Gross Domestic Product. By 1953, the "red gold" was contributing 2 percent to the value of GDP, and by 1962 that figure reached 8.8

percent. The growing significance of bauxite/alumina to the national economy was further underscored by its contribution of 48 percent to total exports and by its employment of over 5,000 workers.

Bauxite production rose significantly between 1954 and 1973, moving from a little over two million metric tons in 1954 to 13.6 million in 1973. The price paid to Jamaica, however, was low throughout the entire period and pitiful between 1954 and 1956. On account of a 1957 agreement the price paid did go up significantly—from US$0.70 cents *per metric tons* in 1956 to US$2.24 in 1957. This higher 1957 price, however, did not change very much and by 1973, Jamaica was receiving a lower unit price (US$2.01) than in 1957. Against this, primary aluminum (the end product of bauxite) maintained a mean price of US$25.54 cents *per pound* (with a standard deviation of 1.82) for the period 1960–1973; in real terms Jamaica was receiving approximately 2 percent of the value of the end product.[22] By 1973, Jamaica was second only to Australia in the world production of bauxite.

The PNP government took the following factors into consideration when it was forming its proposals for the negotiations: (a) the bauxite MNCs are fully integrated companies which control 80 percent of bauxite from the raw material stage to the primary metal (and for some even to end-use fabrication). The concern of the government was that such "tight" vertical integration allowed considerable manipulation of "transfer prices" and directly affected tax and royalty revenues;[23] (b) the revenues paid to the Government by the MNCs were unacceptably low and did not reflect market conditions; (c) the control of bauxite resources by the MNCs was a direct hindrance to development planning; and (d) the industry was completely owned and controlled by foreign countries, a fact which substantively compromised Jamaica's economic sovereignty.

A fifth factor, directly connecting the domestic and international, may be added here. Given the emergence of Democratic Socialism in official discourses, the PNP was under considerable pressure to embark on land reform. This pressure was heightened on account of rising unemployment with no sign of the traditional sectors of the economy absorbing the more than 20 percent out of work. Structural unemployment combined with a severe shortage of housing and high crime in urban areas (primarily Kingston) demanded urgent action. Many sufferers were buoyed by the talk of socialism in Jamaica and felt they had been given the right to seek immediate justice. Some even defined justice in quasi-racial terms. This configuration of circumstances led to *land capture*, a phenomenon whereby thousands of structurally displaced people began to occupy private land without legal consent. This was not simply a situation of squatting, since the main purpose of the "capture" was to secure a farming plot. The captured lands were usually idle, and the legal property of "brown-men." The PNP had already met with stiff resistance from the propertied class on the issue of land reform, and could not afford a frontal assault against this class. Yet something had to be done, especially since the land owners were blaming PNP socialist rhetoric for the land captures. The answer was to be found in the huge amounts of idle land which the bauxite MNCs had under their control. Through reacquisition, the PNP would have land to give to the sufferers without incurring the opposition of the local dominant classes. This is partly why the government was not simply interested in securing revenues.

From a global point of view, the PNP was worried that outright nationalization might be met with retribution from the U.S., transnational capital (outside the bauxite/alumina industry); and multilateral lending agencies. The direction of Jamaican state finances was not very promising, and it was felt that any action which departed from the extant international foreign investment regime might jeopardize future chances of securing multilateral and bilateral aid. The specter of OPEC was still fresh in the minds of the American administration, and nationalization of the North American bauxite concerns would have explicitly politicized the Jamaican gambit. It is for these reasons the Jamaican Government was insistent on informing the U.S. State Department of its intended actions *prior* to notifying the MNCs.

According to Manley himself, the companies did not take the negotiations seriously, despite his insistence that an agreement must be struck before the 1974 government budget. The companies were under the misguided impression that the government would be satisfied with an ad hoc increase of revenues to meet shortfalls in the upcoming budget. The MNCs were clearly working with paternalistic assumptions and failed to gauge the wider historical context in which the PNP had situated the bauxite/alumina industry. In concrete terms, the companies argued the Government's proposed formula for revenues was too costly to them, and that the industry as a whole would be hurt in the long run. Manley subsequently noted that the negotiations were an "exercise in pure farce," given the unreasonable attitude of the companies. The government was also satisfied that the companies were unable to demonstrate both an inability to pay higher revenues, and in what ways Jamaica's proposals would damage the industry.

The failure to arrive at a mutual agreement led the Jamaican Government to unilaterally impose the Production Levy.

The immediate response of the companies was to seek the intervention of the United States' Government on their behalf. Some attempts were made by individual senators and congressmen to flex the economic and political muscles of the United States, but no major act of reprisal came out of Washington. At this point the more overt form of the behavioral/structural power of capital asserted itself.[24]

*Multinational Capital Responds*

Given the mobility of transnational capital, MNCs have a range of behavioral instruments which can be deployed to discipline "recalcitrant states" challenging embedded distortions in the practice of global liberalism. Gill and Law explain the problem thus:

> . . . transnational corporations exert authority across national boundaries, in the way that they allocate resources. The headquarters of such firms often decide on the geographical location of production . . . They make investment decisions on a global scale, *shifting funds from one country to another, so affecting the jobs of millions of workers, and the levels of economic activity in a range of nations.*[25]

The behavior of the bauxite MNCs subsequent to the Production Levy forcefully bore out this problematization of transnational power. Plants were closed, investments shifted to "climates" more favorable to corporate imperialism and, in the end, the level of economic activity in Jamaica was drastically affected.

The reaction of the MNCs notwithstanding, Jamaica did demonstrate that the power of transnational capital is not impervious to being effectively challenged. Although production was scaled down against the wishes of the PNP government, the new revenue formula did significantly increase payments to the country. Moreover, other aspects of the PNP intervention in the industry, such as land acquisition and partnerships, did give Jamaica more control of its national economy. Considerable knowledge about every aspect of the industry was also gained in the process of preparing for the negotiations. In this respect, the Jamaica Bauxite Commission became one of the few, (and certainly the most prominent), institutions specializing in research pertaining to the world bauxite/alumina industry. The Commission became the basis for the Jamaica Bauxite Institute which became the knowledge base for setting up the International Bauxite Association.

## The Multilateral Strategy

The PNP placed considerable weight on multilateralism in its attempt to realize its goals and objectives, bearing in mind that these latter were not fixed. There were two components to its multilateral strategy. First, the government saw multilateral institutions as convenient platforms through which transnational social forces interested in structural change at the global level could be mobilized. In large measure, this entailed a struggle *within* existing multilateral institutions (pace the UN and its specialized agencies) in order to change the extant norms, values, rules, and decision-making process. Secondly, the government contributed to the further development and/or founding of new institutions specifically geared toward countering the economic domination of the northern industrialized nations.

The administration's first address to the United Nations set the scene for an unrelenting attack on the fundamental coordinates of the post-1945 world order, and specifically on the few nations that were interested in its maintenance.[26] After noting that the UN and the General Assembly represent the "highest aspirations of mankind," Mr. Manley, who delivered the address, went on to lambaste the inertia of the organization. He suggested that the difficulty in solving the world's problems does not arise from a lack of ideas "but rather from the stubborn refusal of men to listen." One of the most significant dimension of the speech was an attempt to redefine the principle of "equality of states" in social and economic terms; the legalistic definition ensconced in the principle of sovereignty was deemed insufficient. In Jamaica's judgment, "unemployment and poverty, malnutrition, inadequate housing existing side by side with conspicuous affluence represent an intolerable invasion of the principle of equality. . . ."[27]

In the speech Mr. Manley also called on Third World countries to engage in south-south cooperation and to embark on self-reliant economic strategies. He called for the establishment of a development fund drawn from within the Third World as this would allow "developing nations to *promote the conditions of their own develop-ment* through international cooperation in their own ranks."[28] There was no appeal for foreign aid. Developing states were then invited to Jamaica for a conference in 1973, where such cooperation might be more systematically addressed. This was not mere rhetoric, as important components of the speech later translated into reality.

In this respect, Jamaica appeared to be far more "dangerous" than Cuba, since one could not accuse it of being undemocratic. After all, there were regular, free and fair elections in the country; the PNP itself was democratically elected, and Jamaica was with-out the stigma of a bloody revolution led by "socialist/communist dictators."[29] The Jamaican *danger* lay in the fact that socialism was in the backyard of the United States via the democratic choice of the people. In more global terms, the ideological position of Ja-maica challenged the supposed necessary relation between capital-ism and democracy. On the contrary, the PNP was suggesting that socialism was the answer to the pitfalls of dependent capitalist development which had hitherto been pursued with vigor in Ja-maica and much of the Third World. In other words, ideologically, the PNP presented the view that, as a social system, capitalism was incapable of meeting the social needs of the majority of the population. Consequently, it was necessary for capitalism to be structurally transformed, and for liberal democracy to be democra-tized. According to PNP ideology, these propositions were also ger-mane to the international political economy which both mirrored and contributed to the structures of economic exploitation and political marginalization coeval with the national situation. It is important to recognize, therefore, the way in which domestic and global forces were interpenetrating, and concomitantly the mutual relationship among Democratic Socialism, anti-imperialism, and (Third World) nationalism.

## PNP Third World Leadership Through the IBA

The formation of the International Bauxite Association was perhaps the greatest success of Jamaica's activist foreign policy in Manley's first government. In significant ways, the objectives and actions of the Association represented the PNP's strategic views of Third World solidarity and the possibilities of resisting/countering exploitative (or at least inequitable) aspects of a global economic and political order underpinned by the structural power of western based multinational corporations; their respective home states; and "conservative" social forces in Third World countries. As we shall see presently, the IBA had economic implications outside of the bauxite industry. Its political ramifications have also been of some significance.

Fred Bergsten has pointed out that while oil is more important than bauxite, aluminum which comes from the "red gold" is "second only to steel in importance among world metals."[30] Aluminum is used as a major component in the aircraft and automobile industries, and in a wide range of consumer end products. It is also on the United States' list of strategic stockpiles. There are alternatives to bauxite—alunite, anorthosite, "Georgia clay," coal refuse, and dowsonite, but these are not as economically feasible.[31] Further, the aluminum companies have grown accustomed to bauxite and their plant and equipment are geared to specific types and grades of bauxite.

The nature of the problem here is remarkably similar to those that led to the formation of the OPEC cartel. Bauxite is highly concentrated in a few, mostly Third World countries—Jamaica, Guyana, Suriname, Guinea, Dominican Republic, and Haiti. Australia is also a major exporter. As was the case in oil, the ownership and control of the world's bauxite industry was concentrated in a few North American multinationals—Alcan, Alcoa, Kaiser, Rivere. The industry was noted for extremely high vertical integration and conspicuous oligopolistic practices. What is more is that these practices were condoned by the home governments of the MNC's. Thus Hojman notes:

> ... there is plenty of evidence that the Organization for Economic Cooperation and Development governments are not only aware of oligopolistic behavior in this market, but that these governments positively support these activities and cooperation between these firms, which are seen as a guarantee of stable prices, adequate investment flows, and minimal disturbance to the economies of the industrialized countries.[32]

Such support, however, did not prevent the OECD and especially the United States from maintaining the discourse of free-market enterprise.[33]

Michael Manley and the PNP were well aware of the malpractices of the bauxite MNCs in Jamaica. Since his assumption of the leadership of the party in 1969, the then opposition leader was

keen on increasing revenues from the industry and more fundamentally, altering the relationship between the foreign companies
and Jamaica. One of the first steps in this direction was the creation of the Jamaica Bauxite Institute. In part, the aim of the
Institute was to acquire as much technical, legal, and economic
(especially in the area of marketing) knowledge of the industry as
possible. Prior to the creation of the Institute, this knowledge was
the exclusive preserve of the multinationals.

Consistent with the PNP's strategic view of Third World collective action, the government began discussions with fellow Caribbean bauxite-producing states about a united approach, vis-à-vis
the multinationals. The objectives were to share information about
the industry, discuss their respective negotiations with the MNC's
in order to avoid the latter playing off one country against the
other(s), increase revenues, and tackle the vexing problem of ownership and control. The Caribbean states were in a good position to
initiate actions since they were supplying 80 percent of the U.S.
bauxite/alumina imports. Jamaica was in the best position since it
supplied the lion's share. Collective action, however, was difficult to
formalize since Australia, a major supplier, was only lukewarm to
the idea. Australian trepidation notwithstanding, a number of international and domestic (to Jamaica) factors made "resources diplomacy" viable.

The success of OPEC in 1973–74 demonstrated that it was
possible for relatively weak states to challenge entrenched structures, multinational corporations, and western states without necessarily incurring punitive measures. The fact that western states
did not, or were not able to effectively retaliate against OPEC
countries created both encouragement and political room for similar actions by other commodity producers. The U.S. was also on the
defensive on account of its Vietnam debacle, the effects of which
were both fresh and demoralizing. In addition, this was also the
time when the Third World countries had seized the moral and
political ground for a reconstructed world economic order.

The fact that all but one of the bauxite producers were poor
tended to define the issues surrounding the formation of the IBA in
ideological terms. These countries were not simply interested in
increasing revenues; rather, they saw the challenge in much broader
and structural terms, at times specifically locating the problem in
the hegemonic institutions of Bretton Woods. In an address to the
Geological Society of Jamaica, for example, IBA Secretary General
H. M. Guda reiterated the structural conditions of the global politi-

cal economy which impelled the formation of the Association. He noted that the postwar multilateral framework induced poor countries into uncritically accepting "the terms of reference governing the operations of traditional international economic institutions."[34] According to Guda the consequence of this was that:

> countries emerging to nationhood axiomatically gravitated to membership of the United Nations and its Specialized Agencies, the World Bank and its subsidiaries, the International Development Association and the International Finance Corporation, the International Monetary Fund and the General Agreement on Tariffs and Trade, without seriously examining . . . the fundamental assumptions on which many of these institutions are structured.[35]

The leadership in the IBA had come to the conclusion that these institutions were simply the organizational form of postwar global capitalist expansion, and a corresponding political order. It was also critical of the neo-colonial function of these institutions through which:

> . . . the emergent countries tended to internalise prevailing economic values especially those relating to the continuing economic dominance of technologically advanced countries and the absence of market power by the resource-producing countries of the developing world.[36]

In Jamaica, the PNP had long criticized the former JLP government and even previous PNP governments for uncritically accepting such values which, in another context, Manley described as a "permanent colonial immobility of mind."[37]

Within Jamaica itself there was also a correlation of social forces propitious to "taking-on" the bauxite multinationals. Although the propertied classes were concerned about the leftist rhetoric of the PNP government, they did not have anything to lose from Jamaican leadership in forming the IBA, or from a restructured relationship (and increased revenues) which might come from negotiations with the MNCs which were simultaneously in progress. The impact of imported inflation on manufacturing inputs, the consumer price index, foreign reserves, and the weakness of the Jamaican dollar were of concern. Increased revenues from bauxite could provide a political safety valve by buffering the impact of external economic pressures, while meeting domestic political obligations. The propertied classes were concerned about the increasing influence of the PNP left wing, as well as the rise of anti-imperialist sentiments by the "cultural critics."

At the other end of the spectrum, support came from the labor unions; organized radical groups such as Abeng, WLL, PNPYO; University faculty and students (Sixth Form Association); and the "cultural critics"—Black Power, Rastas, Rudies, and in general the Dread population. Most of these saw the bauxite issue in anti-imperialist terms, and a smaller, but politically important section saw it as "African" people fighting "White Power." Fred Bergsten was constrained to put it that "Jamaica, in fact, moved partly to demonstrate that it was no longer a 'lackey of the imperialists.' "[38]

The dialectic hegemony/resistance-counter-hegemony was very much ensconced in the international politics surrounding the formation of the International Bauxite Association. The anti-imperialist definition of the objectives and "grand strategy" of the Association were prosecuted with such vigor by Jamaica that Australia was moved to demonstrate its distance, and in the end joined the "IBA largely due to the political pressures from its colleagues in the Commonwealth."[39]

The activist role played by Jamaica (and Guyana) in the formation of the IBA was recognized by the U.S. State Department's own reflection on how best to respond to these two countries. It is noteworthy that the major source of comfort for the United States came from the economic dependence of these countries on the OECD states. The U.S. government put it thus:

> The Caribbean producers' limited financial reserves and heavy dependence on the United States, Canada, and Western Europe as markets not only for bauxite *but also their other products* make it unlikely that these countries could withhold their bauxite supplies for an extended period. Jamaica could not readily find other markets for its special type of bauxite.[40]

Of course, this was an accurate description of the situation (i.e., extremely high partner concentration), but was also precisely what Jamaica expected to overcome in its multilateral "resources diplomacy."

Given the expressed intentions of forming a multilateral organization outside the Bretton Woods arrangements, and Jamaica's conscious strategy of multilateral diplomacy, it is important to examine the formal aspects of the IBA. This must be done against the backdrop of its Secretary General's characterization of the Association. He noted that:

> the formation of the International Bauxite Association should be viewed . . . as the formal institutional expression of a nascent economic nationalism currently being witnessed in many developing countries and whose primary purpose is to alter the terms of trade between technologically advanced and backward countries *in the absence of success by traditional economic institutions.*[41]

and again,

> It was only when the emergent countries realised that radical modification in the terms of trade between themselves and technologically-advanced countries could be achieved only by a re-examination and fundamental restructuring of these various multilateral arrangements or by the establishment of new arrangements . . . that serious efforts were made by developing countries to effect beneficial *change outside traditional institutional structures where the dominance of technologically-advanced countries was not institutionally entrenched.*[42]

Some of this "nationalism" was entrenched in the Agreement Establishing the International Bauxite Association.

At the economic level, the IBA was able to make significant industry-wide gains for members and more could have been achieved were it not for Australia's opposition to a floor price for bauxite. The sharing of information enabled most of the producer countries to significantly increase revenues from bauxite. Jamaica's role in this was decisive. Based on thorough research of the industry, the PNP government introduced a levy on bauxite which resulted in a sevenfold increase in revenues. This amounted to "price leadership" in the industry as most of the other producers followed suit.

The Association was also successful in creating a "standard transfer price" pegged to the "American metal market price for primary aluminum." This transfer price of 2 percent to 2.5 percent "amounts to between $33.51 and $41.9 per tonne for bauxite shipped to the eastern seaboard of the United States and Canada." Considerable importance should be attached to this, since collective action by a small group of Third World states was successful in linking revenues to the high value-added end product of their raw material exports.

This structural rearrangement did not go unheeded by the multinationals and the United States government.

A multiplicity of factors informed the response of the Ford Administration. Conservative forces in the U.S.A. were outraged by another Third World threat (following OPEC) and demanded punitive action. The collective actions of Third World countries elicited accusations of "price-rigging," "price-gouging," and threats to American economic prosperity.[43] A discursive chain was constructed as the latter were connected up with supposed violations of the principles of free market enterprise. As such, the ideological offensive of the IBA was countered on the same terrain, namely, as a foreign threat to fundamental American values. The following from the *Los Angeles Times* was typical of the diatribe:

> There is the clear danger that if cartels are successfully organized by exporters of such commodities as bauxite, copper and tin, they, like OPEC, will not hesitate to cross the line between economic justice and price-gouging.
>
> The U.S. Government surely has a responsibility to *resist* the emergence of new cartels whose purposes are at odds with the goal of a prosperous and stable American economy.[44]

The American-based companies in the meantime were also busy organizing action against IBA. The Ford administration supported the companies in bringing the actions of IBA members to international arbitration but, for a number of political reasons, was hesitant to go further. The circulation of threats to America, however, was so diffuse that the U.S. Congress was under pressure to act. Third World solidarity seemed to pose such troubling questions about American "hegemonic leadership" that the legislative branch felt constrained to intervene directly in foreign affairs. U.S. public opinion demanded something be done to discipline these supposedly recalcitrant states, and especially those ones, such as Jamaica, which were playing a leadership role.

Recall that Jamaica, and to a lesser extent, Guyana, were the ideological leaders of the IBA and were eloquent voices for a New

International Economic Order. Both were socialist of some sort, and both openly defended Cuba—America's arch enemy in the Western hemisphere. Just as important, both were heavily dependent on the U.S. markets for their sugar and bauxite exports—that is, for their economic survival. The U.S. Congress was aware of this, and decided to "retaliate by cutting off the sugar quotas of the Caribbean countries in the U.S. market." Of all the "Caribbean countries," Jamaica and Guyana would have been hit the hardest (as was intended), "but the whole quota system died" and thus rendered the Congressional move redundant.[45]

The material capabilities of the United States, however, are so enormous that loss of a retaliatory instrument in one area does not leave it without options. Thus Congress, still under pressure to act, not only found an alternative disciplinary measure, but a much broadened one. It is under these specific historical circumstances that the U.S. Trade Act of 1974 was passed. The Act was aimed specifically at excluding countries that are members of cartels and other producer collectives such as IBA from freely exporting to the United States. The same Act gave the Executive Branch the power to reward countries that do not participate in collective producer arrangements. According to one source, the Trade Act was a major factor in Mexico's decision to stay out of OPEC.[46] The response of the U.S. was such that Jamaica felt constrained to both defend and distance itself from IBA within months of the Association's formation.

The formation of IBA, and its initial success both inspired other commodity producers to follow suit, and strengthened the position of those who had already embarked on collective action. In addition to OPEC and IBA, the early to mid-1970s also saw the formation of the Uranium Cartel (1972); the International Association of Mercury Producers (ASSIMER, 1975); and the Association of Iron Ore Exporting Countries (AIEC, 1974). Further, coffee, rubber, and tea producers also began to adopt "cartel-styled action."[47] By mid-1975, it was clear the collective action of Third World commodity exporters was beginning to make some progress toward a transformed postwar world economic order.

The activism of the Third World via the G77 and Non-Aligned Movement had gathered such momentum that the United States was forced to respond. By mid 1976, Third World pressure was so strong that one commentator was led to suggest, "It may still be an exaggeration to say that a 'new international economic order' already has arrived, without anyone really noticing. But . . . there can be little doubt that the economic order is in a period of flux."[48]

The United States was not oblivious to the challenge presented by Third World multilateral diplomacy both inside and outside of the United Nations system. In July 1975, U.S. Secretary of State, Henry Kissinger, delivered a speech in Milwaukee which echoed the fears of America and tacitly acknowledged that the Third World was gaining ground. He spoke of "troubling trends," "lopsided, loaded voting, biased results, and arbitrary tactics in the UN and its specialized agencies." According to Kissinger, these tactics were used "to coerce the industrialized countries," something which might push the latter to abandon the UN. The Secretary of State expressed fears that the moral rectitude of postwar multilateral cooperation was beginning to perish under the weight of Third World voluntarism. In his words, "Ideological confrontation, bloc voting, and new attempts to manipulate the Charter to achieve unilateral ends threaten to turn the United Nations into a weapon of political warfare."

The U.S. Secretary of State actually ended up in Jamaica (in 1976) to express American concerns, and employed the carrot and stick method of "persuading" the PNP government to desist from some of its Third World activities. The PNP's leadership role was also of great concern to the local ruling classes, and on one occasion the Private Sector Organization of Jamaica (PSOJ), which was formed to coordinate a united opposition against the government, even wrote to the Prime Minister complaining that he (and Jamaica) was too involved with the Third World.[49]

## Multilateralism via the UN System

The criticism of the unbalanced and exploitative economic relations between North and South heightened during the 1970s. Whereas in the 1960s the JLP was satisfied with mere observer status in the Non-Aligned Movement, in the next decade Jamaica became not only a full-fledged member of the movement but one of its leading advocates. The Manley government saw the East-West conflict as secondary to the problems of the Third World, claiming ". . . that it was our duty to avoid its entanglements and *our duty to resist hegemonic pressure wherever and by whomever* it was exerted."[50] But Non-Alignment meant more than simply staying clear of the Cold War.

After the Algiers Conference in 1973, the Non-Aligned Movement increasingly focused on global economic questions. In the language of regime theory, it may be said that the Movement sought to transform the principles, rules, norms, and decision-making procedures of those regimes which underpinned the postwar global political economy. In substantive terms this meant an attempt to re/allocate global resources via "authoritative" rather than purely "market" mechanisms.[51] Unlike the previous JLP government which sought change in "relational power," that is, change *within* the extant structures and institutions of the global political economy, the PNP embarked on a strategy of "meta-power." "Relational power refers to the ability to change outcomes or affect the behavior of others within a given regime. Meta-power refers to the ability to change the rules of the regime."[52]

In its broadest terms, Jamaican foreign policy in respect of the latter was aimed at interrupting the hegemonic nature of world order and, simultaneously, at building solidarity among "the trade union of the poor." As a matter of foreign policy behavior, these aims were articulated in the government's pursuit of the New International Economic Order (NIEO).

At a formal level, the government sought key positions in the Third World movement through which it was able to exercise direct influence on the scope and direction of the challenge to global liberalism. Thus, Jamaica had a seat on the Coordinating Bureau NAM, which allowed it to act as a broker between countries with divergent perspectives and to reconcile their positions with the objectives of the Movement. Often, this meant working outside the purview of the Movement itself. For example, at the Commonwealth Heads of Government meeting in Jamaica in 1975, the main items on the agenda were all pursuant to the NIEO, an issue of fundamental interest to the Jamaican government.

As is well known, Non-Aligned meetings, among other business, were used to prepare the G77 bloc for negotiations in the UNCTAD and elsewhere. Jamaica assumed considerable responsibility in this process, especially as Chair and chief negotiator of the G77 countries. Its ambassador was also chief negotiator on behalf of the G77 on major issues such as the establishment of a Common Fund for commodities. Given its reputation at the negotiating table, it is not surprising that Jamaica was one of a small number of countries invited to the Conference on International Economic Cooperation held in Paris between 1976 and 1977. According to Don Mills, Jamaica's Ambassador to the United Nations at the time, the meeting was instrumental in clarifying issues which had presented major difficulties at previous UN negotiations. More importantly, it cleared the way for the Common Fund for commodities, an issue over which the North and South were hitherto deadlocked.[53]

At times, both regional and global objectives were pursued simultaneously in the government's multilateral strategy, as was the case with the Law of the Sea regime. Thus, Jamaica played a major role at the Third United Nations Conference on the Law of the Sea which led to the UN Convention on the Law of the Sea. In fact, one of the rapporteur of the Conference was a Jamaican, Dr. Kenneth Rattray. According to Rattray, Jamaica exercised considerable influence at the conference, to the point where apart from advancing ideas "we found ourselves courted from all sides —East/ West and North/South."[54] Jamaica thus found herself as a major "broker" at the Conference, and played a key role in "building bridges" among states with conflicting interests and objectives. It also assumed a leadership position for the developing countries in issues such as the Common Heritage Fund. It is interesting to note that Jamaica also pursued some regional objectives at the Conference. In particular, it was one of the countries that advanced the idea of a Common Patrimony in regards to the Caribbean Sea and called for a Regional Economic Zone. This would involve a pooling of living and non-living resources, and a system of reciprocal preferential rights for states in the zone. While the Regional Economic Zone was meant to overcome the limitations of living in a "marine desert," it was also an effort to create an inclusive regime based on regional cooperation within the larger context of the Law of the Sea Convention.

The island's contribution to the Conference and the skill of its diplomacy was partly reflected in securing the site of the International Seabed Authority. According to Rattray, the Jamaican "quest for the latter was not an idle one." There are tremendous benefits to be derived from having an international organization located in a small country. Apart from international prestige, the Jamaican government was especially interested in the technology that the resource-oriented Seabed Authority would attract.

Jamaica's assumption of a leadership position in the Non-Aligned Movement was perhaps well reflected in taking it upon itself to respond to the north on behalf of the Third World. At times, its responses were comprehensive. A sample of this: the ministry of External Affairs released the following official statement in reply to the speech made by U.S. Secretary of State Kissinger admonishing the Third World. It is worth quoting at length since it gives a good indication of how Jamaica saw its role, as well as its conception of substantive issues. The statement read:

Since the United States and other wealthy industrialized countries have been the main beneficiaries of the economic system established at Bretton Woods, it is hardly surprising that Secretary Kissinger should not want to change the basic arrangements on which the present order is based. It is small wonder that his speech should ignore the fundamental need to refashion the structural foundations which govern the availability and distribution of international finance for development; the transfer of real resources and wealth from rich to poor countries; the distribution of gains from trade; and the regime of foreign investment and the operations of multi-national corporations. In all these areas the dice are presently loaded in favor of the developed countries.[55]

This leadership role in the New International Economic Order was also demonstrated by the PNP's strident effort on behalf of the liberation of southern Africa.

## African Liberation

With the overwhelming support of the African descended population, and a modicum of support from some sections of the elite, Manley was empowered to act on the issue of African liberation. Further, he did not feel constrained, at least during the first years of the government, by the structural power of international capital and multilateral financial institutions. His objective, after all, was to diversify the base of Jamaica's international economic network. Under these circumstances, therefore, it is not surprising that Jamaica, and for that matter Manley himself, became "aggressive" about the liberation of Africa.

The significance of the Manley government's leadership in attacking apartheid must not be underestimated. This was more than a matter of fighting for black rights, a phenomenon so pervasive during the period of decolonization that it might be, and often was, brushed aside, or more accurately pushed outside the "table of contents" of international relations proper. But as a matter of historical record, the anti-apartheid struggle was fundamental to the democratization of world order in general. Much later, when the apartheid regime was clearly heading for meltdown, many of the states which had the power all along to intervene had routinely turned their backs. The UN Roll Call votes demonstrate that quite clearly. Abstention in the face of moral indecency is no alibi. So what did the Jamaican government do, that set it apart from the previous JLP record, and from the Western states which fattened and petted the racist regime?

One significant action was to define the anti-apartheid struggle beyond the borders of South Africa and Rhodesia. The issue was seen as national, regional, and global. This meant supporting the liberation movements directly; supporting the Front Line states— Botswana, Tanzania, Zambia, Angola, and Mozambique, and creating "disturbance" at various global fora. In another instance, the Jamaican government cooperated with Cuba which began to intervene militarily in the struggle for freedom in Southern Africa. Only minimal material support was possible, but that did not prevent the Manley government from engaging in sensitive symbolic diplomacy. In this case Cuban planes with troops touched down in Kingston, on their way Southern Africa. There was no objective need for these landings. Rather, the Jamaican government was demonstrating resolve on the issue, and simultaneously providing much needed international political support for Cuba, which itself had been ostracized for so long. The matter did not escape the attention of Washington, and Secretary of State H. Kissinger attempted to exchange the promise of U.S. supported aid for Jamaica, if only the island would turn its back on Cuba and the MPLA.[56]

A distinctive feature of Jamaican policy, vis-à-vis African liberation, was the language that was employed in articulating its concerns. Apart from constructing the problem of African liberation in anti-imperialist and anti-colonial terms, the PNP consistently attacked the hypocrisy of western states who seemed to have claimed universal monopoly rights to the institution of democracy and the language of freedom and justice. In a 1974 address to the General Assembly, for example, Dudley Thompson (Minister of State, Office of the Prime Minister) chastised the "so-called freedom-loving nations" (i.e., the West) for compromising on the liberation of Zimbabwe; Namibia; and South Africa, while freedom and justice were invoked to intervene in other situations. Concluded Thompson:

> Year after year, with monotonous regularity, this August Assembly has passed resolution after resolution condemning the perfidy of that evil spirit otherwise referred to as the Government of South Africa. She remains obdurate and stubborn in her defiance of the United Nations. This intransigence has exposed this body to the charge of shame-

ful impotence. . . . In the case of Zimbabwe and Namibia, there is far more reason and universal support for United Nations troops to settle the question of Freedom and Justice than there seems to be in Korea.[57]

## Bilateralism

The strategic objectives of PNP's foreign policy in this period were also pursued through bilateral means. While there were considerable overlaps in the contents of the multilateral and bilateral tactics, the latter did have some distinctive features. Further, some domestic "groups" which were "silent" on the government's multilateral policies became severely critical of its bilateral policies.

Jamaica's bilateral (foreign) policy during the 1972–1976 period was dominated by new relationships with the United States and Cuba, and by the tensions which attended these shifts. Generally, the PNP government made a concerted effort to build closer ties with Cuba and, simultaneously, to gradually become less American-centric in its foreign relations. These were not ad hoc policies. The double movement just described was part of a deliberate strategy of unhinging the foreign policy "of mendicancy" (vis-à-vis the U.S.) which had hitherto characterized Jamaica's foreign affairs.[58] The ideo-cultural motive was to disestablish the discursive resonance of *America* as the hegemonic *parens patriae*, and replace it with a more historically responsible referential nexus. The stability of America as the authoritative proper noun for freedom/democracy (that is, as a normative fixed-universal signifying world leadership), was critically engaged.

In contradiction to the signifying chain (or system of equivalence)—America = democracy = freedom = progress = defender of the free world, et cetera; the U.S. was re-produced as—America = imperialism = oppressor = supporter of apartheid = the CIA, and so on. Quite the reverse operation occurred in the case of Cuba. In the pre-1972 period the signifier Cuba contained, *inter alia,*—communism = repression = totalitarianism = terror = Castro. The PNP interrupted this chain and, alternatively, reconstructed Cuba as—anti-imperialist = Non-Aligned = Third World leader = freedom fighters = neighbor = Fidel. These processes of disarticulation/rearticulation were *made, pari passu,* through those normal activities associated with bilateral relations between two states. Thus, the dialectic of Jamaican bilateralism has to be understood as massively overdetermined.

There is a sense in which the foreign policy of the PNP toward the United States was very much determined by events leading up to the 1972 Jamaican general elections. The United States government had made a determined effort to keep the JLP in office by supporting Hugh Shearer's campaign. Manley was seen as "...a socialist dedicated to an egalitarian society," a "fact" which the American Ambassador to Jamaica (Vincent De Roulet) saw as inimical to U.S. interest. On the other hand, De Roulet "...noted Shearer was anti-communist, a well-dressed and courteous 'Negro.'" The Ambassador further characterized Shearer as follows:

> In the whole time I dealt with him . . . I never had to listen to a long speech about his little people with withering bellies and the back-to-Africa crap. He was a hard-boiled businessman. He knew where his bread was buttered.[59]

President Nixon listened and acted on De Roulet's advice. Shearer was given an audience with Nixon, and a hefty loan of twenty million (U.S.) dollars was facilitated through the U.S. Agency for International Development. Despite American interference, the PNP won the elections with ease, as discussed earlier. De Roulet's reaction was nasty. The American ambassador "theorized" that Manley was a confused man because of his mixed racial origin. Manley was described as a "latent alcoholic," an "emotional yo-yo," and Jamaicans as "the most spoiled race in the world." Mr. De Roulet was made *persona non grata* in Jamaica in 1973.[60] Upon his return to Washington, the American ambassador is reported to have openly called Jamaicans "niggers" and "idiots." No official apology ever came from Washington.[61]

If indeed De Roulet was afraid the PNP government might pursue a foreign policy inimical to U.S. interests, he was not to be disappointed. Between 1972 and 1974, the Jamaican administration reversed a number of long standing foreign policies, or opened totally new avenues of change. The Manley government established full diplomatic relations with Cuba; broke off relations with Taiwan; sent trade missions to eastern bloc countries and China; made financial contributions to the African States' Liberation fund; banned imports from Portugal and its African colonies; and signed on Jamaica to CARICOM.[62]

The government's recognition of Cuba was a source of both concern and irritation to the United States. Notwithstanding its small size, economic dependency, and its "situation," vis-à-vis the

U.S., Jamaica launched a sustained effort to remove the OAS embargo on Cuba. It teamed up with its "red triangle" partner, Guyana, and together, they convinced Trinidad, Tobago, and Barbados to support "Fidel." The embargo was removed and, predictably, Washington was displeased. Upon securing the lifting of the OAS embargo, a bilateral Air Agreement was signed between Jamaica and Cuba, allowing direct travel between both countries by the national carriers.[63] Apart from the substantive benefits to be derived from the Air Agreement, there was an obvious symbolic statement made. The PNP government was bent on signaling to Washington, and to conservative forces in Jamaica, that it was determined to back up its "speech" with actions. Some of these actions ended up being seen as de facto anti-Americanism.

In 1973, Manley, Forbes Burnham (the illegitimate but "socialist" Prime Minister of Guyana), and Castro, traveled to Algiers on the latter's aircraft. The incident caused a major uproar in Jamaica. The JLP, *Daily Gleaner*, several private sector organizations, and the Catholic Church, criticized the flight and Manley's statement that, he and Fidel, had a fine occasion to talk about the Sierra Maestra. The Cuban flight was situated in the larger picture of the Caribbean Heads of Government delivering "severe blows" against capitalism and imperialism in Algiers. In the meantime, a much closer relationship was being forged between the PNP and the Cuban Communist Party. In January 1974, trade relations were opened with Cuba, with the U.S. responding by threatening to cut off all assistance to Jamaica. One month later, at the Tlatelolco Latin American conference, Jamaican resolve was eloquently stated by Foreign Minister Dudley Thompson, who was moved to tell Secretary of State Henry Kissinger: "Cuba is very close to Jamaica and it is impossible for me to plan Jamaica's foreign policy without keeping that country in mind and without knowing the present U.S. positions toward it."[64]

In July 1975, Prime Minister Manley, Foreign Minister Thompson, and an entourage of PNP leaders, Government officials, some private sector representatives, and the media, paid an official visit to Cuba. The two countries engaged in extensive bilateral talks with emphasis on economic, technical, educational and cultural cooperation, industrial cooperation, and trade. International problems were also examined. The Joint Communique released on the last day of the visit (in both Kingston and Havana) was a congeries of criticism against imperialism, Third World exploitation, the state of international relations, and western myopia:

Both Parties agreed that the international situation favours the struggle being carried out by the peoples of the world against the imperialists, colonialist, and neo-colonialist forces for their national liberation, respect for their sovereignty and for the rescue of their natural resources. They also agreed to condemn the activities of the transnational enterprises. . . .

They stressed the significance of the unity and solidarity of the socialist countries, the progressive countries and national liberation movements for world peace and liberty; these concerted efforts were considered necessary for the long and difficult struggle required to finally eliminate aggression, exploitation and injustice from international relations.[65]

The Communique also called for an "exclusive" Latin American economic system; condemned the existence of colonial regimes in the Caribbean; and reaffirmed the right of "the majority" in Belize, Puerto Rico, and Panama to determine their political future. Statements were also made in support of the people of Chile in their struggle against the repressive regime of General Pinochet; the Revolutionary Government of the Armed Forces of Peru; "the heroic peoples of Vietnam and Cambodia;" and the patriots of Guinea-Bissau, Angola, and Mozambique. The "Arab countries;" the Palestinians; and the people of South Africa were encouraged to keep on struggling against oppression.

The Jamaican government was praised by Castro for its leadership in NAM, the G77, and specifically for its struggle for a New International Economic Order. The Cuban leader further acknowledged Jamaica's efforts on behalf of Cuba at the OAS and other international fora. Manley himself received the National Order of Jose Marti. In return, the Jamaican Prime Minister praised "Comrade Castro" and the Cuban people for their noble struggle against imperialism. In a strong affirmation of the non-negotiability of national and cultural sovereignty, the two leaders stated:

Cuba and Jamaica reject imperialist, neo-colonialist, racist, economic and cultural penetration, which deforms the authentic values of the peoples of Latin America and the Caribbean and proclaim their determination to struggle for the preservation and development of their national cultures.[66]

This cultural critique of imperialism must be taken seriously since it was an internal core element of Jamaican foreign policy. In fact, it is not unreasonable to suggest the PNP was well ahead of its time with regard to the saliency of culture in international relations.

The advances the PNP was recording at the international level were only partly matched on the domestic front. In general, the economy continued to deteriorate after 1973, with little signs of improvement. Nonetheless, some progress was made in what is usually considered "basic needs" in underdeveloped societies, and it may even be argued that meeting some of these needs is what the government should be aiming for in the first place.

# 9

Promise and Defeat:
Hegemony as Structural Power

## The 1976 Election and the Realignment of Social Forces

With democratic socialism in place for nearly three years, and with continuous economic decline, the 1976 general elections amounted to a referendum on ideology.[1] The PNP campaigned intensely on issues of anti-oppression, anti-imperialism, the exploitative nature of capitalism, the liberation of the south from northern economic bondage, a more radical foreign policy, and significantly, the imperative of continuing with the path of Democratic Socialism. Under the leadership of Edward Seaga, the JLP built its platform around issues of anti-communism, PNP economic mismanagement, what it described as an ideology of "nationalism," and perhaps most importantly, the supposed erosion of democracy in Jamaica. The election was intensely contested with sustained media campaigns, thousands attending party rallies, hundreds of deaths on account of political violence, and considerable international attention.

It had become increasingly evident by mid-1976 that the PNP would be unable to maintain the contradictory but hitherto relatively stable class alliance which had served it so well in the past, and not the least in the 1972–1976 period. Realizing that the party had lost significant portions of the bourgeoisie and middle class, the Prime Minister (and the party leadership) made a deliberate decision to reconstitute its political base.[2] This led to an all out effort in recruiting the urban poor, blue collar workers, students, youths, the large section of non-established workers—domestics, higglers, small peasant farmers, clerical and other lower end office workers, and large numbers of unemployed and underemployed.

While the party was keen on stretching its hand below to the marginalized, so to speak, the specificity of the political was still an open question. The problem was compounded because the JLP, despite its decided conservatism, had historically dominated the rural parishes (especially among small peasant farmers), and enjoyed considerable support from the urban working class (mainly through the auspices of BITU), and even the sufferers. What is more, distrust of communism and socialism run deep in Jamaica, as these are invariably associated with dictatorship, poverty, and anti-Christianity; the linking up of these elements into a referent was precisely the discursive strategy of the JLP. Further, being poor, unemployed, exploited, and socially marginalized, does not necessarily translate into antagonism, vis-à-vis the system which had produced these conditions, namely capitalism and racialized marginalization. Social and economic dispossession do not lead to a *logically necessary* political disposition, as Rishee Thakur, in a recent study critical of this reductionist relationship between class and politics has argued. Thakur writes:

> The political, in other words, is not and cannot be reduced to "an internal moment of the social," in which it becomes a "supplement" of the social. If we maintain the latter position, as in classical Marxism, then the political is nothing more than the necessary "correct" strategic moves from "objective" social belonging to a known political interest and outcome.[3]

If indeed the political cannot be derived directly from the social, then the reconstitution of the PNP political base has to be understood in the wider context of a reconstructed interpellative strategy and ideological reconfiguration. In other words, the elections of 1976 cannot be understood simply as a contest between the PNP, which generally took up the cause of the marginalized, and the JLP, which continued to represent the interests of the rich. This was not an election merely about "issues" with each party telling the "voters" where they stand, and how they differ from the other party. This was an election about the very meaning of Jamaica.

The PNP put the election campaign in the hands of the party's most prominent leftist, Dr. D. K. Duncan, a gifted organizer with strong connection to the urban poor and youths. Duncan wasted no time in mobilizing party cadres, especially from the PNP's Youth Organization. The preferred medium of getting the PNP message across was face to face meetings and huge party rallies. This was an effective strategy given Manley's considerable skills as a public speaker. It was especially on these occasions that the PNP leader found his mark in attacking capitalism and alternatively, call on the nation to go "forward with socialism." The intensity and comprehensiveness of these invectives warrant further attention since they played an important part in shaping the terms of reference for the mandate which the party would receive at the polls. Moreover, rhetoric itself would emerge as a major issue in the next few years of the administration's life.

The PNP campaign was launched at Sam Sharpe Square, Montego Bay, on November 21, 1976. In his speech to some 100,000 to 120,000 supporters, Manley himself framed the election as a contest between two different visions of the directions in which the country must go. In launching the election, the Prime Minister railed:

> ... [T]onight we will be launching an election campaign that shall prove to be decisive in Jamaica's history. Tonight we will be launching the campaign that will decide whether our country draws back like a whipped dog to capitalism. . . . Whether we crawl back to be an appendix of other systems . . . or whether we go forward to build the glory of Socialism in Jamaica.[4]

Unlike the 1972 general elections in which the PNP carefully balanced its campaign in order to incorporate all classes and groups in its electoral alliance, in the 1976 election the party clearly made a call to the marginalized social forces. And whereas in the 1972 election Mr. Manley's speeches were eclectic in content, in 1976 the Prime Minister campaigned explicitly for a mandate to continue with the "Glory of Socialism." The word socialism was used thirty-seven times in the Montego Bay speech which launched the election, and "Comrades" was the preferred way of saluting supporters throughout the campaign. The following excerpt from that speech was typical of the discursive strategy through which the PNP framed the election fight:

> And I ask you to bear witness, let them bear witness to the glory of Democratic Socialism (Tumultuous Applause). Let them know some more, keep the glory going my Comrades. Glory to Socialism! Keep the glory going, my Comrades,

> glory to Socialism (Tumultuous Long Applause). Let them
> know we are here in our thousands and our tens of thou-
> sands and our hundreds of thousands to bear witness to the
> glory of Socialism.[5]

The derisive reference to "them" by Mr. Manley left little doubt
that the PNP was now ready to shed its "brown-man world," and
undertake a major offensive against the lingering vestiges of
exceptionalism. Accordingly, the Prime Minister attacked the JLP
and "a small minority" for keeping Jamaica "trapped in a system
that could only operate for the benefit of the few that owned resources," and undertook never to return to the "world of 1972."
Youths, the unemployed, the working class proper, and women were
invited to join the march to the "Glory of Socialism." The race-
conscious social forces were emboldened by the retrieval of heros
and martyrs who had fought against oppression in the days of
slavery and colonial rule, heros and martyrs like Sam Sharpe and
Paul Bogle and Marcus Garvey.

Intellectuals were not left out of the picture and, on November
22, Manley went to Mona to complete the mobilization of all anti-
exceptionalist forces. The Mona speech was a studied and comprehensive attack on: (a) capitalism as a social system wherever it
exists; (b) imperialism and neocolonialism as logical extensions of
capitalism; (c) states in whose benefit it is to protect the world
capitalist economy as constituted; (d) states once connected to slavery and the history of exploitation associated with them; (e) the
minority economic elites in Jamaica who have exploited poor black
people; (f) the established church in Jamaica for resisting change;
(g) the JLP for its "colonial mentality" and slavish deference to the
West; (h) the trade union movement for its "marginal response" in
dealing with the "disease of capitalism" and for "becoming champions of the capitalist system itself"; and not the least, (i) the foreign
policy of previous governments (but especially the JLP from 1962
to 1972) which put so much faith in the capitalist world economy,
and "aid begging."

The foreign policy dimension of the speech needs elaboration
for two reasons. First, the views expressed on the foreign policy of
Jamaica directly cast doubt on the assumption that small/depen-
dent states always "follow the leader." Secondly, it is also interesting to see the ways in which foreign policy is very much the product
of specific configurations of social forces, and further, how indeed
foreign policy discourses figure in the production of a (reconstructed)

national common sense. Mr. Manley noted that all of Jamaican foreign policy in the period 1962–1972 was based on the assumption that "Jamaica is small," and dependent on the "Western economic system." And what was the consequence of this thinking, he asked? His answer is worth quoting at some length:

> The thinking really was this: since we are small and we are poor, we have no real power in the world, the theory is that your only hope is to proceed through life in the posture and with the psychology and the mind of a mendicant. Yes. Mendicancy is the policy. Under the policy of mendicancy the strategy that emerges and was followed from '62 to '72 was literally to seek alms. . . .
>
> The strategy was, since I am going to beg for a redress of the balance of history through aid, to make sure I get it, I am going to be a tame cat in all respects. I am going to be an object of exploitation. I am never going to challenge anything, I am not going to have a position of my own, I am not going to raise my voice in the world. I am going to be a good boy, to be patted on the head from time to time and every time I perhaps deliver the right vote at the United Nations, every time I do not cause any problems in the world, I will hope to get another million dollars for another feeder road.[6]

In contradistinction to the "policy of mendicancy," Mr. Manley insisted the right thing for Jamaica to do is to continue to build a network of relationships with other Third World states and progressive social forces in the developed countries in order to bring about meaningful change in the global political economy. The Prime Minister suggested that no amount of aid can really replace the need for structural changes in areas such as the terms of trade, which are very much tilted against poor countries. He also pointed out that while foreign investment is needed, it must be engaged in a manner consistent with national objectives and the peculiarities of the Jamaican economy; he noted for example that while Jamaica received significant foreign investments in the 1960s, unemployment doubled. In Manley's view, Jamaican foreign policy must be aimed at changing the world, for it is only thus that real changes can be accomplished at the domestic level. In his words, "it is our view that nothing in Jamaica nor indeed in any poor country of the world can be changed internally, successfully or effectively if we cannot find the means to change the world itself."[7] The way in which foreign policy was presented in the election campaign was different from previous elections. The PNP took the position that the injustices which exist in Jamaica cannot be seen as a purely internal matter, since the real problem is with the international capitalist system, and particular states in this system which have been protecting the post-war world order to their own benefit. The PNP asked Jamaicans for a mandate to continue with its efforts in mobilizing Third World pressure to change this world order, since this is the only way progress could be made in Jamaica.

In the end, the PNP scored the greatest electoral victory in the history of Jamaica, winning forty-seven of sixty seats to the House of Representatives. The victory was "historic" in other ways. For the first time since 1944, the middle classes and bourgeoisie deserted the PNP, the party that had always been seen as the bastion of the educated, middle class, "brown-man." These erstwhile "patrons" from the hills surrounding Kingston/St. Andrew either openly identified with the JLP, or left the country for safe havens in Canada and the United States. Whereas in 1972 the party received 60 percent of votes of these wealthy Jamaicans, in 1976 that figure plummeted to 20 percent.[8]

The PNP, however, had succeeded in restructuring its political base. The hitherto marginalized, and now mobilized anti-exceptionalist social forces were now firmly behind the government, while the propertied classes and large sections of the middle classes became even closer to the JLP.

At the beginning of 1977 Jamaica was a deeply divided country. The December 1976 general election had given the People's National Party a solid mandate to press on with Democratic Socialism, but the middle classes, bourgeoisie, church, and media were so adamant about protecting the social order, that the country really entered a period of severe cleavages. The class realignment which had occurred and was accordingly expressed in voting behavior strengthened the influence of the left in the Cabinet. Moreover, these cabinet ministers became "access valves" and conduits for organized left groups in the country. The labor unions and intellectuals took full advantage of this opportunity, especially on account of a new Ministry of Mobilization which was created to establish better communication between "the people" and the government; significantly, the Ministry was headed by D. K. Duncan, former YSL member, committed socialist, and someone not at all liked by the ruling classes. Despite the historic victory at the polls, the PNP

would find it very difficult to carry through with the type of democratic socialist reform it had started in 1974. To a great extent this
was because of increasing pressure from the propertied classes;
multilateral institutions; and the government of the United States
(although there was initial "support" from President Carter). The
most immediate problem, however, was with the economy which
had deteriorated from a condition of weakness to one of crisis.

## The Economy: From Decline to Crisis

The situation facing the government in early 1977 illustrates
the way in which multiple forces—both domestic and foreign—
condition specific foreign policy and behavior. The response of the
PNP also demonstrates why foreign and domestic policies cannot
be separated. To understand these latter, and specifically the circumstances which eventually led to loss of confidence in the project
of social transformation, and then to IMF support, a brief review
of the economic situation in 1976 and early 1977 is necessary.

Practically all aspects of the economy did poorly in 1976. The
most serious problems were in "the deterioration of the balance of
payments and loss of reserves, sluggish production, the increasing
budget deficit, inflation and the maintenance of employment levels."[9]
Gross Domestic Product which entered into a mild decline from
1973, plummeted in 1976. Contractions in the following "industrial
sectors" demonstrate this: Mining and Quarrying –8.9 percent;
Manufacture –6.0 percent; Construction and Instillation –22.5 percent; Electricity and Water –4.6 percent; Transportation Storage
and Communication –3.3 percent; Distributive Trade –15.8 percent; Real Estate –11.1 percent; Miscellaneous Services –6.5 percent. The only sectors that posted gains were Agriculture, Forestry,
and Fishing 2.7 percent; Households and Non-Profit Institutions
3.8 percent; and producers of Government Services 14.9 percent.
Financial Institutions also expanded by 14.5 percent with the Bank
of Jamaica; Commercial Banks, and Insurance companies accounting for most of the growth.[10] Price-driven inflation began to surface
as a serious problem.

Sluggish production resulted in J$165m loss in export rev-
enues, a decline of nearly 23 percent from 1975. While the sub
sectors "Primary Products" and "Manufactured Goods" posted gains
(from J$128.9m to J$140.4m and from J$70.9m to J$82.0m respectively), "Semi Manufactured Goods" dropped from J$527.4m to
J$339.2m—a decline of 35.6 percent. This sharp decline was largely

due to depressed world market prices for sugar which resulted in revenues dropping from J$139.7m to a paltry J$55.9m. Further, while the unit price of alumina increased from J$163.83 to J$173.47 per ton, labor unrest resulted in lower production and loss of J$106.1 millions in foreign exchange.[11]

The consequences of lost export earnings would have been considerably harsher were it not for demand management which the government had put in place in early 1976. Given the deteriorating Balance of Payments which began to surface in the third quarter of 1975, certain monetary and fiscal measures were adopted to stabilize the situation. Among the monetary instruments of effective deflation were the tightening of Central Bank credits, foreign exchange control, and higher liquidity requirements for the commercial banks. Fiscal instruments included higher taxes— especially on upper income (over J$8,500), wage restraint, a property tax policy of "tax what you see" (designed to circumvent tax shelters on money income), and "consumption duties on motor vehicle licences."[12] Physical limits were also set on the import budget.

The measures adopted by the government resulted in a 18.7 percent contraction of imports from 1975. While raw material imports remained within a predictable annual fluctuation band (dropping by 5.4 percent.), imports of Consumer and Capital Goods fell dramatically—29.6 percent and 32.3 percent, respectively. The relatively sharp reduction in food imports elicited the wrath of the working poor who were faced with rationing some staples, such as flour. The only comfort came from increased domestic food production, but this was mostly beneficial to rural communities. The shortage of capital goods was met with considerable criticism from the business sectors. The JLP went on an international campaign to discredit the government, and found warm support in the U.S. media. Calculated "bad publicity" only served to deepen the Balance of Payments problems by forcing a deficit in the "Invisible Trade" category.

A spate of articles in some of America's well respected newspapers and magazines circulated stories of a new Jamaican-Cuban danger, and of wanton violence in Jamaica. Potential tourists listened, and in the end the results were damaging for the Jamaican economy. Against a steady upward trend over the past decade, 1976 was the first year (since 1968) that fewer tourists than the preceding year went to Jamaica; 82,544 fewer, or a decline of 14.9 percent. Apart from the absolute magnitude of the decline, the category of "Stay three nights and over" suffered the heaviest loss.

Of the 82,544 loss, 63,904 were from the latter—which is the most profitable group.[13] During the same period, American tourists to the Caribbean Area increased by 5 percent.[14]

The sustained effort of the U.S. media and the JLP resulted in 17.8 percent loss of foreign exchange in the tourist industry.

At the end of 1976, the current account showed a deficit of J$291 million compared to the J$257 million deficit in 1975. The real problem for the Balance of Payments, however, came from short falls on the capital account which recorded heavy losses. The previous strategy of financing the current account through net capital transfers collapsed.

While the rate of increase of the Gross External Debt was on a downward trend, it still remained high enough for serious concern. Thus, the success in cutting the ratio of external debt to total national debt by 5.4 percentage points in 1976–77 still left a situation where 33.6 percent of the national debt was *foreign owned.* The inertia of net productive capital inflows in conjunction with difficulties in raising foreign financing (both public and private) forced the government to rely on significant increases in domestic borrowing and further expansion of the public sector. As a result, while the external debt situation was stabilized (although still unacceptable) the annual increase of Gross Internal Debt increased by 53.5 percent in 1976–77.

Of course the JLP was also aware of the acute hemorrhaging of the economy and the disillusionment of the middle classes. Edward Seaga, in fact, had correctly "predicted" that if the PNP won the election, the Jamaican dollar would be devalued by 40 percent, a charge which the incumbent government was quick to deny. The economic situation in the country clearly warranted decisive action. Senior members of the cabinet were aware of this well before December 1976 and, as mentioned above, secret negotiations with the IMF had already begun. The magnitude of the election victory and the concomitant mandate received, however, made it politically difficult to proceed through IMF macroeconomic adjustments. What options did the government have?

### The People's Plan

It is now well known that the "tam pack" were at D. K. Duncan's house celebrating the victory for Democratic Socialism.[15] On this occasion, the indefatigable Minister of Mobilization (to be) was prevailed upon to abandon the "imperialist route," and instead, embark on the road to social (read socialist) transformation. The UWI social scientists were concerned that IMF management would visit excruciating economic burdens on the working poor and unemployed, and would reverse the gains the PNP had secured since 1972. The intellectuals also offered their services to the government. This was the beginning of the Emergency Production Plan (EPP), tabled in parliament as the People's Plan.[16]

The EPP was researched and written from mid-January through March 23, 1977, when it was presented to the PNP government. The Task Force put together to bring forth the Plan was headed by the National Planning Agency (NPA), and included several government Ministries, para-statals, and UWI social scientists.[17] The Plan was based on a truly national effort in which thousands of recommendations and suggestions were sent in to the NPA, hundreds of meetings held throughout the country, and a genuine national debate about the direction in which the country should go.[18] Without doubt, this was a socialist Plan, the elements of which were neatly summarized in a section headed, "What Needs to be Done." Under this heading, the Plan called for the following: (1) disengagement from the international capitalist system; (2) redistribution of wealth and income; (3) socializing the means of production and exchange (internally and externally); (4) redistribution at (2) to benefit the peasants and working class, and to expand the productive capacity of the society, by; (5) placing the society's resources in the control of the people organized for collective productive activities; (6) the above measures would further realize the boxed-in creative energies of the dispossessed and alienated who comprise the bulk of our human resource base.[19]

The development strategy proposed was based on increasing Jamaica's self-reliance, diversification of the country's foreign economic relations, and "changing the structure of the Jamaican economy."[20] A foreign policy of increased cooperation with socialist countries and other Third World states was also proposed.

The document noted that development is much more complicated than "economic development" and, as such, there should be a more comprehensive approach to "socialist transformation" in which the productive base of the economy would: (1) promote more uniform and strategic growth of state capital in areas that cater to basic needs of the population, and in areas which are critical to the functioning of the economy; (2) promote and facilitate the establishment of socialist modes of production at the people's level.[21]

The Plan also recommended State control of banking and finance, acquisition of the flour mill, cement plant, oil refinery, and other industries critical to national development. More importantly, the PNP government should make a determined effort to "embrace co-operative and socialist principles" of production relations through Co-operatives, Community Enterprises, and land acquisition and redistribution. At the same time, all incentives to foreign and local "big private capital" and joint partnerships with the latter should be discontinued.[22] In April 1977, Prime Minister Manley put forward a People's Plan in parliament, a Plan which did draw on the recommendations of the EPP. But, the conservatives in the PNP were still influential, and the EPP was so watered down that "it took the heart out of the document—the emphasis on self-reliance."[23] The combination of pressing economic problems; the strength of the "moderates" and conservatives in the PNP leadership; and the election of Jimmy Carter as President of the United States, led the PNP leadership to basically ignore the EPP and instead, turn to the IMF. As it would turn out Jimmy Carter's "toleration" of ideological pluralism in the Caribbean would actually (in part) lead to the fall of Democratic Socialism.

*The Turn to the IMF*

In June of 1977, the Fund and Jamaica struck an agreement on a Stand-by Agreement which provided for US$75 million. The terms of the agreement were not as hard as is usually associated with IMF policies. In what amounted to a reversal of political influence in the international system, the Jamaican government exerted considerable pressure on the IMF to come to an agreement favorable to this "small, dependent, democratic socialist state"! While the negotiations were in progress, Manley contacted the Prime Ministers of Britain, Canada, and Australia, asking them to use their influence in getting Jamaica what it wanted. These Commonwealth colleagues of Manley sent messages to the IMF Board of Directors in support of Jamaica's case. In a letter dated 26 July, 1977, Australian High Commissioner J. H. A. Hoyle wrote to Manley saying:

> I have been instructed by the Prime Minister of Australia, the Rt. Hon. Malcom Fraser, to pass the following message to you. The message reads:

"When I wrote to you on 6 July, 1977, I mentioned that I had asked my colleague, the Treasurer, to look at the situation regarding Jamaica securing an IMF tranche to assist the balance of payments. The treasurer has advised me that agreement has been reached between the IMF and Jamaica on a standby arrangement. *In these circumstances, I have asked the Australian Executive Director to support the Jamaican request when it comes before the Fund Board.* I am pleased that this matter looks like being resolved to your satisfaction...."[24]

The matter was indeed to Jamaica's satisfaction, by and large. The Government was allowed to keep a dual exchange rate system which was introduced in 1977 and which the Fund wanted to suspend. A basic rate was used to cover essentials, Government transactions, and the bauxite industry, while a more market-driven rate (called a "special rate") was allowed to penalize unnecessary imports.[25] Secondly, the government was allowed to continue its "liberal wages policy," an arrangement which the Fund was not too pleased about. On the IMF's behalf, the following were secured: (a) reduction of government expenditure by $140 million; and (b) quarterly targets for Net Domestic Assets, Net International Reserves, and Net Banking System Credit to the Public Sector.[26]

The July Agreement was short lived. Jamaica made a drawing of US$22 million in September, but this was not sufficient to stem the tide of continuing inflation in the world economy, loss of tourist revenues, and net outflow on the capital account as payment on previous loans. In December 1977 the Government failed the IMF test on Net Domestic Assets. Although the margin of failure was insignificant—$9 million or 2.6 percent—the IMF suspended the Stand-by Agreement and proposed a three-year Extended Fund Facility Program (EFFY). The Fund's "prior action" demands for the latter included devaluation of the Jamaican dollar and a crawling peg to be instituted later.

In May of 1978 a three-year EFFY program was entered into. The negotiations were entered into because of the economic crisis, but also because of pressure from local business interests, and from moderates within the cabinet. Unlike the 1977 Stand-by Agreement, the terms and conditions of the spring 1978 for US$220 million were severe. Even the "moderates" in the cabinet who had encouraged a new IMF Agreement were taken aback, and some were "shocked."[27] "[T]he feeling was widespread among participants and observers that there was an element of revenge in the IMF team's approach for Manley's audacity to mobilize political pressure for the first agreement. . . ."[28] Michael Manley came to the same conclusion, noting that "it is almost as if it wished to punish Jamaica for daring to mobilize international support. . . ."[29] The dual exchange rate system was abolished and a 15 percent devaluation was forced on the new unified rate; this in effect was a 47 percent devaluation of the old rate. The crawling peg of 1–1.5 percent monthly installment (amounting to 15 percent devaluation for the period May 1978–May 1979) was also put in place. The structural thrust of the EFFY also meant a decreased role for the public sector and simultaneously, incentives offered to the private sector. Price controls were lifted and the private sector was guaranteed a profit rate of 20 percent. The liberal wages policy which the government managed to continue in the 1977 Agreement was reversed, and a 15 percent cap on wage increases was put in place.[30] In the second year of the EFF, the PNP agreed to limit both wage and price increases to 10 percent through a social contract. Foreign exchange and domestic credit to the public sector were tightened even more, but the IMF agreed to expand the EFF to US$426 million (up from US$240 million).

The government followed the Program, but was unable to stem the tide of international inflation (which averaged 8.5 percent–14 percent through 1978–1979); increases in international interest rates and oil prices; real recession in the U.S. which had negative consequences for bauxite/alumina exports and tourism, and was unable to secure new commercial bank loans. While the *rate* of decline in the GDP was stabilized, the budget and current account deficits narrowed, and domestic public sector credit streamlined, serious structural problems still existed in the areas of the total debt and severe foreign exchange shortage.[31] By December 1979, Jamaica was having considerable difficulties in meeting the objectives of the EFFY. It failed another IMF test.

This December 1979 failure put the government in a precarious position. To enter into a new agreement would mean even more drastic measures which would have completely compromised the political credibility of the PNP. Accordingly, the government sought a waiver of the test by suggesting it had followed the principles and norms of the EFF and that the shortfalls were caused by circumstances outside of the government's management of the economy. The IMF disagreed and asked for new negotiations, which began in early January 1980.

The negotiations were difficult and in the judgment of the PNP, the IMF was making unreasonable demands and setting unreachable targets. On the current account, the Fund wanted cuts or eliminations of several basic needs programs; massive layoffs of Government workers (to the tune of 11,000); and drastic cuts in Government subsidies of essentials. Among the programs that would have been affected were: JAMAL, the Special Employment Program, boarding grants to students, the Cultural Development Commission, a Ministry of Education's program which targeted Grade 10 and 11 students, and the Institute of Sports. The demands on the capital side were equally harsh and would have amounted to $250 million in cuts. This would have led to closing down of the Jamaica Omnibus Service, Air Jamaica, the Jamaica Development Bank, the Small Enterprises Development Company, the Agricultural Development Corporation, the Tourist Board, Jamaica Vacation Sales, the Jamaica Industrial Development Corporation, Cornwall Dairies Development Limited, and the expansion program of the Jamaica Broadcasting Corporation.[32] These unacceptable and politically unsustainable demands resulted in the PNP abandoning the IMF route in March 1980 by discontinuing negotiations all together.

The several agreements which Jamaica and the International Monetary Fund entered into between July 1977 and 1980 shed considerable light on the ways in which a small underdeveloped state embarking on an alternative course of social and economic development might become disciplined by the global hegemony of embedded liberalism as practiced through multilateral institutions. To begin with, and according to Manley, "the IMF made its distaste for Jamaica's policies clear from the start of the discussions. . . ."[33] The IMF deepened and broadened its demands for market oriented policies with each new agreement. One thing is for sure—the IMF used its resources to compel Jamaica into adopting a "development strategy" more conducive to neoliberal orthodoxy, and decidedly against the path that the Jamaican government wished to follow. The differences between the government and the Fund were fundamental.[34]

The IMF and the Manley government differed on the most crucial aspects of economic policy. As Manley himself saw it, the major disagreements were over the following: (a) the "expansionary fiscal and monetary policies of the government"; (b) "the exchange rate and the profitability of tradable goods"; (c) excess demand in the economy, especially with respect to the level of real wages; (d) the dual exchange rate which the government had introduced in 1977; (e) "the general question of intervention by the government in the free market system," especially concerning import controls and the government's State Trading Corporation; and (f) "the question of whether the government favored the public sector in terms of available credit in the banking system and in servicing the debt."[35]

The IMF policies of the period were not without consequences for the major sections of Jamaican society. The mix of policies rewarded capital by increasing profit margins, on the one hand, and put severe pressure on the poor on the other. A combination of wage restraints, budget contraction, and increased taxes, either made essentials considerably more expensive, or not available at all. No matter how ideologically neutral one is (if that is possible at all) it was not difficult to fathom the general strategy of neoliberal discipline. If taxes on profits are frozen, as they were, and if price support (in the form of subsidies) for essentials are eliminated (as they were), there is a definite class content to the process of restructuring. That said, it must be acknowledged it was the PNP which in the final analysis, made the turn to the International Monetary Fund.

The about-turn of the PNP in 1977 was shocking, especially in light of the mandate which the party had received to continue with Democratic Socialism. The party had, after all, asked Jamaicans to make a choice between returning to "capitalism like a whipped dog" and the path adopted in 1974. Certainly, the left wing of the PNP (the PNPYO and Women's Arm in particular) and the full spectrum of radicals (Sixth Form Group, WLL, the New World Group, Rudies, Rastas, Abeng) thought the party had not only a social, but also political and democratic obligation to fulfil. To the "lower classes," the about-turn of the PNP here was nothing short of staggering. In Jamaica, class "betrayal" is easily translated into "race betrayal," and in fact some suggested that it was the latter at work in the turn to the IMF. Beckford and Witter, two of the most prominent scholars in Jamaica (and both contributing authors of the People's Plan) put the "blame" squarely on the shoulders of the Prime Minister thus:

> We are of the view that the fundamental explanation lies in his lack of confidence in the capacity of the masses of black Jamaican people to assert their productive creativity. It is a position that derives from a brown Jamaican petit-bourgeois perspective.[36]

The "race question," vis-à-vis the turn to the IMF had another dimension. The most socially progressive members of the PNP were outside the party leadership. They were younger, and had a strong identification with their African heritage. These foot-soldiers of the PNP were critical to the mobilization effort undertaken by Duncan, and certainly contributed to the massive electoral victory in December 1976. They were the ones who knocked on doors and delivered thousands of supporters to PNP rallies. And significantly, they were also the ones who tended to define Democratic Socialism very much in terms of black liberation as much as in class terms. Along with PNP-linked labor unions, it was this section of the party which fiercely resisted the adoption of an IMF plan.

It is quite clear that while the government's foreign policies were pursued very much as a "proactive" PNP agenda in the first period, these policies became far more reactive and defensive in character in the second. At the multilateral level, Manley and his cabinet were essentially forced to go against what they stood for in principle as a party, namely, turn to the International Monetary Fund for financial assistance. The general strategy (and objective) of "self-reliance," which was the clarion call of the PNP since 1972, collapsed under the weight of IMF demands. In what almost amounted to an international parody, Jamaica, which saw itself as one of the leading critics of an oppressive world economic order encoded in the institutions of Bretton Woods, was constrained to negotiate secret deals with the IMF. While the government continued to deploy the rhetoric of Democratic Socialism at home and champion the cause of Non-Alignment and NIEO abroad, there were visible signs of abatement in its critique of imperialism, multinational corporations, and the United States. Between 1977 and 1980, the administration which once proclaimed that size is no measure of resolve, was battered by the economic orthodoxy of the Fund. As a result it would not be an exaggeration to suggest that Democratic Socialism became effectively disciplined by the hegemony of global liberalism. What were the implications for foreign policy?

## Bilateral Policies

In the 1977–1980 period, the bilateral policies of Jamaica were aimed at achieving two principal objectives. First, much emphasis was placed on normalizing relations with the United States. This was made easier because of the entry of the Carter administration which adopted a more benign policy to Third World countries in general. Normalization was also important to Jamaica on account of badly needed financial support from the United States. Secondly, the government continued to build bilateral relations with countries outside the North Atlantic triangle in an effort to diversify its external opportunities. This diversification, however, was also aimed at a more strategic purpose, namely, to counter the imperialism of the "North." Jamaican policy to Cuba was the most significant aspect of this broader politicized foreign policy.

*Policy to the United States*

The normalization of Jamaican-American relations was directly related to a shift in U.S. policy to the Caribbean as a whole. There were four broad shifts to the new policy. The U.S.: (a) acknowledged it had neglected the region and to correct that, undertook to "spend more time and be much closer to those that are closest to us"; (b) recognized that strained relations with Cuba had presented difficulties for the U.S. in the region and, based on this, pledged to normalize relations with the little "communist" country; (c) took stock of the fact that previous U.S. administrations had supported governments which did not respect the rights of their own citizens, and alternatively, would base its policy on respect for human rights; and (d) adopted a general policy of tolerating ideological pluralism in the region.[37] In effect though, this amounted to less reliance on "dominance" and more on forging "consensus" from above.

The emphasis on normalization of relations with the United States was underlined by frequent visits made to Washington and New York by top ranking officials of the PNP government. The Carter administration had barely settled in when foreign minister P. J. Patterson paid a visit to Washington. It was an important visit. The Jamaican government was at the time negotiating with the IMF, and worried about devaluation of the (Jamaican) dollar and suspension of the dual exchange rate system recently introduced. There were serious concerns also with bad press in the U.S. media which was wreaking havoc in the tourist industry. Given the dire situation of the Jamaican economy, it was crucial that Washington be "brought on board."

While in Washington, Patterson met with Secretary of State Cyrus Vance and Under Secretary of State for Political Affairs Philip Habib. It is significant that a government which prided itself so much on self-reliance and breaking out of "western imperialism" should find it necessary to explain its problems to the United States with such urgency. In the end, even such acquiescent behavior was not sufficient to avoid the devaluation. Patterson's visit, however, did set the stage for two important visits from Washington.

In May of 1977, Rosalyn Carter paid a visit to the island, and this was followed up in August with a trip by Andrew Young, U.S. Ambassador to the United Nations. Judging from a White House letter to Prime Minister Manley, it seems as if the Jamaican government made a deep impression on Mrs. Carter on bringing about reform in international institutions. Thus, President Carter wrote to Manley stating, "As Rosalyn said to you, I believe that the international economic institutions, which were established by the industrialized countries after World War II, need to be reexamined to take into account the interests and concerns of the developing countries of the world."[38]

This was indeed a significant statement from the President of the United States. Jamaican officials also had some success in convincing the Carter administration to tolerate Democratic Socialism, albeit under the broader rubric of ideological pluralism in the Caribbean. In the said letter to Manley, Carter expressed his tacit "approval" of Democratic Socialism as follows:

> Like you, I am eager to find a bridge which unites the various social and economic systems in the world in a way which will enhance the lives of all humankind. The "human rights," which concern me and all Americans, *include not just political rights, but also our belief that all governments have the responsibility to see that the basic human needs of their people are satisfied.*[39]

This was a major diplomatic accomplishment for the PNP government at a time when the private sector and other domestic forces were criticizing Democratic Socialism. Ironically, therefore, a socialist/Third World government was getting some measure of ideological support from the President of the United States, while such support was difficult to mobilize from the dominant classes internally. This seeming contradiction continued for a while.

In August 1977, Ambassador Andrew Young visited Jamaica. Among other issues, the PNP government made a strong case for its support of African liberation movements and particularly its support of Cuban troops in Angola. Such support had previously incurred the admonishment of former Secretary of State Henry Kissinger, who had threatened reprisals. The ruling classes in Jamaica were also severely critical of Jamaica's Cuban-African foreign policy. Against this, Young wove a complex web of cultural and political connections among the United States (especially Black America), the Caribbean, and Africa. He acknowledged Jamaica "as essentially the most outspoken leadership in the Third World," and accepted Jamaica's "thesis" of Cuban intervention in Angola.

The Jamaican policy of getting the United States to understand and accept its role in Third World leadership was obviously being met with some success. In December 1977, a high-level Jamaican team which included Prime Minister Manley visited the United States to further its foreign policy objectives.[40]

According to an internal PNP document, the U.S. administration took the visit "extremely seriously" and "made it clear that they did not welcome Jamaica so much as Jamaica, but as a pivotal figure in the Third World. . . ." This must have been welcomed news to the Jamaican mission given its perceived role of representing the problems of the Third World to the United States Government. Indeed, the seriousness the Carter administration attached to the visit was underlined by the absolutely "first eleven" team which met the Jamaican delegation. The American side consisted of President Carter, Vice President Mondale, Secretary of State Cyrus Vance, National Security Advisor Z. Brzezinski, Under Secretary of State for Latin American Affairs—Ambassador Todman, Special Economic Advisor Dr. Cooper, Special Economic Advisor to the Security Council Bob Pastor, and Ambassador to Jamaica Fredrick Irving.

The Jamaican delegation outlined to the Americans what it considered the "non-negotiable" aspects of its foreign policy. Among these were the island's support of African liberation movements; its relations with socialist bloc countries; and its quest for a New International Economic Order. A strong position was also taken on Cuba. Prime Minister Manley insisted that Jamaica's close relationship with Cuba is a determined policy, and called on the U.S. to lift its embargo on the Castro government. Foreign Minister Patterson also made a strong statement in support of Belize, which was seeking independence from Great Britain.

The delegation also met with the Joint Foreign Relations Committee of Congress and again defined its foreign policy "non-negotiables." By now, it was clear Jamaica saw its bilateral relations with the U.S. in a twofold manner. On the one hand, the PNP government was seeking closer ties with the U.S. on account of domestic political pressure and the need for bilateral assistance. On the other hand, the government was also seeking to establish its credibility as a Third World leader on multilateral issues.

Jamaica's foreign policy toward the United States under Carter began to achieve immediate results. As the table below shows, bilateral aid jumped sixfold in 1977 and was maintained at uncharacteristically high levels through 1978 and 1979.[41] In the area of politics (narrowly defined), the Americans also showed more respect for Jamaican international initiatives and expressed less concern over the "third path." The Jamaican government was particularly satisfied with the relaxation of pressure on Cuba, an issue in which the PNP government had invested much diplomatic effort. This *rapproachment* between Washington and Kingston, however, was short lived and began to come apart in 1979.

The turnaround of Carter's policy towards Jamaica, was only indirectly linked to the island's foreign policy to the United States; a number of complex factors were also at work in the U.S. itself, in Jamaica, and globally.

First, there were some significant international events in 1979 that did not bode well for America's global interests. The Soviets invaded Afghanistan in order to prop up an unpopular regime which claimed to be Marxist, and which was decidedly pro-Soviet in posture. The Carter administration took this matter seriously, and as

### Table 1
### U.S. Loans and Grants to Jamaica, 1971–1981. US$m

|  | 1971 | 1972 | 1973 | 1974 | 1975 | 1976 | 1977 | 1978 | 1979 | 1980 | 1981 |
|---|---|---|---|---|---|---|---|---|---|---|---|
| Total Econ. & Military | 23.1 | 6.1 | 8.4 | 13.2 | 4.3 | 5.1 | 32.2 | 23.8 | 18.1 | 14.6 | 75.1 |
| Loans | 20.0 | — | 4.4 | 9.9 | 1.4 | 2.4 | 28.5 | 19.5 | 12.7 | 10.0 | 69.4 |
| Grants | 3.1 | 6.1 | 4.0 | 3.3 | 2.9 | 2.7 | 3.7 | 3.8 | 5.4 | 4.6 | 5.8 |
| Other U.S. Loans | 0.9 | 17.5 | 7.3 | 15.9 | 16.1 | 0.2 | 0.5 | — | — | — | 7.4 |
| Ex-Im Loans | 0.9 | 16.7 | 7.3 | 15.9 | 16.1 | 0.2 | 0.5 | — | — | — | 6.4 |
| All Other | 0.8 | — | — | — | — | 0.5 | — | — | — | 1.0 | — |

*Source: Adapted from J. D. Stephens and E. H. Stephens, 1986, p. 397.*

a symbolic registration of its concern, withdrew from the upcoming Olympics. 1979 was also the year that the Iranian revolution occurred, and the credibility of the Carter government itself was tied to the fate of American hostages. Closer to the U.S., the Sandinistas in Nicaragua finally toppled the dictatorship of Somoza and set up an essentially Marxist-inspired government. The FSLN were "threatening" to do much the same in El Salvador. In the Caribbean itself, the New Jewel Movement dislodged Sir Eric Gairy in Grenada, and declared a socialist government.

In the United States itself there was a reconfiguration of social forces and the emergence of an authoritarian-populist political culture, underwritten by hyper-liberal economic orthodoxy. Accompanying the rise of monetarism were strong feelings of American jingoism. There were serious concerns about the loss of American leadership, and grave doubts about Jimmy Carter's commitment, (if not ability), to deal with the perceived hegemonic decline. The election of Margaret Thatcher in the United Kingdom only added to Carter's now beleaguered leadership. The President had to act, and that he did. Andrew Young was fired from his position as Ambassador to the UN in August 1979, and soon after, Secretary of State Cyrus Vance was replaced.

Against this backdrop, the Sixth Non-Aligned Summit (attended by Heads of State) was held in Havana. The Summit was very ideological in character. On the one hand, Castro was attempting to redefine the very meaning of Non-Alignment. In his judgment, the principal struggle of the movement was seen as anti-imperialism and global capitalist exploitation. So defined, Castro saw a natural alliance of the Third World with all socialist states, including those "forces" which are not from the Third World. Substantively, this was a decidedly anti-western (and particularly anti-American), pro-Soviet formula. Well respected Non-Aligned states such as Tanzania and India rebuffed Castro's gambit.[42] The Jamaican Prime Minister did quite the opposite.

Manley not only accepted Castro's thesis but went on to attack the United States directly. Knowing fully and well that Marxists were at the forefront of the Puerto Rican independence movement, he declared support for the island's sovereignty. Various Marxist movements were praised for their dignified struggles at home, and against "western imperialism" abroad. In welcoming Grenada and Nicaragua to the Non-Aligned Movement, Mr. Manley hinted at "a common thread of radicalism which reflects the need for change in our hemisphere."[43] At a time when the U.S. was on the defense in world politics, the Jamaican Prime Minister went on to extol V.I. Lenin, Gamal Abdul Nasser, Marcus Garvey, and Fidel Castro, among others. Cuba and Castro were specifically invoked as models of anti-imperialist struggle to be emulated in the western hemisphere. The Prime Minister said:

> No area of the world has had a more extended exposure to, experience of, *nor proximity to imperialism than Latin America and the Caribbean.* We have seen forces of progress extinguished in Guatemala, snuffed out like a candle in the Dominican Republic, undermined and finally overwhelmed in Chile, and yet, I dare to assert that, despite these tragic reversals, the forces committed to the struggle against imperialism are stronger today than ever before. We believe that this is so because our hemisphere has had a Movement and a Man: a catalyst and a rock; and the Movement is the Cuban Revolution, and the Man is Fidel Castro.[44]

This peculiar form of socialist, pro-Cuban/Soviet Non-Alignment was not well received in Washington. The U.S. Ambassador to Jamaica charged that Manley's Havana speech seemed "unfriendly to non-authoritarian and non-communist nations generally and the United States in particular." According to Ambassador Irving, the speech also "appeared to indicate a distinct shift of Jamaica's foreign policy towards a position unfriendly to the views and interests of the United States." The State Department sought a "response" from the government of Jamaica "as soon as possible." In responding to the concerns expressed, Foreign Affairs Minister P. J. Patterson essentially reiterated the "non-negotiable" aspects of Jamaican foreign policy, albeit under the diplomatic cover of the Non-Aligned Movement as a whole. The Movement, wrote Mr. Patterson, "has always confirmed its anti-imperialist, anti-colonial, anti-racist and anti-hegemonic character." Patterson also rejected the charge of a shift in Jamaica's foreign policy, or the harboring of any "unfriendly attitude" toward the United States. The damage, however, had already been done.

In light of Manley's Havana speech, and given the shift from the Vance to the Brzezinski faction in Washington, Jimmy Carter could not very well continue his "lenient" policy toward Jamaica. This was particularly damaging to Jamaica at a time when the IMF was about to review the island's economic performance. Kari Levitt explains:

The Carter administration withdrew its previously lenient and mildly supportive position of Manley in the councils of the Fund. IMF officials who were inclined to bend the rules to give Jamaica one more last chance at economic recovery were criticized for being soft on Jamaica.[45]

The commercial banks and financial institutions affiliated to U.S. foreign policy followed suit. The commercial banks flatly refused to entertain any discussion of rolling over Jamaica's huge debt servicing, and instead openly sided with opposition leader, Edward Seaga.[46]

## Other Bilateral Policies

Jamaica's relationship with the United States directly affected its bilateral relations with other states. First, the more accommodative attitude of the early Carter administration made it easier to foster substantive ties with non-traditional partners, including eastern bloc countries. From approximately September 1979 onwards, however, these ties became more a matter of necessity on account of strategic non-cooperation from Washington. The drying up of bilateral and multilateral aid and loans from the north increasingly pushed the PNP government into finding economic resources elsewhere. During the second period the issues of anti-imperialism; global anti-racism; Third World sovereignty; and global economic justice were combined in a sustained attack against the ontological assumptions of the extant world order. It should be noted forthwith, however, that the extent to which the Jamaican government could, and did, develop new bilateral relations, was nonetheless circumscribed by the threat of reprisals from the domestic ruling classes, as well as by Washington.

The diversification and deepening of Jamaica's relations with socialist countries should not, however, be understood in purely instrumental terms. While it is true that "resource diplomacy" was dictated by the combination of a sick economy and the discipline of global liberalism, the PNP was also consciously attempting to break Jamaica's historical embeddedness in the logic of North-Atlantic exploitation. Seen this way, the diversification of foreign policy was a double movement. In the first instance, the attempt was to formulate a linkage among the West, slavery, and neo-colonialism, as a unified/noncontradictory chain of equivalence. In short, America (as a signifier of the West) had to be "*re*-produced" as the current trafficking symbol of a longer historical narrative of global oppression. The second "act" of the double movement (occurring simultaneously, as it were), was to position Jamaica as a critical actor in the subversion of hegemonization and Othering. The specificity of a counter-hegemonic space was to be constituted in, and through, the concrete practice of actively dealing with "the forbidden," i.e., Cuba, and other socialist states. This foreign policy which purposefully engaged the "dangerous supplements" of America's global hegemony became the *method* for disestablishing and renegotiating national sovereignty.

Jamaica's foreign policy toward Cuba in the period after 1977 became very politicized. Whereas in the first period relations between the two countries was largely restricted to governmental interaction, in the second period closer ties were forged at the party level. In addition, the National Workers Union and the PNP's Women's Movement established closer links with non-governmental groups in Cuba. Cuba also became an intermediary between Jamaica and eastern bloc states, and thus, Jamaican policy toward the little socialist state to the north had much wider implications than would normally be associated with bilateral relations. Put differently, Cuba was the springboard for Jamaica's ideological and political diversification at the international level. The first step in this larger foreign policy was the continuation of the policy of "defending" Cuba.

As noted earlier, the PNP government took it upon itself to represent the interests of Cuba to the United States. Representations were made at various levels, including direct "depositions" to the U.S. government. Manley took such personal interest in Cuban-American relation that he had to be "restrained" by his own Cabinet in "fighting for Cuba."[47] There is little doubt that the "defense of Cuba" allowed the Jamaican Prime Minister to attack imperialism, and specifically to criticize the United States' role in reproducing an unjust world order, without incurring the stigma of being anti-American.

For its part, the Jamaican government made great efforts to establish closer economic linkages with its closest northern neighbor. The Manley government organized meetings between Cuban officials and leading Jamaican capitalists (and their organizations). "Business trips" to Cuba were also facilitated.[48]

The slight warming of relations between the private sector and Cuba was not total. Throughout the "summer" of 1979, the PSOJ (in conjunction with the *Gleaner* and JLP) attacked the PNP government and the Cuban Embassy. The following charges (labeled "allegations" by P. J. Patterson) were made against the "Jamaican-Cuban connection":

- Political indoctrination of the Brigadistas trained in Cuba.
- The creation of a Cuba-trained force based at Jamaica House.
- The provision of Cuban guns to the Home Guard.
- The operation of Soviet and Cuban Intelligence Officers in Jamaica.
- The grant of special wireless facilities to the Cuban Embassy in Kingston.
- The use of police groups to watch and to destabilize the Opposition.
- The existence of a "Death Squad" within the Police Force.
- The *bona fides* of the Cuban Ambassador-designate to Jamaica.
- The association of Ministers of Government with Cuban and Soviet diplomats.[49]

Patterson rejected these "allegations" as baseless, and reiterated "that the relationship between Jamaica's domestic interests and Jamaica's foreign policy interests is a close, critical and dynamic one, and the two cannot be separated."[50] The Deputy Prime Minister and Minister of Foreign Affairs went on to scold the critics for reviving the "bogey of communism."

Yet, it must be noted, that only thirteen days after Patterson's public rebuke, Roy Mc Gann, Parliamentary Secretary in the Ministry of Defense, was invited to Cuba (along with Chief of Staff, Colonel R. J. Neish) by Cuban Army General Raul Castro Ruz. The content of the letter makes it clear that discussion about forging closer military links had long begun. The letter in part read:

Regarding the *continuation of the conversations initiated in December 1977,* related to the possibility of training personnel from the Jamaica Defense Force at our military training centers, it is a pleasure for me to invite you and Colonel R. J. Neish, Chief of Staff, to visit Cuba in the

present year. This visit will contribute to get a higher reciprocal knowledge and to increase the relations between
our two Armed Forces.[51]

There could be little doubt that the PNP government was indeed redefining some aspects of its security network. Further evidence of this came from Patterson himself, who acknowledged that
Jamaican police personnel were being trained in Guyana. Guyana
itself had developed an ongoing security relationship with Cuba. In
the eyes of the United States and conservative groups in Jamaica,
Kingston was part of a "red triangle" along with Havana and
Georgetown. Edward Seaga's "theory" that Manley, Castro, and
Burnham had an agenda of converting the whole region to socialism won much respect in Washington. The Opposition leader also
insisted that there were attempts to link the region into the "Soviet
loop." Again, there were grounds for such "speculation"; the PNP
was indeed making every effort to develop economic, political, and
ideological linkages with Moscow.

In September 1978, Jamaica's Ambassador to the USSR, Ben
Clare, met with Nikolai V. Mostovets (Chief of the Sector of the
International Department of the CPSU Central Committee) "to
stress the importance which [Jamaica] attach[es] to . . . relations
with the Soviet Union and the importance to [the Jamaican] economy
of the technical co-operation and key projects. . . ." Mr. Clare reported back to Kingston that the Soviets were ". . . showing increasing interest and understanding of the policies and approaches of
the Party and Government." Mostovets led a small delegation to
Jamaica late in September 1978.

On the economic front, the Jamaican government was keen on
securing technical assistance from the USSR. There were specific
discussions, for example, about setting up a cement plant. Of course,
in and of itself, there is nothing political or ideological about such
a project. If, however, "Soviet cement" is used by Cuban Brigadistas
and Jamaican technicians in constructing schools and low cost
housing, the latter financed by state loans, there were some obvious connections to be made. The same was true of the sale of
alumina and bauxite to the Soviets. In 1979, the Soviets agreed to
buy 50,000 tons of Jamaican alumina (for fiscal 1980) and, beginning in 1984, to increase that to 250,000 tons. These agreements
were partly meant to be, and were seen as, a statement against the
North American MNCs.

Negotiations were also begun in 1978 to obtain loans from the Soviets. The initiatives were undertaken through the Moscow Narodny Bank. Although the Bank is headquartered in London, communications were routed to Moscow, probably for the approval of the Soviet Government. The PNP government could not and did not give any public indications of these negotiations.[52]

If the PNP was secretive about its negotiation of a loan with the Soviets, this was certainly not the case on the more political front. In April 1979, Manley and a Jamaican entourage paid an official visit to the USSR. The Prime Minister was loud in his praise for Leonid Brezhnev, whom he described as "a true friend of all national liberation movements." Garvey and Lenin were "sutured" as champions of anti-imperialism. The Soviets were equally comradely in their response. Jamaica was linked to "the army of peace in the arena of international relations" through its activist foreign policy and internal struggle against colonialism. In the words of A. N. Kosygin (Prime Minister and Chairman of the Council of Ministers of the Soviet Union):

> It is with great sympathy that the Soviet people follow the persistent efforts made by the people of Jamaica to remove from their path once and for all the onerous heritage of the colonial domination and to build a new life worthy of man.[53]

Apart from developing closer relations with the USSR, the PNP government also made a concerted effort to establish economic cooperation with other eastern bloc countries. In early 1977, a Hungarian team visited Jamaica and negotiations were begun for economic cooperation. Discussions centered around Jamaican exports of spices, sauces, liqueurs, cured tobacco, clothing, citrus products, processed foods, jams, aluminum sulphate, sulphuric acid, perfumes, and bauxite. In return the Hungarians would export pharmaceutical and chemical products, and provide lines of credit to Jamaica.

A more comprehensive proposal was tabled by the Romanians who were willing to provide assistance in:

> (a) the expansion and development of the livestock industry, including the provision of facilities for processed dairy produce, agricultural machinery, and the development of crops such as sorghum and sunflower;

(b) the development of a local livestock feed facility;

(c) soil conservation;

(d) developments pertinent to the tourist industry;

(e) fisheries;

(f) scholarships for training personnel in agriculture and management; and

(g) lines of credit.

Of course, there is nothing inherently revolutionary about any of the above agreements. What is important, though, is that the PNP government was beginning to develop bilateral relations with the decidedly forbidden in terms of Jamaica's past foreign policy. Indeed, the sensitivity of these bilateral gambits was such that secrecy attended a good deal of the negotiations. Secrecy was of such importance that even the internal PNP documents which outlined the parameters of the talks with the Hungarians were not for open circulation within the government. In part, this may be the result of the determination that:

> In respect of criteria for obtaining assistance from the CMEA, the recipient country must demonstrate a serious commitment to the pursuit of economic development as well as an *alignment with the anti-imperialist stance in international relations.*[54]

This acceptance of "aligned assistance" was clearly contradictory in terms of what NAM represented ideologically.

## The Opposition Groups

During the 1977–1980 period, the social forces in Jamaica became even more polarized, with direct consequences for foreign policy. The following were arrayed against the government: the media (especially the *Gleaner* newspaper), the dominant classes which formed an umbrella organization ( the Private Sector Organization of Jamaica—PSOJ), the JLP and its affiliated union—BITU, some factions within the police and military, and a significant section of the middle classes; the established Church also complained about Jamaica's slide to socialism as they had done previously. The *Gleaner*, PSOJ, and JLP formed a cohesive bloc and worked closely with each other and with anti-PNP interests in the United States.

The PSOJ became an extremely powerful influence in the country. Among their members were: Jamaica Manufacturers Association, Jamaica Chamber of Commerce, Jamaica Exporters' Association, Small Business Association, Masterbuilders Association of Jamaica, Manchester Chamber of Commerce, Advertising Agencies Association of Jamaica, Lions Club of Kingston, Jamaica Insurance Advisory Council, Building Societies Association of Jamaica, Hardware Merchants Association, Jamaica Bankers Association, Custom Brokers Association of Jamaica, Jamaica Developers Association, Master Printers Association, Professional Societies Association of Jamaica, Life Insurance Companies Association of Jamaica, Jamaica Banana Producers Association, Importers and Distributors Association of Jamaica, Life Underwriters Association of Jamaica, Jamaica Employers' Federation, and Jaycees of Jamaica. Judging from this list, it is not unreasonable to suggest the entire Jamaican ruling class was arrayed against the government. Further, if you add the leading national newspaper, the JLP, and one of the most powerful trade unions (BITU) to this list, it is not difficult to see the magnitude of the PNP's problems.

The PSOJ adopted a three dimensional strategy in fighting Democratic Socialism. First, it demanded and secured regular meetings with the Prime Minister and senior members of the Cabinet. These meetings covered every aspect of government domestic and foreign policy. The Government was often forced to modify or abandon specific policies, and more generally to pursue broad lines of economic policies which were acceptable to the private sector. It is also important to recognize that the PSOJ did not confine itself to narrow economic issues which affected its membership directly.

The PSOJ took it upon itself to *intervene* in "extra-economic" affairs as well. A good illustration of this happened on 28 August, 1979 at one of the regularly scheduled meetings of the Organization and Cabinet. After much discussion of policies relating to maternity leave, education, Industrial Tribunals and their Awards, tax, smuggling, and illicit importation, S. Carlton Alexander (President of PSOJ) attacked the government's attitude toward multinational corporations, and particularly the recent treatment of Coca-Cola and Bata. The exchange between Mr. Alexander and Prime Minister Manley provides a good example of the kinds of differences which usually surfaced at these meetings. Mr. Alexander said:

> Multi-national corporations were needed; they were big professional Managers with all facilities built-in to give marketing, technology and services aimed at development and were guided by high ethics and a code of behavior.[55]

Mr. Manley agreed it was important to work with MNCs, but was less convinced about their ethics. In reply to Mr. Alexander he stated:

> [T]here was widespread international concern about the implications of their behavior in individual poor countries. There was the tendency of a totally callous indifference to resultant effects in periods of slowing down and a way had to be found to get a logical response from them.[56]

The debate over "ideology" was not always as cordial. On a number of occasions the PSOJ or one of its members wrote harsh letters of condemnation of government policy and ideology. The most caustic invectives concerned Jamaica's relations with Cuba and other socialist/communist countries on the one hand, and the country's deteriorating relationship with the United States, on the other. In February 1979, for example, the organization wrote a strongly worded letter condemning the use of Cuban construction workers for building schools in Jamaica. The private sector saw a grave threat to Jamaica's way of life from Cuban penetration.[57]

At times, the field of PSOJ's criticism was expanded so as to accommodate the articulation of "international communist threats," the PNP Government, and local protest groups. The government was accused of facilitating links between radical local interests and international counter-hegemonic movements. More pointedly, the PSOJ was convinced that the government's foreign policy agenda was to take Jamaica into the world's socialist/communist camp. A good illustration of the PSOJ's ideological (counter) warfare surfaced in March 1979, when the PNP Women's Group (led by Beverley Manley, wife of the Prime Minister) joined forces with the Committee of Women for Progress to sponsor a rally in honor of International Women's Day. The Committee of Women is affiliated with the Workers Party of Jamaica, a Marxist-Leninist party, which had declared "critical support" for the PNP in fighting "IMF imperial-

ism." In a letter to the Prime Minister representative of the
Organization's penchant for linking local groups; the Government;
and "foreign threats," Alexander pointed out:

> We have always contended that all political or other groups
> have a right to organize and to express themselves with the
> full protection of the law, but we hold a very strong view that
> our Government ought not to link itself with communist
> organizations as appears to be the case on this occasion.
> The communist movement in Jamaica was small and
> insignificant until recent years when it has expanded its
> indoctrination and organization through Government owned
> media and using several platforms of the People's National
> Party. We are very well aware that in those countries where
> Democratic Socialism is accepted, communists are regarded
> with the same horror as Fascists, and are offered no facili-
> ties by the Democratic Socialists.[58]

Mr. Alexander went on to acknowledge that it was this type of
ideological linkage which led to massive amounts of money being
withdrawn from Jamaica in 1975. The PSOJ president also issued a
veiled threat of capital strike, by noting the revival of the economy
is "impossible . . . if we continue to have this fear that your Government and Party are slowly but surely linking themselves to the
International Communist Movement. . . ."[59] The ideological warfare
between the PNP Government and the private sector intensified
after the breakdown of talks with the IMF in 1980. The PSOJ had
put considerable pressure on the government to come to some kind
of agreement with the Fund, and was openly critical when this did
not materialize. On the Government side, an intensive public campaign of public education about counterrevolution was undertaken.
The Government-controlled Jamaica Broadcasting Corporation (JBC)
aired a number of shows which supported the Cuban, Nicaraguan,
and Grenadian revolutions as historically responsible projects of
structural transformation. On the other hand, a documentary series
on the CIA and destabilization was aired. This "public education
campaign" saw a combined response from the *Gleaner*, JLP, and
PSOJ. The Government was accused of "brainwashing" the population, "abusing freedom of the press," and "inciting revolution." Avis
Henriques, Director of PSOJ and President of Jamaica Chamber of
Commerce, wrote to the Government outlining the charges. Apart
from demanding an end to the various "brainwashing" projects,

Henriques also wanted a better image of the United States portrayed. The exchanges between conservative forces and the Government were vitriolic in nature. Manley's reply to Henriques epitomized the tenor and pitch of the ideological feud as the following excerpts shows:

> What makes your letter profoundly disturbing is the fact that the *Daily Gleaner* has in recent years carried out a policy of concentrated propaganda, distortion and character assassination that is without precedent in modern Jamaican history. They have had columnists openly inciting people to consider the overthrow of the democratically and constitutionally elected Government of Jamaica. They have maintained a veritable flood of propaganda against a friendly neighbor, Cuba, that beggars description. Not once, so far as I am aware, has your voice been raised in protest against this as "an abuse of press freedom" or as "an incitement of our people to violence." Not once have I heard your protest against the seeds of bitterness, division and hatred that have been sown by the *Gleaner* and its columnists without let and hindrance over the last four and a half years. . . .[60]

With respect to the problem of the image of the United States, Mr. Manley pointed out that considerable airtime of public television in Jamaica is devoted to shows like "Dallas"; "Love Boat"; "Little House on the Prairie"; and "Public Eye," (among others) which romanticize America. The Prime Minister suggested the nine hours of film on the CIA (aired on the JBC) was necessary because "there is in Jamaica today, as there was in 1976, a striking similarity between events unfolding around us and the documented methods that have been developed by the C.I.A."[61]

The campaign against the PNP was also taken outside Jamaica, with Opposition Leader Seaga and other JLP officials teaming up with anti-communist elements from Cuba and the United States, in the U.S.A. The network of people and organizations in this anti-PNP/Castro front was extensive, and drew support from top ranking politicians in the U.S. At a breakfast in Washington attended by right wing "elements" sometime between 25th–28th September 1977, Mr. Seaga called for the formation of a conservative equivalent of the Socialist International (of which the PNP was a member), and surmised "here was another area of leadership and another area of influence for the United States."[62]

Working along with Mr. Seaga was Anthony Mackenzie, who ran as a JLP candidate (Upper St. Andrew) in the 1976 general elections, but was defeated. Mackenzie went to the U.S. and made contact with Howard Phillips and Richard Vigoury, both of whom had impressive anti-communist credentials. Phillips was founder of the "Conservative Caucus" and "Young Americans For Freedom"; Vigoury was also a member of Young Americans, with extensive connections in publishing, broadcasting and fundraising for right-wing projects. The Mackenzie-Phillips-Vigoury "group" recruited a Mr. Dalbert Williams, who had published anti-PNP materials. Seaga's associates included Dr. Roger Fontaine, Director of the Latin American Division for the Center for Strategic and International Studies, Georgetown University; Ray Klien, Director of that Center, and former Deputy Director of the CIA; and Congressman Dan Marriot. Other participants in the network were Peter Whittingham (a suspected Jamaican drug dealer); Stanton Evans, who was connected to right-wing broadcasting; and last but not least, Ronald Reagan, who would soon become the President of the United States. Anti-Castro "operatives" were also part of the network. On the "PNP side" was Philip Agee who went to Jamaica in September 1976 and "kept in touch" with the situation in Jamaica through the Covert Action Information Bulletin.

What emerged from the Washington-Miami-Kingston (JLP) network was an organization called "Friends for a Free Jamaica," with Williams as the head, and Phillips as Co-Chairman. Williams himself published a pamphlet with the same title as the organization, in which he sounded the Red Triangle alarm; Evans and Reagan made radio broadcasts about communist threats in the Caribbean and infiltration in Jamaica; Marriot sent a letter to President Carter listing eight reasons why the U.S., IMF, and World Bank should not "support" the PNP. His list of charges included the following: (a) the PNP has taken over the education system from primary to university level; (b) there are "government owned collective farms" in Jamaica; (c) the state has taken over the transportation system and key industries, including multinationals; (d) the PNP has taken over the economy; (e) the United States is constantly denounced; and (f) the PNP has "avowed relations" with Castro, China, and the Soviet Union.

Opposition Leader Seaga used the "Friends for a Free Jamaica" to call for investigations by Amnesty International of alleged human rights abuses in Jamaica. He also intimated the general elections of 1976 were rigged and requested the assistance of a

Commission of Jurists to investigate the improprieties (despite the fact that the only irregularities reported were more votes [for him] than eligible voters in his own riding). As the 1980 elections neared, Seaga and the JLP circulated rumors that the PNP was planning to cancel the elections and declare a one party state. The "Friends for a Free Jamaica" gave these rumors credibility by repeating them in the U.S., buoyed as it were by the Gleaner's total war on the PNP.

On November 8, 1977, Foreign Minister Patterson moved a Motion of Censure against Opposition Leader Seaga "for reprehensible conduct and acts inimical to Jamaica." In presenting the case, the Foreign Minister accused Mr. Seaga of having "the servile mentality of an Imperialist mind," a statement which drew loud applause from the Gallery of the House of Representatives. Mr. Patterson also had strong words of condemnation for those in the United States who had joined the JLP in attempting to topple the PNP government. One such condemnation read: "there was Ronald Reagan who did two successive broadcasts damaging to Jamaica and one only shudders to think what could have happened to a small country like Jamaica, if peradventure he had emerged as President of the United States."

Mr. Reagan, of course, did become President of the United States and, in October 1980, the PNP was defeated by the JLP. Mr. Seaga became the new Jamaican Prime Minister, and Jamaican foreign policy quickly reverted to the pre-1972 "philosophy" of "following the West." In substantive terms this meant deference to the United States Government and to the ideas and global institutions which supported America's global "leadership." The "new mendicancy" of the JLP did not go unnoticed, as the Reagan Administration and multilateral financial institutions (particularly the IMF) came to the "aid" of Jamaica.

Mr. Seaga was the first head of a foreign government received in Washington by President Reagan. This was not an innocent or meaningless fact. It was indicative of the new American administration's resolve of reinvigorating the old Truman Doctrine of supporting anti-communist forces. Jamaica under Manley was not communist, of course, but developments in the Caribbean and Central America positioned Jamaica (through Seaga) once again to take up the mantle of regional leadership, only this time, for a project of ideological and political reversals. In short order, the new Reagan government would initiate a long and drawn-out policy of supporting counter-revolutionary activities against the Sandinistas in Nicaragua, and the FMLN in El Salvador. And when the United States invaded Grenada, Jamaica was at the ready to supply troops!

President Reagan and Prime Minister Seaga would also hatch a new regional strategy of hegemonization. This was done by forming the Caribbean Basin Initiatives (CBI) which was intended on providing economic incentives to stay close to the United States. In the context of the second "Cold War," the CBI was the Reagan equivalent of the earlier Alliance For Progress, which was one instrument in a broad strategy of beating back local mobilizations against imperialism.

Regarding Jamaica itself, the United States pulled up the stop signs to foreign economic assistance. American support of Jamaica at the IMF and other multilateral agencies would result in increased aid. There was also significant increase in direct foreign aid to Jamaica, so much so, that the island was among the highest recipient (in per capita terms) of American assistance. President Reagan was also instrumental in forming the U.S. Economic Committee on Jamaica, and through his own efforts, got David Rockefeller to chair the group.

The full extent of the new hegemonization which commenced in the 1980s with the rise on monetarism and a pervasive neoliberal orthodoxy would surface later when the once illustrious champion of the marginalized in Jamaica, and the "trade union leader" of the poor of the world, Michael Manley himself, would declare himself for market society. The global social forces had won, but not everything. For during these years Jamaica had gone through a cultural revolution of sorts, and the intellectual preparation developed in the awakening of the marginalized may yet be the only basis for meaningful change.

# 10

---

## Onwards with Critical Theory

The claims for a critical approach to international theory, as much of the earlier chapters suggest, are to be found at the levels of ontology and epistemology, and more broadly, through a philosophy of *praxis*. These latter themselves have been situated in the larger historical and sociological contexts of what theorists of the new historical materialism call "perspectives." It is precisely on the basis of linking both theory and practice to broader perspectives that this work has attempted to go beyond the extant approaches to the foreign policy of the Third World.

First, the *fixed-universals* characteristic of much of international relations theory have been found to be wanting. In contradistinction to transhistorical truth claims usually produced and articulated through the master concepts (or tropes) of state, power, and national interest, the emphasis in this study has been on arresting the specificities of what R. G. Collingwood calls the "a priori imagination."[1] It is only in the *act of movement* that forces which are improperly deemed to be universal and timeless have any meaning. To begin with the concepts themselves have to historicized.

Problem-solving conceptualizations of state and national interest (and by implication, the concept of power also) have been jettisoned. The state is not a static thing-institution which simply adapts to changing interests, while remaining the same state. Rather, as has been shown, and consistent with the stress on social forces, the state may be seen as a configuration of power, conditioned by specific economic, socio-political, and ideo-cultural forces present at a given conjuncture of history. On account of this, the concept "forms of state" as developed by Gramsci and Cox, and as applied here, seems to be more analytically useful and historically accurate. This analysis of Jamaica clearly shows the ways in which

201

the different state forms can exist even while the legal shell of government has not changed.

The analysis of foreign policy as a function of "national interest" in which the latter is equated with state interest is clearly inadequate. All too often national interest is taken as a given reality since, by definition, that is to say as a fixed-universal, all states have *national* interests. This understanding of national interest, which is privileged as the *raison d' etre* of state behavior (and by implication of history), reduces extremely complex historical phenomena to mere self-aggrandizement, the latter itself based on assumption of human nature in the abstract.

In chapters 3 and 4, considerable emphasis was placed on developing an alternative to the static and ahistorical assumptions rife in problem-solving international relations theory. Pregiven realities which are extrapolated out of assumptions of human nature and then given"scientific sanctity" through positivism are rejected. On the contrary, an important thesis of this book is that reality is made, manufactured, produced, or constructed, on the basis of material and cultural conditions in historically determinate periods. In particular, national interest is understood as the official, authoritative, and public expression of a way of life, that is to say, of culture. In the reconstructed historical materialist or social forces approach advanced here, the position that this culture is fundamentally based on social relations defined by social classes is only partially accepted. Rather, culture is posited as an overdetermined complex of class and non-class elements. Thus, while production has a generative capacity, the specific forms that elements of the superstructure take depend on historically concrete mediation(s). As such, ideas and institutions have a *contingent* rather than a *necessary* relationship with the substructure.

As a general point of departure it is important to recognize that the new historical materialism, and specifically the method of historical structure, is flexible and antidogmatic. In the analytic framework developed around the categories ideas, institutions, and material capabilities, there is no privileging of any of these categories as a point of departure. The emphasis of historical structure is more keen on understanding the relationship among the constituent parts of the analytic triad with particular attention given to the overdetermination of each element by the other two. Clearly, the emphasis is on apprehending the structure and social reproduction of social formations in their totalities. Epistemologically, it is precisely this openness and holism that allow for the incorporation of other discourses. Closer examination will in fact show that some aspects of poststructuralist analysis have remarkable similarities with the new historical materialism and vice versa.

First, both the new historical materialism and post-structuralism adhere to a nonpositivist and nonreductionist epistemology. As such, neither approach strives toward nomological generalizations (as a form of reliable knowledge), or aims at establishing some originary presence (as a founding moment or privileged point of departure). Both approaches see knowledge as a key element in any configuration of power and consequently insist on treating it (that is, knowledge itself) as an object of problematization. Thus knowledge, like reality, has no ontological *isness*; rather it exists only *in its movement* within historically determinate structures/discourses. Cognizant of the way in which power operates as a constitutive presence in the making (production) of knowledge(s), considerable emphasis is placed on reflexivity of theoretical practice.

Gramscian historical materialism and poststructuralism are also remarkably similar in the way in which they deal with time, and the relationship between time and knowledge. Both place emphasis on the transient character of social reality and, correspondingly, the "time-boundedness" of knowledge. For Gramsci himself, as Esteve Morera argues, transience is expressed through the concept of "historicity," meaning the non-permanentness and fluidity of all elements of history. Not only are the material conditions of history transitory, but so are thoughts, ideas, spirituality, and consciousness.[2] On account of the historicity of constitutive properties, therefore, reliable knowledge may also be gained through the *specific historical and social forms* of the objects, not only through nomothetic extrapolation. Moreover, this antipositivity (hinged as it were on an absolute historicism) makes it impossible to establish general (historical) laws. This is precisely the poststructuralist critique of fixity and closure.

The lengthy analysis of the role of social forces in the making of foreign policy points to, *inter alia*, the limitations of state-centric approaches to international theory. While it is the state (or components of the state) that *acts* in the international arena, it is also the case that the state is not a given. The state is always underpinned by a specific balance of forces and it is the balance, per se, that defines the way in which the national interest is formed. In the case of Jamaica, it is precisely a structural shift in the balance of class and other forces that produced the conditions for the emergence of Democratic Socialism and the corresponding foreign policy of the PNP government.

An important dimension of the analysis of social forces is that race becomes an important factor in international relations. This book has shown the way in which the primordial category "race" becomes historically active (or activated) in the constitution of the social structure of plantation economy and continues, albeit in more complex ways, under the regime of "export-led development." Norman Girvan sums this up neatly:

> Evidently although the structure became more differenti- ated and the simple master/slave-white/non-white correspon- dence was broken, the relative ranking of the different racial groups remained the same and ethno-cultural racism con- tinued to be an important characteristic of intra-national and inter-national relations and also an important instru- ment of exploitation.[3]

By including race as an important social force in Jamaican politics, some subtle aspects in the making of foreign policy have been revealed. To begin with, it has been shown that hegemonic practice is veritably overdetermined. The racial dimension of what Rishee Thakur calls Anglo-Christian hegemony, which defined the common sense of daily life under colonialism, was not divorced from the way in which "the economy" per se functioned. In the postindependence period, the racial inscription of hegemony went through a palingenesis, such that, while the racio-spatial division of the social structure was maintained, it took the form of demo- cratic citizenship. During the 1960s, the contradictions of this le- gal-cultural configuration began to burst at the seams. Democratic citizenship began to be articulated in institutional forms diametri- cally opposed to the accepted order of things. The counter-hege- monic social movements of the 1960s and 1970s unhinged the Anglo-Christian *weltanschauung*, and with it the coordinates of Jamaica's international relations.

The temper of the political-cultural displacement was such that the very "proper subjects" of Jamaican foreign policy became redefined. The liberation of African people (in the continent of Af- rica) from foreign (often white) domination was given top political priority. Instead of the lip service paid to supporting the liberation movements in Africa before 1972, the Manley administration, mind- ful of the PNP's support base, found it necessary to prosecute lib- eration from racial oppression with costly material and political involvement. Even a personal visit by U.S. Secretary of State

Kissinger could not dissuade the PNP from openly "standing behind" the MPLA (in Angola). One conclusion that may be drawn from this, of course, is small states, whether weak and/or dependent, do act with some autonomy in the international system, the costs notwithstanding.

Apart from demonstrating the scope with which a small/weak, relatively poor, and dependent state can act, the Jamaican case is a poignant illustration of the amorphousness, fluidity, and indeterminacy of national interest. That "race" was a key factor in the country's foreign policy during the 1972–1980 Manley governments cannot be doubted. The fact of the matter is that there is nothing axiomatic about this. This dimension of policy did not come about because, and only because, the majority of the population is of African ancestry. Obviously, if this were the case, one would have to explain why the preceding JLP governments did not adopt similar policies. The point is, national interest is not fixed, nor is it simply a matter of self-interest. On the contrary, it is constantly negotiated through political struggles. In Jamaica's case, this took the form of cultural redefinition in which the African heritage of the nation was asserted. As such, the national component of the equation "nation-state" was the determinant instance in the country's foreign policy pertaining to African liberation. It is thus not unreasonable to conclude that national interest and state interest are not necessarily complementary (if a narrow conception of state is maintained).

It is also necessary to include the notion of global civil society in attempts at understanding the transnational dimensions of the global political economy. The nation-state as the proper boundary within which culture, identity, interest, and power revolve, is clearly inadequate. In fact, Marcus Garvey had challenged the strictures of the nation-state since the early decades of the twentieth century when he formulated a Pan-Africanist ideology aimed at the cultural, political, and economic regeneration of people of African ancestry. During the 1960s and 1970s, Garvey was—so to speak—"awoken from the dead" and deployed in the bitter cultural war of position in Jamaica. In this very process, however, those social movements committed to fracturing Anglo-Christian hegemony pointed to the limitation of Jamaica per se, as the theater of war (sometimes literally so). For the Rastas, Jamaica (that is to say Jamaican sovereignty) is merely the political/institutional expression of a world imperialist system dominated by a handful of western countries. Moreover, Jamaica is the legal form within the

Westphalian system which keeps them from returning to Africa. This transnationalization of identity is not restricted to the category of race/culture or to the Rastas.

The thrust of the Non-Aligned Movement during the heights of the 1970s also appealed to a kind of isothermal identification. While it is true that capital and technology are far more mobile than labor, the Movement sought to redefine space and identity. Leaders like Michael Manley insisted that the global political economy was sharply divided between North and South and that this division matched an equivalent maldistribution of power. Accordingly, a subtle aspect of the political strategy of the Non-Aligned leadership was geared toward the production of a transnational identity on the part of the South. It is for this reason Third World leaders adopted a distinctive kind of global rhetoric, much of it impugning the sense of justice and morality extant in the global political economy. Jamaican foreign policy, of course, went much beyond rhetoric. Despite its small size, relative weakness, and structural dependence, Jamaican foreign policy during the 1972–1980 period was quite forceful, challenging as it did some of the entrenched structures of power. As a general observation it is interesting to note that policies were pursued at different levels, employing different methods. This is significant given the popularly held view that foreign policy works like a gigantic monolith in service of the national interest.[4]

Three "tactics" (or components) of engagement were employed, namely, unilateral, bilateral, and multilateral policies. While it is generally safe to say the three components had considerable unity of purpose, it is also the case that some policies pursued at one level were in contradiction or, at least inconsistent with, policies pursued at the other two.

At the unilateral level, the material highlight of the government policy was the institution of a levy on bauxite/alumina. This action increased the government's revenue from this industry sevenfold and gave Jamaica a more significant role in the management and control of the country's most important foreign exchange earner. At the diplomatic level, Jamaica won an important victory here insofar as the response from the United States and Canada was not as hostile as might have been reasonably expected. The implication of the bauxite levy was far reaching, prompting similar action from other bauxite-exporting states. In the larger picture of "north-south" relations, the levy also demonstrated an alternative way in which dependent states might seek "economic justice" without using the extreme measure of outright nationalization. The levy was also consistent with the government's bilateral and multilateral policies.

The government's bilateral political policies were quite controversial, especially given the attempt on the one hand to "manage" its relations with the U.S.A. in a benign manner, while on the other, pursing very close relations with Cuba. The difficulty of balancing a proCuban policy while maintaining friendly relations friendly with the U.S.A. also reflected deep political divisions internal to Jamaica.

The PNP did have a mandate to pursue Democratic Socialism which, in part, meant challenging imperialism and, by implication, the historically structured and institutionalized relationship between the U.S.A. and Jamaica. The fact of the matter is that much of PNP support came from sections of the population which saw such a challenge as necessary to the very definition of Democratic Socialism. The "Third Path" meant redefining not only Jamaica's economic relations with the U.S.A. (and the North in general), but also the cultural foundations upon which modern Jamaica had been built. For elites in Jamaica this was a "declaration of war" against liberal democracy; free market enterprise; and against Western civilization.

The PNP government was unable to resolve this structural problem and its foreign policy reflected the contradiction. An important lesson may be extrapolated from these tensions. Against the accepted division of domestic and foreign policy rife in problem-solving approaches to international relations, the Jamaican experience clearly demonstrates the ways in which the two are indeed mutually related. As such, democratic socialist transformation at home, well nigh implied anti-imperialism at the international level and vice versa. "Foreign policy," therefore, must not be seen simply as a mere extension of "domestic policy"; rather the two must be understood as structurally related dimensions of a historically specific configuration of forces. In the case of Jamaica, this configuration was the consequence of development through growth, and the attempt to go beyond the circle of Puerto Rican type modernization.

The PNP administration placed considerable emphasis on its multilateral policies. The thrust of these policies sought to realize two sets of objectives, but operated in contradictory spheres. First, in economic terms, the government sought to navigate itself within the confines of existing international regimes with the aim of extracting economic resources. Despite the declared objective of breaking Jamaica's traditional relationship, vis-à-vis the Bretton Woods (inspired) financial regimes, the government nonetheless sought development funding from the World Bank, Inter-American Development Bank, bilateral aid from the United States, and balance of payments support from the International Monetary Fund.

Concerted attempts were also made to maintain and/or extend preferential trading arrangements with the United States and EEC. Whenever guaranteed quotas for bauxite/alumina and sugar (the two principal exports) were threatened, the PNP government was quick to point to imperialism. Yet, if indeed the overall structure of the trading relationship between Jamaica and the North was "imperialist" (inscribed in the terms of trade differentials of which M. Manley was a great critic), it would appear as if his fight to maintain significant aspects of that relationship effectively amounted to a plea for a more benign, if not benevolent imperialism. More than that, it is not unreasonable to suggest that for Democratic Socialism to have succeeded in Jamaica, the "imperialist heartland" would have had to cooperate in substantial ways. This contradiction is characteristic of so many governments in the Third World which are interested in breaking the chains of neocolonialism but find themselves at the doorsteps of "imperialism" asking for more of the same.

Certainly, the other hand of the PNP's multilateral policy was explicitly aimed at subverting key aspects of the global political economy which were found wanting in justice. The government's policies with respect to the International Bauxite Association, African liberation, regional integration, south-south cooperation, and the New International Economic Order, all bear testimony to a campaign for global political change. While Jamaica cannot claim ownership to whatever gains were in fact made on these global issues, it can legitimately take some responsibility for sustaining them on the global agenda. What then of Jamaica's declared policy of wrenching itself out of, and working toward transforming a neocolonial/imperialist world order?

There is no doubt these objectives were pursued with considerable seriousness and resolve. Unlike many other Third World countries, the Jamaican challenge to key elements of the existing world order was not merely to deflect domestic political problems onto the world stage where a ready made alibi could be found for the country's woes. There is indeed sufficient evidence to demonstrate a foreign policy informed by a societally-driven conception of counter-hegemony. Such evidence, however, would only make sense within a *theoretical problematic of counter-hegemonic practice.*

## Counter-Hegemony in Theory and Practice

At its broadest level, counter-hegemony refers to a total way of life lived outside the ontological and philosophical system of meaning *exercised* in hegemonic interpellation. This is a kind of ideal-typical way of life, and may be seen as integral counter-hegemony. The latter is not fantastic in character, for several cultures over broad periods of time have aspired to this mode of living. With respect to modern capitalist societies, such consciousness may involve the attempt to empty oneself of commodified desire, or by renouncing what liberal economics calls "want." For the Third World, it also means renouncing the cultural legacies of colonialism and the more recent forms of consumerist penetration which have become so central to the strategy of global corporations.

From a more sociological standpoint, decommodification would require an understanding of the socio-cultural agenda of late-capitalism which constructs *self-worth* through hyperconsumption. Of course, the reproduction of the fetishized self is not the result of mere "empirical consumption" but the ontological privileging of the idea of consumption itself. The project of late capitalism, it seems, is to advance a social system based on generalized commodity production, and to the production of a generalized self underwritten by commidified desire. Integral counter-hegemony would involve the *disarticulation of the signifying chain* which produces a commoditized imaginary by constantly bringing the self and commodities into a social relationship. The specific task is to wrench one's self-worth out of the "world of commodities."[5]

At the level of "international relations," transnationalization *per force* involves the *homogenization* of commodified desire on a global scale. The strategic project of corporate expansion is to subsume geographical space into cultural space, by systematically introducing marketized common sense on a global scale. This subversion of space is absolutely necessary for late-capitalism to reproduce itself since globalization, in effect, means the erasure of cultural specificities. On the other hand, it is precisely the resistance to the making of a global (commodified) subject that might be the basis of strategic counter-hegemony. It is for these reasons the particularity of identity and the concomitant rejection of Universalism have become important in recent debates. Apart from selling "world products," corporate global expansion inadvertently also sells a way of life, a culture. It goes without saying that the real questions are: what way of life, and whose culture should form the template of global humanity? The answer seems to be a consumptive culture regulated by *meum et tuum* (a 16th century principle of private property law which meant what is mine is mine, and what is yours is yours. Each should have the right to enjoy his/her own property). This is why, the problematic of civilizations is crucial to a critical approach to global political economy. From a Third Worldist perspective, counter-hegemony should involve a long-term project of cultural decolonization.

In Jamaica the "culture of Dread" systematically eroded the foundations of Anglo-Christian hegemony and put the commodified self on defense. The lived experience of the Rastas as well as the philosophical implications of their "alternative practices," were so diffuse that it would not be farfetched to conclude that Jamaica went through a cultural revolution during the 1960s and 1970s. Of course it would be inaccurate to suggest Dread culture has been successful in obliterating commodified desire in Jamaica. That is not the point. What is important from the perspective of counter-hegemony are the types of questions that emerged during the period under consideration. In some significant ways "the limits of the possible" were redefined, and self-worth was reposed in larger historical dimensions. Simply put, the majority of those who make up Jamaica became recognized by undermining what Edward Said calls the "gigantic caricatural essentializations" which had hitherto constructed the (colonized) facts of national common sense.[6]

At a historically concrete level, counter-hegemony involves the forging of strategic alliances among otherwise unconnected subaltern groups. In terms of theory, by unhinging social class from an economic reductionist base and by depriveleging it as the fulcrum of social transformation, the working class will be only one element, albeit a key one, in the formation of a broad front against the exercise of hegemonic practices. The general ideological strategy of counter-hegemonic fronts would be to develop constant "discursive readiness" through what Laclau and Mouffe call "popular democratic interpellation."[7] Within particular nation-states, such a front may become sufficiently powerful that it might considerably influence the balance of social forces. Further, by occupying strategic institutional spaces, a subaltern front can play a decisive role in the forms of state and world orders that emerge.

## Some New Directions

A great deal has happened since the early 1980s. In Jamaica itself the PNP would follow the electoral cycle and replace the JLP.

There was one major difference though: the PNP, again under M. Manley, and then under the former Foreign Minister, P. J. Patterson, would embrace the orientations and policies which it had fought against with such vigor. The shift in Jamaica itself is part of a broader pattern of global change, and like Jamaica, Third World foreign policies will have to be retooled to deal with the rapid changes occurring. One way to understand the nature of the current transformations is to examine pressures emanating from both the world order level and domestic levels. Combined, these latter will no doubt continue to shape the forms of state which are emerging.

The structural reconfiguration of the global security order, the impact of economic globalization, and the proliferation of liberal democracy have had, and will continue to have major implications for Third World foreign policy. In the realm of security, the demise of a tight bipolar world has given rise to new forms of multilateral intervention. Third World countries will find it much harder to treat violation of human rights; ethnic cleansing; or even civil wars as purely internal matters. Haiti; Somalia; Nigeria; Indonesia; and for that matter, even Chile, are good illustrations of this.

Specifically, Third World foreign policies will need to meet new challenges of transparency and accountability vis-à-vis the "international community." Put differently, new normative pressures consistent with democratic governance which have become part of the operational code of multilateral institutions, the UN Security Council included, will impact upon state sovereignty. In the Caribbean, CARICOM'S "intervention" in Guyana may be seen as a regional variant of the increasing tendency for the world community to take action in cases of civil disturbance.

Economic globalization is having, and will continue to redefine Third World (but not only the Third World) sovereignty. This has to be understood in two dimensions. Firstly, the emphasis on liberalization, privatization, and deregulation, combined with the structural power of internationally mobile capital, has introduced new forms of economic "discipline" for Third World economies, most of which are still resource oriented. Governments that become too defensive against what Stephen Krasner once called "global liberalism," will be punished by "the market."

In addition, International Financial Institutions which are driven by monetarist policies, and which share the ideology of "free markets," will work with those states that embark on "marketization," and adopt a more hands-off stand with those that pursue, or return to various forms of protection. There is strong evidence to suggest that a distinctive form of market hegemony, combined with multilateral intervention has emerged in the post "cold war" period.

The "new hegemony," as this writer would like to call it, however, cannot be fully explained without factoring in social forces at the domestic, local level. The first thing to recognize is that the response from civil society has not been, and will not be uniform. The reason for this is that these world order pressures are having differential impacts on the various groups which compose society. Within the working class itself, for example, there is an increasing division between those who have secure employment, and a growing mass of "contingent" and informal workers. The first group is generally connected to the upper rung of manufacturing, the high-end of the service economy,"idea-based value"production, and government jobs. These groups are increasingly being recruited in domestic coalitions which support "globalization," the latter itself understood as submission to global market forces, and more broadly, market ideology. Other groups, with less secure employment, however, are falling into poverty, and are becoming part of a movement of discontent.

These groups are likely to constitute a counter-hegemonic force, or at minimum resist the pace and depth of restructuring. But domestic counter-hegemonic forces need not be so mechanically related to the economic, qua economic. The reason for this is that political action is often informed by cultural identity as argued throughout this book. Economic hardship, for example, might be translated into racial oppression, or global liberalism might be seen as an assault on national pride.

The specific way in which discontent is expressed depends on both the conjunctural forces of change, and the collective historical memory of subjects. The Rastafarian movement in Jamaica has, for example, been on the upsurge of recent. In their interpretation, the current situation in Jamaica, propelled by various instruments of neoliberalism, is the result of neocolonial racial oppression. The same may be said for the "resistance movement" in Chiapas, Mexico and elsewhere. Local/domestic forces, therefore, at a minimum, are engaging the pressures which are emanating from the world order level.

Finally, world order pressures and domestic/local forces will continue to affect the *forms of state* that emerge. The pressures from above are powerful, but run into limits that are placed on account of mobilization from below. Popular mobilization is more effective today precisely because of changes at the world order level described above, and particularly due to the rise in democratic governance. During the "cold war," resistance from below was more "effectively" dealt with by the Third World state. In general, authoritarian-developmentalist states manipulated the "cold war" rivalry; invoked sovereignty; and took cover under various international institutions.[8] It is a bit more difficult to do that today, although it must be stated forthwith that the record of interventions shows a disturbing pattern of showing up where the dominant states have vested interests. The changes that have occurred of recent must be understood in terms of the continuing patterns of entrenched power on the one hand, and generalized marginalization on the other. Clearly, the bases for the dialectics of hegemony-resistance/counter-hegemony are very much alive.

# Notes

## Chapter 1. Introduction

1. Obika Gray (1991).

2. Antonio Gramsci (1971), p. 353.

3. Stephen R. Gill (1993), p. 30.

4. S. Gill (1993), p 30.

5. S. Gill (1993), p. 24.

## Chapter 2. Approaches to Third World Foreign Policy

1. Claude Levi-Strauss (1962), p. 15.

2. Levi-Strauss uses the notion "right pending disproof" to acknowledge the merit of intuition as the "primordial" basis for classification. He writes: "It seems probable, . . . that species possessing some remarkable characteristics, say, of shape, colour or smell give the observer what might be called a 'right pending disproof' to postulate that these visible characteristics are the sign of equally singular, but concealed, properties." C. Levi-Strauss (1962), p. 16.

3. Whereas foreign policy is concerned with goals and intentions, foreign policy behaviour focuses on the action, and the consequences of those actions, undertaken by the state. See Furiol (1984).

4. As used here, perspectives "refers to the basic concepts and assumptions which underpin theoretical explanation." See Stephen Gill and David Law (1988), p. 17. This is somewhat similar to the notion of "frame of reference" put forward by Snyder, Bruck, and Sapin (1962), p. 26.

5. While the dependency/world systems approach does not have an explicit theory of foreign policy per se, the literature is sufficiently developed

215

to allow us to extrapolate some general propositions which can act as a guideline for what such a theory might look like. A number of studies have in fact used the concept of "dependency" in the analysis of Third World foreign policy. See, for example, Franklin B. Weinstein (1972); Timothy M. Shaw (1985); Christopher Clapham, ed., *Foreign Policy Making in Developing States: A Comparative Approach.* London: Saxon House, 1977; Bruce E. Moon, (1985, 1989) W. J. Biddle and John D. Stephens (1989).

6. Bhagat Korany (1974), p. 70.

7. Michael Handel (1981), p. 3.

8. Although there are strong grounds for putting mini/micro states in a separate category, as some authors do, others continue to use small, weak, and mini/micro synonymously.

9. While there is considerable disagreement over the categories small and weak states, this is not the case for the associated categories great and middle powers and mini states. More importantly, most scholars accept the division of the international system into classes of states.

10. For a good discussion of size as a variable, see Maurice A. East (1973), p. 557.

11. N. Amstrup (1976), p. 165.

12. For an interesting discussion of characteristics other than size, which might be used to separate small and great powers, see Bjol Erling (1971).

13. Colin Clarke and Tony Payne (1987).

14. R. P. Bartson (1971), p. 41.

15. See M. Handel (1981), p. 31.

16. Ibid.

17. David Vital (1967), p. 8.

18. Ibid., pp. 8–9.

19. Guyana and Jamaica also have similar international "outlooks." For a discussion of outlooks, see Daniel S. Papp (1988), ch. 12.

20. For an excellent discussion on nomothetic generalizations in international relations, see J. Rosenau (1971). For an elucidation on nomological explanation in general, see Carl G. Hempel (1968). On the problem of comparative analysis, see Neil J Smelser (1973), pp. 42–86.

21. A. Przeworski and H. Teune (1973), p. 121. Marx uses the concept of "general equivalence" in his analysis of the money form of value.

22. For an informative discussion of "core interests and values," see Kal J. Holsti (1983), pp. 129–131.

23. Handel (1981), p. 36.

24. Ibid., p. 10.

25. Ibid.

26. Ibid., pp. 10–11.

27. R. L. Rothstein (1977); Annete Baker Fox (1959); D. Vital (1967).

28. R. L. Rothstein (1968).

29. Ibid., p. 4.

30. Marshall R. Singer (1972).

31. Stephen Gill and David Law define ontology as follows: "ontology refers to the nature of reality and its underlying units which form the starting point for theoretical explanation." S. Gill and D. Law (1988), p. 19.

32. Robert G. Gilpin (1986), pp. 304–305.

33. Kenneth Waltz states the problem as follows: "with many sovereign states, with no system of law enforceable among them, with each state judging its grievances and ambitions according to the dictates of its own reason or desire-conflict, sometimes leading to war, is bound to occur." Kenneth N. Waltz (1970), p. 159. For another classic statement of this argument, see Hans J. Morgenthau (1973).

34. Hans Morgenthau (1973), pp. 107–155.

35. See Kenneth Waltz (1979), p. 131.

36. Ibid., p. 98.

37. Ibid., p. 192.

38. Waltz makes the point as follows: "The parts of a system are related to one another in ways that are determined both by their functional differentiation and by the extent of their capabilities. The units of an anarchic system are functionally undifferentiated. The units of such an order are then distinguished primarily by their greater or lesser capabilities for performing the same tasks." K. Waltz (1979), p. 97.

39. Ibid., p. 98.

40. Ibid., p. 97.

41. Handel rejects the idea that small states are only peaceful and have only defensive capabilities. See M. Handel (1981), pp. 37–38. David

Lowental argues that small states play an international role far beyond their size. This is especially true of their activities in the United Nations and other world bodies. See his essay, "Social Features" (1987).

42. D. Vital (1967), p. 87.

43. For a thorough discussion of the position of weak states in different international systems, see M. Handel (1981), ch. 4.

44. George Liska (1968), p. 27.

45. Annete Baker Fox suggests that small states have the tendency to align with the stronger. Small state foreign policy behavior is, therefore, "anti-balance of power." See Fox, *The Power of Small States,* p. 187.

46. For a sound discussion of the conditions under which small states are most likely to resist the pressures from great powers, see A. B. Fox (1959), pp. 181–184.

47. For a rigorous analysis of the rational decision making process in modern bureaucracy, see Graham Allison (1971), chapters 1 and 3.

48. P. J. McGowan and Klaus-Peter Gottwald (1975), p. 470.

49. Ibid., p. 472.

50. These categories of foreign policy behaviour were originally put forward by J. Rosenau in his seminal article, "Pre-Theories and Theories of Foreign Policy." See J. Rosenau (1971). P. J. McGowan and Klaus-Peter Gottwald (1975), p. 472.

51. P. J. McGowan and K-P Gottwald (1975), p. 475.

52. Ibid.

53. Ibid., p. 476.

54. Ibid., p. 478.

55. Derived from their diagrammatic representation of an adaptive conception of foreign policy. McGowan and Gottwald (1975), p. 276.

56. K. J. Holsti, "National Role Conceptions in the Study of Foreign Policy," in Stephen J. G. Walker, ed., *Role Theory and Foreign Policy Analysis.* Durham: Duke University Press, 1987. This essay was originally published in *International Studies Quarterly,* Vol. 14, 1970.

57. K. J. Holsti, 1987.

58. Ibid., p. 5.

59. Ibid.

60. Ibid., p. 6.

61. See J. Rosenau (1987).

62. Ibid., p. 45.

63. Robert Jervis (1976), p. 18.

64. K. J. Holsti (1987), p. 7.

65. Ibid., p. 8.

66. Margaret G. Herman (1987), p. 162.

67. See, in particular, his (1974, 1975, 1978, 1984).

68. B. Korany (1974), p. 82.

69. For a discussion of these assumptions and the concept of "situation," see B. Korany (1975) pp. 67–72.

70. B. Korany (1974), p. 83.

71. B. Korany (1975), p. 73.

72. B. Korany (1974), p. 85.

73. Naiomi B. Wish (1987), p. 96.

74. Ibid.

75. B. Korany (1974), p. 83.

76. Ibid.

77. B. Korany (1974), p. 84.

78. See Nye and Keohane (1989), pp. 8–11.

79. N. R. Richardson (1976), pp. 10–11.

80. N. R. Richardson (1976), p. 5.

81. A. Armstrong (1981), p. 461.

82. N. R. Richardson (1976), p. 70.

83. M. Nichloson (1989).

84. Richardson (1976), p. 64. See also C. Barner-Barry and R. Rosenwein (1985), p. 170.

85. Bruce Moon (1985), p. 304. Emphasis added.

86. B. Moon (1983), p. 315.

87. B. Moon (1985), p. 306.

88. B. Moon (1985), p. 306.

89. B. Moon (1983), pp. 320–21.

90. Biddle and Stephens (1989), p. 423.

91. Biddle and Stephens (1989), p. 414.

92. J. A. Braveboy-Wagner (1989), p. 7.

## Chapter 3. A Social Forces Approach to Foreign Policy

1. R. W. Cox (1986), p. 217.

2. Cox (1986), pp. 217–225.

3. Cox (1981, 1986, 1987).

4. Cox (1986), pp. 217–225.

5. Cox (1986), p. 220.

6. Cox (1986), p. 220.

7. For a clear statement of Waltz's criticism of the irrelevance of states and societies as units relevant to the theorization of the "international system," see K. Waltz (1979), chapter 3.

8. J. V. Femia (1981), p. 37.

9. Femia (1981), p. 39.

10. Cox (1992), p. 140.

11. S. Gill and D. Law (1988), chapter 7.

12. For more on "fixed universals," see R. B. Persaud (1997).

13. Cox (1992), p. 140.

14. For a brief introduction to hegemonic stability theory, see Robert O. Keohane (1989), chapter 4. For more comprehensive studies, see Robert Gilpin (1981); Paul Kennedy (1988); and Robert O. Keohane (1984).

15. Cox (1989), p. 140.

16. Gramsci (1971), p. 350.

17. Femia (1981), p. 46.

18. As Femia points out, Gramsci saw postrevolutionary France as a close approximation of such a "paradigm case." See Femia (1981), p. 46.

19. Femia (1981), p. 47.

20. Femia (1981), p. 47.

21. Femia (1981), p. 47.

22. Cox (1983), pp. 165–166.

23. Gramsci (1971), p. 106.

24. Anne Showstack Sassoon (1987), p. 210.

25. This formulation is partly based on a note from R. W. Cox to the author.

26. Louis Althusser also developed an extended concept of state in which he included institutions such as the school and church as arms of the state. See Louis Althusser (1971).

27. Althusser (1971), p. 178.

28. For an excellent analysis of the impact of the international states system on different forms of state, see Theda Skocpol (1979).

29. Cox (1987), p. 6.

30. It should be noted that Cox has addressed this problem. In his influential 1979 essay on ideologies and the NIEO, for example, he pointed out that "... the articulation of counter-ideologies becomes a part of the action...." This dimension of his general approach to the dialectic of hegemony-counter-hegemony is extremely important but needs to be a lot more explicit. Cox (1979), p. 257.

31. W. I. Robinson (1999), p. 63.

32. In a 1979 article on ideologies and the New International Economic Order, for example, Cox argues that "... it is possible to see, for each category or perspective [on the NIEO], an intellectual framework or ideology that serves to define a particular problematic peculiar to that perspective." In this case, the "framework or ideology" of each category corresponds to certain objective interests. This is an important point in that it dispels the artificial division between "science" and "ideology" by suggesting that all perspectives, or more accurately all knowledges, have some fundamental ontological assumptions which makes purely "objective" social science well nigh impossible. The problem with the formulation, however, is that it places too much emphasis on a direct relationship between interests and ideology, when in fact that is a relationship which has to be explained. In the article, for example, Cox notes that "The ideological quintessence of the establishment perspective" was expressed by Harry Johnson who "flays Prebish-style economics" and alternatively posited an economics based on "... rational behaviour by individuals and economic groups confronted with possibilities of substitution." Two paragraphs below Cox observes that "the fundamental commitment of the establishment perspective is to an open world market with relatively free

movement of capital, goods, and technology. Government interventions should be of a kind that supports this goal, and such interventions as would impede it are to be condemned" (p. 201). Now, while both of these are accurate statements about the "establishment perspective" (as defined by Cox), there is no way of knowing how the second statement (i.e., the goals etc.) become represented as economic science, if indeed the latter is the "ideological quintessence" of the former. The key point here is that the peculiar ideological representation of the "establishment perspective" as scientific knowledge does not have any inherent relationship with the interests represented. This claim to science rather, is to be explained largely against the *credible counter-ideologies* which had surfaced at the time and which were threatening the hegemonic position of bourgeois economics. Specifically, therefore, H. Johnson took establishment interest and the knowledge underpinning it, from which he produced a particular discursive narrative (of economic science) in a specific historical contestation. In this instance, economics as a *rational science*, was the "trafficking symbol" (or the authoritative sign) of the knowledges from which policy should be derived. Further, used this way, "economic science" was not merely an (ideological) justification for policies already formed (or even in the making), but a discursive moment in the constitution of legitimacy of the "science." See Robert W. Cox, "Ideologies and the New International Economic Order: Reflections on Some Recent Literature," *International Organization* 33, no. 2 (1979).

33. Adam Watson (1992), chapter 4.

34. R. B. Persaud (1995), p. 209.

35. S. Gill (1990), p. 49.

36. Other notable examples of the relationship among capitalist modernization, regimes, and passive revolution are to be found in "aid regimes." The Alliance for Progress and Caribbean Basin Initiatives are poignant testimonies to this case.

37. David Campbell (1992), chapters 2–4.

38. Hedley Bull (1984), pp. 220–221.

39. Hedley Bull put the point thus: "The dominance of the European or Western powers at the turn of the century was expressed not only in their superior economic and military power and in their commanding intellectual and cultural authority but also in the rules and institutions of international society." Bull (1984), p. 217.

40. See Robert H. Jackson (1990), chapter 1.

41. T. Skocpol (1979), p. 29.

42. Cox (1986).

43. David Campbell (1992).

## Chapter 4. Ideology, Culture and National Interest

1. As such, realism as the dominant paradigm of international relations, sees interest (defined as power) as universal and unaffected by time and circumstance; an assumption which by definition privileges the concepts of interest and power over all other concepts in international relations, ideology included. For a classic statement of this proposition, see H. J. Morgenthau (1978), chapter 8.

2. Warner Levi makes this argument quite explicitly stating that "ideology plays subordinate role in deciding the state's objectives and plan for action to reach them, and a more important role in justifying the decision *once it has been made.*" Warner Levi (1970), p. 5, emphasis added. In a much bolder statement of this position he suggests that "every insight permitted an outsider—through memoirs, memoranda, interviews—into the making of foreign policy confirms that in the deliberate designing of foreign policy the chronology is interests first, ideology second or not at all." Levi (1970), pp. 9–10.

3. See for example, Bayless Manning (1976); Seweryn Bailer (1978); Mark A. Stoler (1987).

4. Hans Morgenthau describes the process thus: "For if A enters the arena of political combat with the open declaration I want power over B, he will alert B and the friends of B and may well discourage his own potential friends who are afraid of his power. If he is able to conceal the actual essence of his aspirations in the political arena by political ideologies, if he can make it appear that what he wants is not primarily power over B but something else, such as the common good or the realization of some other objective value to which most or all members of this particular segment of society can adhere, then he has already won one battle in the political combat. He has already half disarmed his opponents and the prospective objects of his power and weakened their resistance by making it appear that what he wants is something else but power and that for this reason there is no moral or rational justification for opposing him." H. J. Morgenthau, in Schawb (1978), p. 119.

5. Hans Morgenthau (1978), p. 117.

6. Clifford Geertz (1964), p. 47. Vojtech Mastny captures the ideologized meaning of ideology when he states "in Anglo-American parlance, the very word ideology has an unsavoury ring. For most people, it connotes either sinister goals dressed up in fancy phrases or, scarcely more reassuring, a starry-eyed devotion to abstractions incompatible with sound politics." V. Mastny, in Schawb (1978), p. 7.

7. Cox (1987), p. 395.

8. Louis Althusser (1971), p. 159.

9. Clifford Geertz (1973), pp. 45–46.

10. C. Geertz (1973), p. 218.

11. Geertz (1973), p. 62.

12. Ernesto Laclau (1977), p. 94.

13. Laclau (1977), p. 99.

14. Ernesto Laclau and Chantal Mouffe (1987), p. 105.

15. Laclau and Mouffe (1987), p. 105.

16. See Louis Althusser and E. Balibar (1970), Part One.

17. Edward W. Said (1979), p. 94. This perspective has also been developed by some historians who have imported discourse analysis into historiography. See, for example, K. Jenkins (1991), pp. 8–9.

18. The author benefited greatly from discussions with Rishee S. Thakur on the problem of the "open political frontier."

19. See Karl Mannheim (1985), pp. 78–84.

20. Perry Anderson argues, for example, that the coercive aspect of hegemony cannot be separated from the problematic of hegemony. In his judgment, the threat of violence is crucial to social and political control. See P. Anderson (1976/1977).

21. See Enrico Augelli and Craig Murphy (1988) chapters 7–9; Robert A. Mortimer (1977), chapters 4–7.

22. For more on "relational" and "meta" power, see S. D. Krasner (1985), chapters 2 and 3.

23. For a full exposition of this notion of a "transnational imagined community," see Akhil Gupta (1992). The idea of "imagined communities" received its fullest development by Benedict Anderson. See Benedict Anderson (1983).

24. Cox (1992), p. 143.

25. Miliband goes on to argue, and properly so, that "capitalist-democratic regimes" do not take "hegemony for granted." He explains: "The whole history of these regimes, since the achievement of an extended suffrage, the creation of national working class movements, and serious political competition between bourgeois and labor or socialist parties, has been marked by a determined 'engineering of consent' on the part of the conservative forces, and by their fierce striving to win the hearts and minds of their subordinate populations. The sources of these struggles

have been extremely varied, and their forms have ranged from the most sophisticated and subtle to the most stridently demagogic. The purpose, however, is always the popular ratification of the prevailing social order, and the rejection by the working class . . . of any notion that there could be a radical and visible alternative to that order." R. Miliband (1990), p. 346.

26. Gupta (1992), p. 63.

27. Gupta (1992), p. 64.

28. Craig N. Murphy (1983), p. 60.

## Chapter 5: The Making of Modern Jamaica and the Emergence of Exceptionalism

1. W. O. Jones, quoted in George Beckford (1972), p. 6. Emphasis in the original.

2. Beckford (1972), p. 8.

3. Beckford (1972), p. 9.

4. Philip Curtin (1968), p. 22.

5. Beckford (1972), p. 11.

6. Beckford (1972), pp. 13–14.

7. Beckford (1972), p. 35.

8. See J. D. Stephens and E. H. Stephens (1986), pp. 21–25.

9. See Fred Block (1977), chapter 3.

10. Owen Jefferson, in N. Girvan and O. Jefferson pp. 109–121; G. Backford and Michael Witter (1982), chapters 6 and 7.

11. Carl Stone (1989), p. 27.

12. Government of Jamaica, *Five Year Independence Plan, 1963–1968,* 1963, p. 39.

13. Government of Jamaica, *Five Year Independence Plan, 1963–1968,* 1963, p. 39.

14. Government of Jamaica, *Five Year Independence Plan, 1963–1968,* 1963, p. 17.

15. See Colin G. Clarke (1975), chapters 5 and 6.

16. Government of Jamaica, *Five Year Independence Plan, 1963–1968,* p. 36.

17. Government of Jamaica, *Five Year Independence Plan, 1963–1968,* p. 36.

18. Government of Jamaica, *Five Year Independence Plan, 1963–1968,* p. 24.

19. Approximately 38,000 East Indians were taken to Jamaica as indentured laborers in the period 1845–1916. For more on the East Indian indentured immigrants, see Verene A. Shepherd (1999/2000), pp. 93–115.

20. See, for example, Gordon K. Lewis (1969), chapter 7.

21. Rex Nettleford (1978) p. 3.

22. This characterization is taken from Anthony J. Payne (1988), p. 2.

23. See M. G. Smith (1974), especially chapters 1–4.

24. M. G. Smith (1974), p. 162. Emphasis added.

25. M. G. Smith (1974), p. 65.

26. Aggrey Brown in fact argues that skin color was part of the strategy of divide and rule in slave society, a technique which ironically valorized the premium put on skin color. The latter became the " . . . most important criterion for measuring an individual's worth." Thus, "the lighter the skin pigment of the colored creole, the greater the possibilities of obtaining manumission or favours from the whites." Further, it was the acceptance of the colonizer's "strategy" that set the stage for race and color to evolve as part of the hegemonic imagination. As Brown points out, "it is thus not surprising that the colored and domestic slaves considered themselves better than the blacks and aspired toward those positions that would bring them into close social relations with the whites. This was particularly the case of colored women who were thrilled at the prospects of being the mistress of a white man of whatever status." Brown (1979), p. 32. See chapter 2 of Brown (1979) for a full exposition of the strategy of "divine and rule."

27. Quoted in Terry Lacey (1977), p. 34.

28. See Carl Stone (1973), p. 8. His other criticisms of cultural pluralism pluralism are (a) " . . . the accuracy of its description of the determinants of social status"; and (b) " . . . its relevance to the subjective definition of contending strata in the society" and (c) " . . . its accuracy in defining the main objectives and goals over which conflict occurs." Stone (1973), p. 8.

29. C. Stone (1978), p. 19. See his *Democracy and Clientelism in Jamaica* (1980).

30. See Adam Kuper (1977), pp. 111–149.

31. Kuper (1977), p. 120.

32. The color gradation from least to most prestigious that Taylor found was as follows: hugly (*sic*) black, black, Negro, cool black, dark, dark brown, brennet brown, coolie royal, sambo, brown, colored, light brown, Chinese royal, light colored, mulatto, gogran, high colored, fair skinned, play white, Jamaica white, buckra, and white. The last four categories reveal a great deal about the complexity of color, status, and power. Thus although "play white" is very high in the scheme, the term is rather sarcastic; that is ridiculing someone who is very light but with sufficient color to question the authenticity of their whiteness. This comes out more clearly with the notion of "Jamaica white." In this instance it is not a question of *color qua color;* rather this category of white is marked down a couple of grades because it is *local whiteness.* The most authentic, that is highest and most desirable ranked categories, are those whites associated with foreignness. Buckra used to be a patently derogatory term for the white *man* during slavery. Ironically, the depth of colonialism in Jamaica and the specificity of its race, class, and color articulation is such that the term is now an emblem of status. Council Taylor (1955), pp. 44–45.

33. Carl Stone (1973), p. 49. It is important to note that while he does insist that race cannot be analyzed outside of class and vice versa, and further, explicitly calls for class analysis, he means this only in a restricted sense. Class for him is defined more in terms of occupation and possession of material goods, or lack thereof. See chapters 1 and 3 of his *Democracy and Clientelism in Jamaica,* for a more detailed exposition of the meaning of class.

34. Charles Mills (1987), p. 72.

35. Stuart Hall (1977), p. 154.

36. Hall (1977), p. 154.

37. For a systematic exposition of the concept "structural combinatory," see Louis Althusser and Etienne Balibar (1979), Part III. Briefly, the concept refers to a totality produced through an articulation of different elements, where the elements become modified through their "combination" with other elements, and the whole becomes more than the sum of the parts.

38. For an excellent discussion of the influence of Christianity in Jamaican slave society, see Mary Turner (1982).

39. Nettleford (1978), p. 19.

40. W. Bell and J. W. Gibson (1978).

41. Bell and Gibson (1978), p. 27.

42. Bell and Gibson (1978), p. 16.

43. Bell and Gibson (1978), p. 18.

44. Marlene Cuthbert (1976), p. 51.

45. Cuthbert (1976), p. 53.

46. Stephens and Stephens (1986), p. 55.

47. Stephens and Stephens (1986), p. 55.

48. Morris Cargill, for example is a planter and regular columnist in the *Gleaner*. During the 1970s he waged a sustained "campaign" against the Manley government.

49. Stephens and Stephens (1986), p. 92.

50. For a good description of these tactics by the *Gleaner*, see Cuthbert (1976).

51. Jack Johnson-Hill (1981), p. 12.

52. Edward Seaga holds a bachelor's degree in sociology from Harvard. Michael Manley's training in economics at the London School of Economics was never mentioned and ". . . the democratic socialism he represented became vulnerable to accusations of ignorance—of *not knowing* how to do this or that—particularly, and ironically, in the economic sphere." Quoted from Johnson-Hill (1981), p. 8.

53. Johnson-Hill (1981), p. 13.

54. Ibid.

55. Obika Gray (1991), p. 54.

56. Gray (1991), p. 54.

57. Quoted in Gray (1991), p. 54. The "early days of Jamaica's social and economic revolution" here refers to the rapid increase in industrial production and infusion of foreign capital during the late 1940s and 1950s.

58. Quoted in Gray (1991), p. 56.

## Chapter 6. Counter-Hegemonic Forces

1. Ferdinand Braudel, translated by M. Kochan (1973), p. xii.

2. For most of the decade 1962–1972, approximately one fifth to one quarter of the Jamaican labor force was unemployed, with Kingston always having a higher rate than the national average. Toward the end of the 1960s the national unemployment rate started to climb even higher, reaching historic highs of over 30 percent from late 1966 through 1969. These figures would have been considerably higher were it not for heavy emigration to the United Kingdom until about 1965. See Terry Lacey (1977),

pp. 16–18. For an examination of unemployment problems for the next decade, see John S. Gafar (1988).

3. Gray (1991), p. 72.

4. Rex Nettleford (1978), p. 201.

5. Gray (1991), p. 117.

6. Gray (1991), p. 73.

7. Gray (1991), p. 68.

8. Gray (1991), p. 68.

9. Gray (1991), p. 68.

10. Gray (1991), p. 77.

11. According to Stuart Hall, "Rastafarianism thus came to be the 'language' in which the rising aspirations of the popular black masses of the society were expressed. It succeeded in shifting the index of cultural hegemony in Jamaican society and began to substitute for the dominant cultural system of white bias an alternative regime 'grounded' on the African connection, blackness, and the vernacular culture. . . . Jamaica became for the first time in its history, culturally black." S. Hall (1985), p. 288.

12. The reader should keep in mind that Garvey was still living in colonial society and thus not only had direct experience of white domination, but also a relatively fresh memory of the Morant Bay uprising during which a large number of blacks were slaughtered or subsequently hanged by white colonial officials. Clearly, Garvey took the real-concrete *historical agents* of imperialism very seriously. This is one area where Garvey, the Rastafarian, and the Black Power movements placed more emphasis than other critiques of imperialism, Marxism included.

13. Horace Campbell (1991), p. 168.

14. Barry Chevannes (1991), p. 130.

15. Errol Miller (1973), p. 112. Emphasis added.

16. According to some accounts, Bedward—who was a "revivalist and healer," is reputed to have given the following warning—"Hell will be your portion if you do not rise up and crush the white man . . . there is a white wall and a black wall and the white wall has been closing around the black wall but now the black wall is becoming bigger than the white and they must knock the white wall down." Pronouncements of this sort were not unusual during the early parts of this century in Jamaica and must have had a strong interpolative effect on poor, dispossessed blacks. V. Pollard (1982), p. 17.

17. M. G. Smith, R. Augier, and R. Nettleford (1967), pp. 7–8.

18. The idea of "Anglo-Christian hegemony" is taken from Rishee Thakur. See Rishee Thakur, *Politics and Hegemony in Guianese Nationalism, 1945–1965*. (Ph.D. Dissertation, York University, 1994). Chapters VIII and IX of this study examine in great detail, what Thakur calls, an "Anglo-Christian ethic."

19. M. G. Smith, R. Augier, and Rex Nettleford (1967), p. 4.

20. Smith, Augier, and Nettleford (1967), pp. 17–18.

21. The Catholic Church was very upset with the findings of the investigation and suggested the report submitted by Smith, Augier, and Nettleford was "unworthy" of scholarly research. The real fear of the Church was that the report not only vindicated the Rasta movement, but also provided fuel for growth. Of course, the position of the Church also has to be understood in the larger historical and cultural context of what was happening; the movement had launched a major "offensive" against the privileged position which "European Christianity" occupied in Jamaica and directly linked this Christianity to the oppression of *black people* in their own country.

22. Smith, Augier, and Nettleford (1967), p. 18.

23. Smith, Augier, and Nettleford (1967), pp. 18–19.

24. In its widest sense Babylon refers to all oppressors, irrespective of race or national identity. Whites have been especially singled out on account of the history of slavery and the continuing position of "ethnic minorities" in Jamaica. Babylon is also a "myth" which serves to conceptualize oppression across time and space and simultaneously to provide an intellectual framework and organizing principles for liberation. In a more immediate sense the concept designates the forces of state coercion, and especially the police.

25. Letter to "His Excellency, The Governor General, Constitutional and Executive Representative, Regina Elizabeth II, U.K., & Gt. Rt.," dated August 22, 1979, and signed by "Illect of JAHRASTAFARI" and "Illect of Records." *PNP Archives*, Kingston Jamaica.

26. Quoted from Obika Gray (1991), p. 240. Gray makes the interesting observation that this letter, *inter alia*, is indicative of the "close attention" the brethren give to "international affairs." Gray also notes that the effect of the letter ". . . was electrifying, especially among the middle classes. Not since the Morant Bay rebellion in 1865 had a group of Jamaicans taken up arms against the state. As if that was not enough, here was a group of people who wore their contempt for society by their hair and even facial expressions. It was time to put a stop to the lunacy that was Rastafari. The police were not slow to take their cue from the general public, as a

wave of intimidation, shaving of locks, arrests, beating, and imprisonment, descended on all Rastafari, in unprecedented scale and scope." Gray (1991), p. 72.

27. Semaj (1980), p. 27.

28. Semaj (1980), p. 27.

29. Semaj (1980), p. 28.

30. According to the UWI Report, the only parts regarded by the brethren as "the true word of God" are: Psalms 18, 21, 29, 48, 87, 137; Genesis 18; Numbers 6; Leviticus 11, 21; Deuteronomy 16; Isaiah 11, 43; Jeremiah 23, 8; Malachi 1; Hebrews 11; I Corinthians 4; I Timothy 6; I John 4; 2 Thessalonians 3; Ezekiel 5, 13, 23; and Revelations 13, 15, 17, 18, 19, 22. Smith, Augier, and Nettleford (1967), p. 19.

31. Smith, Augier, and Nettleford (1967), p. 22.

32. Erna Brodber (1984), p. 55.

33. Smith, Augier, and Nettleford (1967), p. 22.

34. Ken Post (1978), chapter 6.

35. Semaj (1980), p. 26.

36. Pollard (1982), p. 20.

37. Thus Barry Chevannes notes that "By keeping alive the issue of identity and forcing it on national consciousness, the Rastafari movement has helped to expose and by so doing overturn certain assumptions of the ideology of racism, particularly among the middle classes." Chevannes (1991), p. 60.

38. Gray (1991), p. 155.

39. Norman Girvan makes a strong case for the imbrication of race in Caribbean discourses of liberation. He writes for example—". . . in so far as an ideology of physical and cultural racism is used to legitimize the socio-economic order, ideologies of racial pride and self-assertion are essential to the generation of the collective self-esteem amongst the population at large which is a psycho-cultural precondition to their challenging the system. We believe therefore that black nationalist ideologies remain relevant not only in the Caribbean but all over the Americas where black communities are found. . . ." N. Girvan (1975), p. 30.

40. Gray (1991), p. 152.

41. Gray (1991), p. 154.

42. In this vein, N. Girvan argues ". . . that the process of capitalist expansion in the Americas in the nineteenth and early twentieth centuries

required and generated a new expression of the racial division of labour both within countries and in the hemisphere and between them." N. Girvan (1975), p. 20.

43. Gray (1991), p. 155.

44. H. Campbell (1987), p. 132.

45. Gray (1991), p. 171. "Abeng" was the name of the horn used by the Maroon warriors (the earliest of Jamaican slaves who constantly fought the Spanish colonialists and who had set up independent communities before British arrival in 1655) and as Campbell points out, its use by the intellectuals was ". . . itself a reflection of the new sense of importance of the people's history." Campbell (1978), p. 132.

46. H. Campbell (1987), p. 173.

47. H. Campbell (1987), p. 173.

48. George Sorel (1961), p. 54.

## Chapter 7. Facilitating Passive Revolution

1. V. Lewis (1981), p. 44. In a speech to the Parliament in May 1974, Prime Minister Manley underlined this passivity by pinpointing four assumptions which had informed Jamaican foreign policy prior to 1972. According to the Prime Minister these were: (1) that the economic relationship with the developed countries was fixed in dependence; (2) that we were lucky to have foreign capital and know-how; (3) that we need foreign capital and it was acceptable to "trade" national sovereignty to achieve this; and (4) that metropolitan countries owed us aid or soft loans. M. Manley, Address to Parliament, May 1974. File: Speeches, Manley, M. *PNP Archives*.

2. Lewis (1981), p. 1972–1977.

3. Government of Jamaica, *Policy Statement to the UN General Assembly*. XVII Session, 1962. Ministry of Foreign Affairs, Kingston, Jamaica.

4. Quoted in George E. Eaton (1975), p. 202.

5. Michael Manley would later characterize JLP policy as "mendicancy." In his own words: "The thinking really was this: since we are small and we are poor, we have no real power in the world. The theory is that your only hope is to proceed through life in the posture and with the psychology and the mind of a mendicant. Yes. Mendicancy is the policy." See "Prime Minister, The Hon. Michael Manley at U.W.I., Nov. 22, 1976." File: Speeches, Manley, M. *PNP Archives*.

6. D. K. Kumar (1988), p. 115.

7. The PNP government would later severely criticize JLP "behavior" in the United Nations. In a speech delivered at the University of the West Indies (Mona campus), M. Manley intimated that the JLP was like a "tame cat" ready to "deliver the right vote" in exchange for economic aid and to demonstrate its faithfulness to the West. See "Prime Minister, The Hon. Michael Manley at U.W.I., Nov. 22, 1976." File: Speeches, Manley, M. *PNP Archives*.

8. Cox (1987), p. 7. Emphasis added.

9. Quoted in Lewis (1981), p. 46.

10. Government of Jamaica, *Five Year Independence 1963–1968*, p. 11.

11. Government of Jamaica, *Five Year Independence Plan 1963–1968*, pp. 121–123.

12. Government of Jamaica, *Five Year Independence Plan*, p. 126.

13. Government of Jamaica, *Five Year Independence Plan*, p. 35.

14. Carl Stone (1989), pp. 27–28. Emphasis added.

15. H. Shearer, *Policy Statement to the UN General Assembly,* XVII Session, 1962.

16. Harry G. Matthews (1968), pp. 85–86.

17. Quoted by D. Mills (1989), p. 140.

18. George Eaton (1975), p. 203.

19. H. Campbell (1987), p. 139.

20. Campbell (1987), p. 135. Emphasis Added.

21. Michael Kaufman (1985), p. 113.

22. Stephens and Stephens (1986), p. 57.

23. Lacey (1977), p. 94.

## Chapter 8. From "Exceptionalism" to Democratic Socialism

1. John S. Gafar (1988), p. 64.

2. The "Rod of Correction" refers to a cane reportedly given to Michael Manley by Emperor Haile Selassie. Manley usually waved the "Rod" at election rallies much to the delight of Rastafarians and the "Dread"

*Notes*

population as a whole. The Rod carried religious symbolism, especially
since Manley was dubbed or adopted the name, Joshua. In the context of
Jamaican society and politics, the Rod also symbolized Manley's professed
commitment to moral redemption of the country which had been "squan-
dered" during the 1960s under the JLP. During the 1976 general election,
the JLP circulated a rumor that Manley had lost the "Rod," thereby inti-
mating an equivalent loss of power with which the Rod was associated.
Soon after the rumor began, Manley turned up at a huge rally, trium-
phantly "brandishing" the Rod.

3. Quoted in Stephens and Stephens (1986), p. 66.

4. Darrell E. Levi (1989), p. 126.

5. Levi (1989), p. 126.

6. Levi (1989), p. 131.

7. Some of the most influential persons in important positions were:
Mayer Matalon (from one of the "twenty–one families") was Chair of the
Urban Development Corporation and member of the National Bauxite
Commission (NBC); Eli Matalon (also from the Matalon family) became
Minister of Education and Security; Pat Rousseau, Chairman of Life of
Jamaica headed the NBC; K. Hendrickson, head of National Continental
Corporation became Chair of Jamaica Public Services; R. D. C. Henriques
(from the *Who's Who* family) and director of Jamaica Mutual Life and the
Bank of Nova Scotia (Jamaica) ". . . was placed at the helm of the Cocanut
Industry Board and was a director of the Sugar Industry Capital Rehabili-
tation Board; D. Williams, President of Life of Jamaica (and later a leading
member of the PSOJ formed to represent business interests against the
PNP) chaired the Jamaican Association for the Advancement of Literacy
(JAMAL); and A. U. Belinfanti, "a well off cane farmer," became Minister
of Agriculture." See Kaufman (1985), p. 75.

8. Stephens and Stephens (1986), p. 82.

9. Information gathered from "Policy Aims and Performance of the
PNP Government, 1972–1974," Kingston: PNP Archives, File: "Foreign
Affairs—Foreign Policy, 1972–1974"; Government of Jamaica, Economic
and Social Survey, Jamaica, 1973; Stephens and Stephens, 70–71; and
Kaufman, xii–xiii. Not all programs are included here.

10. A good representation of this argument is made by Fitzroy
Ambursley. See his "Jamaica: From Michael Manley to Edward Seaga," in
*Crisis in the Caribbean* (1983).

11. "Statement to the House of Representatives by the Prime Minister, The Hon. Michael Manley, Wednesday, November 20, 1974." *PNP
Archives.*

12. In Manley's judgment ideology ought to ". . . reflect our experience as a party, our understanding of our country and its needs, our analysis of the world, and provide a framework for the determination of policy." M. Manley (1982), p. 121.

13. Manley (1982), p. 123. What is interesting here is the range of factors representing different social forces which were *actually considered* in the naming process. And although Manley disassociates the PNP from African one-party states here, he does acknowledge the influence of Nyerere's African Socialism on his own thinking about an alternative vision. Further, the fact that "democratic socialism" was launched during Nyerere's official visit to Jamaica is of some cultural/political import. It should also be borne in mind that at the time of this address the National Executive Council of the PNP had endorsed democratic socialism. The document, however, was cause for considerable controversy within the party and was not adopted.

14. M. Manley (1982), p. 125.

15. In fact the PNP official position on this states that "the foreign policy seeks the application to international affairs of the same principles upon which our domestic policy is based." See *The Principles and Objectives*, p. 52.

16. This is a telling and significant characterization of Jamaican foreign policy prior to 1972 given that the PNP had been in office before. What is more, is the apparent contradiction between this characterization and Michael Manley's claim that the PNP has always been socialist. If indeed the PNP has always been socialist, how can the party account for a "servile relationship with imperialism" when it was in office under the leadership of Norman Manley. This contradiction is left unresolved as far as party explanation is concerned. It is more reasonable to suggest that in the post-1972 period, PNP foreign policy became decidedly more anti-imperialist.

17. *Principles and Objectives,* p. 52.

18. M. Manley, Address to the Parliament, May 1974. File: Speeches, Manley, M. *PNP Archives.*

19. The two following statements by the Prime Minister give adequate testimony to this conclusion. First he states that "it must be understood that the great economic forces of history did not reverse themselves by accident. If you are to modify them at all, they have to be modified by the marshalling of enormous political forces." Secondly, he then goes on to describe the nature of the struggle in global terms, by pointing out that "the struggle of the world is between those who seek to organize support for justice on the one hand, and those who can employ power to defeat justice on the other." M. Manley, Address to the Parliament, May 1974. File: Speeches, Manley, M. *PNP Archives.*

20. M. Manley, Address to Parliament, May 1974. File: Speeches, Manley, M. *PNP Archives*. Emphasis added.

21. M. Manley, "Address to Parliament," May 1974.

22. C. E. Davis (1989), p. 257.

23. Transfer pricing is an accounting technique used by MNCs in intrafirm trade in order to reduce payments to the host government. Generally, the firm in the host country would over-invoice the headquarters for inputs and services, thereby lowering book profits (for the host firm), and as a result would pay less taxes. David Goldsborough (1987), pp. 217–218.

24. Gill and Law (1988), chapter 7.

25. Gill and Law (1988), p. 90. Emphasis added.

26. The Prime Minister put it thus: "Simply put, this Assembly has become known as a place where torrents of words that burn with urgency and truth fall upon deaf ears—ears that are closed by the narrowest considerations of national self-interest. The continuing inability of the United Nations to mediate situations of international crisis and reduce the inequalities between nations does not reflect any lack of desire or skill among the staff of this organization or its various Agencies. The inadequacies of the United Nations precisely reflect the misplaced priorities of its member nations—and *especially of the most powerful and wealthy ones* among them." Quoted from Statement by Hon. M. Manley at the 27th Session of the United Nations General Assembly, October 2, 1972.

27. Statement by Hon. M. Manley at the 27th Session of the United Nations General Assembly, October 2, 1972.

28. Statement by Hon. M. Manley at the 27th Session of the United Nations General Assembly, October 1972. Emphasis added.

29. The question of democracy began to take on added significance after the 1976 general election on account of a spirited campaign by Opposition Leader Seaga to tarnish the election results. Seaga did not let up on the issue and by September the matter was of such concern that Prime Minister Manley wrote the following note to P. J. Patterson (who was a one of the most senior Cabinet Ministers): "Dear P. J., Could you give thought to the point that Seaga has mounted quite an offensive in the Canadian, U.K., Trinidadian and U.S. Missions, for certain, that our Election was bogus, that we are going to destroy freedom of the press, etc., etc. A counter-offensive may be needed. Consider and comment please." Letter from Prime Minister Michael Manley to Minister of Foreign Affairs, P. J. Patterson, dated 14th September, 1977. *PNP Archives*.

30. Fred Bergsten (1976), p. 12.

31. Bergsten (1976), p. 17.

32. David E. Hojman (1980), p. 290.

33. Rhetoric as used here refers to the discursive *form* through which "free-market" is reproduced as common sense, not in the pejorative sense as is customary.

34. Henri A. M. Guda (1975), p. 2.

35. Guda (1975), pp. 2–3.

36. Guda (1975), p. 3.

37. Manley, Budget Debate Speech, 1973.

38. Bergsten (1976), p. 13.

39. Bergsten (1976), p. 13.

40. U.S. State Department Memo., January 1974. Emphasis added.

41. Guda (1975), p. 4.

42. Guda (1975), p. 3.

43. As early as July of 1974 Manley found himself defending the formation of IBA. In an address to the ACP/EEC Ministerial Meeting held in Kingston (15 July, 1974), the Prime Minister noted on behalf of the Third World that "sometimes we are almost dumbfounded by the insensitivity of our metropolitan friends." In a more specific defense of IBA he said: "In the end, we have been driven to construct simple groupings of mineral or raw material producers like the International Bauxite Association. Immediately, masking economic self-interest behind the irrelevant phrases of classical economic jargon, we are accused of forming cartels. And every kind of specter and bogey of another time and situation are invoked to spread fear and confusion. Yet an association like that of the bauxite producing countries is simply evidence and expression of a common will on the part of those producing countries which recognize their community of interest." Consistent with the ideological thrust and discursive strategy of PNP foreign policy Mr. Manley moved on to situate IBA within the parameters of international economic justice and equality of states: "Our aims are positive and have to do with *organizing a new relationship between producing and consumer countries; new methods of bringing the productive process into harmony with social purpose; and new and just relationships between those who own resources, those who control capital, those who control technology, those who supply labor and those who consume the final product." PNP Archives.* Emphasis added.

44. *Los Angeles Times*, reprinted in *Jamaica Daily News*, Wednesday April 2, 1974. Emphasis added.

45. Bergsten (1976), p. 19.

46. *Los Angeles Times,* reprinted in *Jamaica Daily News,* Wednesday, April 2, 1974.

47. Fiona Gordon-Ashworth (1988), p. 88.

48. Paul Lewis (1976), p. 744.

49. Letter from Prime Minister M. Manley to Mr. Anthony Johnson, Executive Director, PSOJ, dated 23 February, 1979. *PNP Archives*: File: "PSOJ."

50. Michael Manley (1982), p. 106.

51. Stephen Krasner (1985), p. 14.

52. Krasner (1985), p. 14.

53. C. Mills (1987), p. 147.

54. Telephone interview with Dr. Rattray, December, 1993.

55. Government of Jamaica, Press Release. Statement by Ministry of External Affairs on Recent Speech by U.S. Secretary of State, Dr. Henry Kissinger. *PNP Archives*, File: External Affairs: Correspondence, 1975.

56. J. Phillips (1980), p. 479.

57. Statement by The Hon. Dudley J. Thompson, Minister of State, Office of the Prime Minister of Jamaica—Before the Twenty-Ninth Session of the United Nations General Assembly, October 2, 1974. Government of Jamaica Publication.

58. Manley had previously described Jamaican foreign policy prior to his first government as "a slavish obedience to the U.S. and the countries of the NATO alliance." Quoted in Kumar (1988), p. 127.

59. Levi (1990), p. 139.

60. Levi (1990), p. 140.

61. De Roulet was not a career diplomat. His selection for the ambassadorship to Jamaica was based on what the *Times* called "an auction." He and other members of his family apparently made regular donations to the Republican Party. In 1968–69 he gave $44,000 and in 1972, $32,000. His father-in-law Charles S. Payson gave $28,000 in 1968, $32,000 in 1970, and $88,000 in 1972. Before his appointment to Jamaica, Mr. De Roulet was listed in the *Congressional Quarterly* as mayor of North Hills, New York. See *The Miami Herald,* Tuesday, July 24, 1973. The *Herald* chastised Mr. Roulet for interfering in Jamaican domestic affairs. Apologies to Mr. Manley and the Jamaican people came from private sources. An American sociology professor wrote to Manley apologizing for De Roulet's "boorish-

ness and ignorance." M. Buddy Martin, President of Local 3959 (Toronto), United Steel Workers of America also wrote an open letter to the Prime Minister and the Jamaican people affirming that Jamaica was "the only place on the earth where a black man can stand ten feet tall regardless of his position or stature." See Levi (1990), pp. 140–142.

62. Georges A. Furiol (1984), p. 174.

63. PNP, "Developments in Jamaica's Foreign Policy." *PNP Archives*, File: "Foreign Affairs—Foreign Policy, 1972–1974."

64. Furiol (1984), 178.

65. "Joint Communique of Cuba and Jamaica." *PNP Archives*. July 13th, 1975, Kingston and Havana.

66. "Joint Communique of Cuba and Jamaica." *PNP Archives*. July 13th, 1975. Kingston and Havana.

## Chapter 9. Promise and Defeat Hegemony as Structural Power

1. As used here, ideology refers to the basic assumptions which would govern the society in the foreseeable future.

2. In a letter to Willis O. Issacs (Jamaica's High Commissioner to Canada and a top ranking conservative member of the PNP), Mr Manley in fact acknowledged that the party had lost the middle classes since 1974. He nonetheless admonished Mr. Issacs for his pessimism and insisted that there were still people in the PNP who were willing to fight, and will "fight." The Prime Minister did not take too kindly to the suggestion that the party should have stayed away from the "title"—"Democratic Socialism." Letter from Prime Minister M. Manley to Mr. W. O. Issacs. *PNP Archives*. (Date not decipherable).

3. Rishee S. Thakur (1994), p. 34.

4. Speech delivered by the Prime Minister, The Hon. Michael Manley at Sam Sharpe Square, Montego Bay, November 21, 1976.

5. Ibid.

6. Quoted from "Prime Minister, The Hon. Michael Manley at U.W.I., November 22, 1976." *PNP Archives*.

7. Ibid.

8. Kaufman (1985), p. 125.

9. Bank of Jamaica, *Report and Statement of Accounts*, 1976.

10. Government of Jamaica, *Economic and Social Survey Jamaica, 1976.* Kingston: National Planning Institute of Jamaica.

11. Government of Jamaica, *Economic and Social Survey, 1976,* pp. 47–48.

12. Bank of Jamaica, *Report and Statement of Accounts,* 1976.

13. Department of Statistics, *Statistical Yearbook of Jamaica,* 1979, pp. 541–547.

14. Government of Jamaica, *Economic and Social Survey: Jamaica, 1976.* p. 149.

15. The "tam pack" was a phrase given to progressive social scientists attached to the University of West Indies, Mona and who were severely critical of what has been described as "Jamaican exceptionalism." The "tam" is a head gear with a mix of colors very much resembling the ones worn by Rastas and other "Black conscious" movements.

16. The Plan was later published as (1985) *Pathways to Progress: The People's Socialist Plan—Jamaica 1977.* Kingston: Maroon Books.

17. The EPP was written by G. Beckford, N. Girvan, Louis Lindsay, and Michael Witter, all of them Marxist or left-leaning social scientists.

18. Kaufman (1985), pp. 133–136.

19. G. Beckford, N. Girvan, L. Lindsay, M. Witter, and "The Jamaican People," *Pathways to Progress,* 1977, pp. 21–22.

20. Kaufman (1985), p. 135.

21. G. Beckford, et al. (1985), p. 35.

22. Ibid., pp. 35–37.

23. Kaufman, 138.

24. "Finance—International Monetary Fund." *PNP Archives.*

25. The dual exchange rate system was adopted on 22 April, 1977. The original rate of J$1.00 = US$1.10 was kept as the basic rate. The new "special rate" was fixed at J$1.00 = US$0.80 or US$1.00 = J$1.25. According to the Bank of Jamaica, the special rate meant an effective devaluation of 37 percent (for that category of transactions) and an overall devaluation of 24 percent when the basic and special rates were combined. See Bank of Jamaica, *Report and Statement of Accounts,* 1977.

26. The reduction of Net Banking System Credit to the Public Sector was perhaps warranted (from the IMF's perspective) on account of a definite pattern of progressively increased public sector credit with the reverse being true for the private sector. With increasing Central Bank interven-

tion in 1976, net domestic credit to the government jumped by 81.3 percent or J$540.9 million. The corresponding figure for the private sector was 4.3 percent. Increased credit to the government resulted in a significantly higher budgetary expenditure in 1976, so much so that it accounted for 47.2 percent of total GDP for fiscal year 1976. See *Economic and Social Survey Jamaica, 1976.*

27. Stephens and Stephens (1986) p. 200.

28. Ibid.

29. Manley (1987), p. 160.

30. In macro-structural terms the EFF Program called for: (a) policies to stimulate output and growth; (b) incomes and prices policies to adjust the relative prices without creating runaway inflation; (c) policies to put the fiscal budget on a sound basis and to create adequate levels of public sector savings and investment; (d) policies to control monetary conditions; and (e) policies to reorganize the balance of payments and external finance. Bank of Jamaica, *Report and Statement of Accounts*, 1978.

31. Government of Jamaica, *Ministry Paper No. 26*. File: "Finance—International Monetary Fund." *PNP Archives.*

32. PNP, "What the IMF was Demanding." File: "Finance—IMF." *PNP Archives.*

33. Manley (1987), p. 154.

34. See Richard L. Bernal (1984).

35. Ibid., p. 146.

36. G. Beckford and M. Witter (1982), p. 93.

37. United States Information Service, Interview with Ambassador Andrew Young. File: "Foreign Affairs Correspondence—1977." *PNP Archives.*

38. Letter from President Jimmy Carter to Prime Minister Manley, dated 24 June, 1977. File: "Foreign Affairs Correspondence." *PNP Archives.*

39. Ibid. Emphasis added.

40. The team consisted of Prime Minister M. Manley and his Permanent Secretary, Gordon Wells; Minister of State, Richard Fletcher; Jamaica's Permanent Representative to Geneva and the Common Fund Talks and later Governor of the Bank of Jamaica, Herbert Walker; Jamaica's Permanent Representative to the United Nations and Chairman of the Group of Seventy-Seven, Don Mills; Ambassador Alfred Rattray; Minister of Foreign Affairs, P. J. Patterson; Chairman of the Jamaican Bauxite Institute, Pat Rousseau; Permanent Secretaries in the Ministry of Foreign Affairs, Keith Rhodd and Frank Francis; and representing the Women's Movement, Beverley Manley.

41. The 1971 amount of US$23.1 was, in fact, given to the Hugh Shearer government specifically to avoid M. Manley's accession to the office of prime minister.

42. Gwyneth Williams (1987), p. 68.

43. Levi (1990), p. 212.

44. Quoted in Levi (1990), p. 211. Emphasis added.

45. K. P. Levitt (1983), p. 252.

46. Ibid., p. 252.

47. A good example of this occurred in March 1977 when the foreign affairs minister forwarded a confidential appraisal of American-Cuban relations. By this time, the Carter administration was showing concrete signs of relaxing the grip on Cuba. Referring to the appraisal Patterson wrote to Manley: "It certainly goes toward fulfilling our wish to make progress and emphasize that at this time we in *Jamaica cannot benefit by trying to prove more royalist than the King.*" Letter from P. J. Patterson to Michael Manley, dated 29 March 1977. File: "Foreign Affairs Correspondence." *PNP Archives*. Emphasis added.

48. For the five-year period 1974–1978, total Jamaican exports to Cuba was $2,630,827.31; Cuban exports to Jamaica for the same period was $3,500,212.17.

49. P. J. Patterson, "Statement by The Hon. P. J. Patterson, Deputy Prime Minister and Minister of Foreign Affairs and Vice President of the People's National Party." File: "Speeches: P. J. Patterson, July–December." *PNP Archives*.

50. Ibid.

51. Embajada De Cuba (Jamaica). Letter from General Ruz to Mr. Roy Mc Gann. (Unofficial Translation), dated City of Havana, July 18, 1979. Emphasis added.

52. A letter from Clare to Manley leaves little doubt as to the extent to which Jamaica was becoming "involved" with the Soviets, without the knowledge of the Jamaican public. Wrote Clare: "I got the impression that the approach would be handled with great discretion by Narondy and all we would need to do is to ensure the appropriate secrecy at our end." Letter from B. Clare to Prime Minister M. Manley, dated 26 October 1979 (Embassy of Jamaica, Moscow). File: "Foreign Affairs Correspondence, 1978." *PNP Archives*.

53. Speech by A. N. Kosygin at the Official Dinner in Honor of Prime Minister Manley. Moscow, April 10, 1979.

54. Quoted from "Notes on Hungary [on the Occasion] of Visit of Hungarian Officials—January 24, 1977." File: "Foreign Affairs. Emphasis added. Correspondence, 1977." *PNP Archives.*

55. Minutes of Meeting with the PSOJ Held at Jamaica House, August 28, 1979. File: PSOJ. *PNP Archives.*

56. Ibid.

57. In a letter dated 8 February 1979, the PSOJ president catalogued a long list of complaints against the PNP government which included criticisms of the State Trading Corporation, Jamaica Development Bank, government handling of crime, the situation in prisons and public hospitals, the government's poor relationship with the military (specifically the sudden retirement of Major-General Green), shortage of foreign exchange, and shortage of fertilizers. Alexander then went on to state: "While we have all been reeling from this unfortunate and depressing catalogue, commentators of open communist sympathies have been continuing to denounce and attack every institution in our country, using the Government-owned media. In addition, there are reports of Cubans using high-powered transmitters throughout rural Jamaica, raising the gravest suspicion as to their intentions." The PSOJ president then called on Prime Minister Manley to discontinue the Cuban-Jamaican program through which Cuban construction workers were building schools. PSOJ, Public Statement and Letter to The Hon. Michael Manley. PSOJ Reference—SCA/sa. File: "PSOJ." *PNP Archives.*

58. PSOJ, Letter to The Hon. Michael Manley, dated 21 March 1979. *PNP Archives.* File: "PSOJ."

59. Ibid.

60. Letter to Mrs. Avis Henriques, Director, PSOJ; President, Jamaica Chamber of Commerce, dated 15 July 1980. File: "PSOJ." *PNP Archives.*

61. M. Manley, "Draft Letter to PSOJ." This letter has no date, but the incidents the Prime Minister referred to would indicate the letter was written sometime in 1980.

62. Quoted in "The Hon. P. J. Patterson on Censure Motion—November 8, 1977." File: "Speeches of P. J. Patterson . . . 1977." *PNP Archives.* Mr. Patterson suggested the organization may very well be called "Capitalist International" or "Imperialist International."

## Chapter 10. Onwards with Critical Theory

1. R.G. Collingwood (1956), pp. 231–249.

2. Esteve Morera (1990), pp. 36–37.

3. Norman Girvan (1981), p. 21.

4. This problem is largely the result of assuming that the state is a single rational actor bent on maximizing benefits and reducing costs. G. Allison and J. D. Steinbruner, in two separate works, have roundly criticized this so called rational actor model. See Allison (1971) and Steinbruner (1974).

5. My understanding of the commodification of the self, and the cultural strategies and tactics of embedding the same in culture, is very much influenced by the thinking of Rishee S. Thakur, Arnold Harrichand Itwaru, Walter H. Persaud, Elarick R. Persaud, and Lameharshine Singh.

6. Edward W. Said (1993), p. 307.

7. Laclau and Mouffe (1985), chapters 3 and 4.

8. In the case of the Caribbean, for example, Guyana's Forbes Burnham earned quite a reputation for delivering salvos against imperialism and neocolonialism. His repressive rule in his own country was defended as an internal matter. Interestingly, Mr. Manley in response to a question from this author defended Burnham under the identical rubric.

# References

## Primary Sources and Official Government Publications

*A Guideline to Jamaica's Foreign Policy, 1972–1974.* No date.

Bank of Jamaica, 1972–1980. *Report and Statement of Accounts.*

Bureau of Mines, United States, 1982. *Minerals Yearbook, Volume I: Metals and Minerals.* Washington, D.C.: United States Department of Interior.

Carter, Rosalynn, June 18, 1977. Handwritten note to Prime Minister M. Manley. Subject: Mrs. Carter's Visit to Jamaica.

Chin, L., Managing Director, October 17, 1978. Henkel Chemicals Ltd. and Past President of Jamaica Exporter's Association. Letter to Prime Minister M. Manley. Subject: Private Sector /Government Co-operation.

Department of State (USA), January 22, 1974. Memorandum. Subject: Raw Materials Other Than Oil as Economic Weapons against the United States and Other Major Consumers.

Department of State (USA), July 14, 1975. Speech by Secretary of State Henry A. Kissinger before the Institute of World Affairs of the University of Wisconsin. Washington: Bureau of Public Affairs, Office of Media Services.

Embajada De Cuba (Jamaica), September 20, 1979. Statement made by Ambassador Ulises Estrada to J.B.C. (Radio and TV) and R.J.R.

Embajada De Cuba (Jamaica), July 18, 1979. Letter to Mr. Roy Mc Gann, Parliamentary Secretary, Ministry of Defence, Jamaica. (Unofficial translation). Subject: Military Co-operation between Jamaica and Cuba. Letter written by General Raul Castro Ruz.

Embajada De Cuba (Jamaica), September 18, 1979. Transcript of Press Conference by Cuban Ambassador, H. E. Ulises Estrada.

Embassy of Jamaica (Moscow), September 8, 1978. Letter to Prime Minister M. Manley. Subject: Jamaican-Soviet Relations. Letter written by Ben Clare.

Embassy of Jamaica (Moscow), October 26, 1978. Letter to Prime Minister M. Manley. Subject: Soviet Arranged Loan to Jamaica. Letter signed by Ben Clare.

Girvan, Norman. August 17, 1979. Letter to Prime Minister Manley. Subject: Human Rights in Guyana.

Government of Jamaica, 1973. *Budget Debate Speech, May 2.*

Government of Jamaica, 1978. Statement by The Hon. P. J. Patterson, M.P. Minister of Foreign Affairs of Jamaica, to the Conference of Foreign Ministers of the Non-Aligned Countries. Belgrade, July 25–29, 1978.

Government of Jamaica, Statement by The Honorable P. J. Patterson, M.P. Deputy Prime Minister and Minister of Foreign Affairs, to the Fifth Session Of UNCTAD, Manila, Philippines, May 9, 1979.

Government of Jamaica, *Economic and Social Survey Jamaica, 1973.* Kingston: National Planning Agency.

Government of Jamaica, 1973–1980. *Economic and Social Survey Jamaica,* Kingston: National Planning Agency.

Government of Jamaica, *Five Year Independence Plan, 1963–1968: A Long Term Development Programme for Jamaica.*

Government of Jamaica, *National Income and Product, 1980.* Kingston: Department of Statistics.

Government of Jamaica, 1987. *Policy Statements of Jamaica at the United Nations, 1962–1987.* Kingston: Information Division, Ministry of Foreign Affairs.

Government of Jamaica, 1983. *Production Statistics.* Kingston: The Statistical Institute of Jamaica.

Government of Jamaica, *Statistical Yearbook of Jamaica,* Various years.

Government of Jamaica, 1978. Statement by The Hon. P. J. Patterson, M.P. Minister of Foreign Affairs of Jamaica, to the Conference of Foreign Ministers of the Non-Aligned Countries. Belgrade, July 25–29, 1978.

Habib, Philip C., September, 1979. Senior Advisor to the Secretary of State, Department of State, Government of the United States of America, Letter to Prime Minister M. Manley. Subject: U.S. Support for Caribbean "Development Process."

Harrington, Michael. May 4, 1978. Letter from the President, Institute of
Democratic Socialism (New York), to Mr. P. J. Patterson, Minister of
Foreign Affairs. Subject: IDS Visit to Jamaica.

Hill, K. G. A., December 4, 1979. Ambassador, Permanent Mission of Jamaica to the Office of the U.N., Geneva. Letter to P. J. Patterson,
Deputy Prime Minister and Minister of Foreign Affairs. Subject:
Eastern Europe, World Energy Situation, Colonel Qadhafi, Iran, and
the International Monetary System.

International Bauxite Association, 1981. *Agreement Establishing the International Bauxite Association.* Kingston: IBA.

Issacs, Willis O. (no date). High Commissioner to Canada, Letter to Prime
Minister M. Manley. Subject: The Thirld World, United Nations,
Israel, and the USA.

Issacs, Willis O., February 18, 1975. "Personal and Confidential" letter to
Prime Minister M. Manley. Subject: PNP Political Strategy.

Jamaica Union of Tertiary Students, July 11, 1979. Letter to Prime Minister M. Manley. Subject: Appeal to Recognise the "Provisional Government of National Reconstruction Set up by the Sandinista Front
of National Liberation.

Jamaica Women's Bureau, 1979. *Jamaica Women's Bureau Report,* April
1978 to March 1979.

Jamaican Ambassador (to Cuba), March 21, 1977. Confidential Telegram
(No. 46) to Minister of Foreign Affairs, Jamaica. Subject: "U.S.-Cuba
Relations."

Joint Communique of Cuba and Jamaica, July 13, 1975.

Kiwanis Club of Kingston, September 25, 1979. Letter to Prime Minister M.
Manley. Subject: Dispute Surrounding Cuban Ambassador to Jamaica.

Kiwanis Club of Kingston, October 19, 1979. Letter to Prime Minister
M. Manley. Subject: Dispute Surrounding Cuban Ambassador to
Jamaica.

Kosygin, A. N., April 10, 1979. Speech by A. N. Kosygin, Prime Minister
and Chairman of the Council of Ministers of the Soviet Union at the
Official Dinner in Honour of Prime Minister Manley, Moscow,

Lago, Manuel Gonzalez, Frente Amplio of Uraguay, October 17 and 29,
1979. Letter to Prime Minister M. Manley. Subject: Jamaica's Policy,
vis-à-vis the "Anti-Fascist Struggle" in Uraguay.

Ministry of Foreign Affairs, May 15, 1975. "Press Release." Subject: Statement by Ministry of External Affairs on Recent Speech by U.S. Secretary of State, Dr. Henry Kissinger.

Ministry of Foreign Affairs, June 15, 1976. Statement on Russia.

Ministry of Foreign Affairs (Economics Division), January 24, 1977. Visit of Hungarian Officials. Notes on Hungary.

Ministry of Foreign Affairs, September 26, 1979. Speech delivered by members of Vietnamese Delegation to Jamaica. Subject: Jamaican-Vietnamese Relations; Anti-Imperialist Struggle. (Non-Official Translation. File: 58/103.)

Ministry of Foreign Affairs, November 2, 1979. Notes of meeting between HMFA and Ethiopian officials, Friday October 26, 1979. Subject: Discussion Leading to Closer Ties between Jamaica and Ethiopia.

Ministry of Foreign Affairs (Economics Division), April 23, 1980. Report of the Visit of The Hon. Deputy Prime Minister and Minister of Foreign Affairs to Haiti and the Dominican Republic, April 1–3, 1980.

Nkomo, J. M., November 23, 1979. President, Zimbabwe African Peoples Union. Letter to Prime Minister M. Manley. Subject: Support for Liberation Struggle.

Oakley, Leo, November 19, 1979. Ambassador, Permanent Mission of Jamaica to the Organization of American States. Letter to Prime Minister M. Manley. Subject: Jamaica's Policy, Re Anti-Fascist Struggle in Uruguay.

Office of the Prime Minister. Notes on a meeting at the Inter-Continental Hotel, Montego Bay on Thursday, February 17th, at 1.30 p.m. between H.P.M., the American Ambassador Mr. Summer Gerrard, and Senator Daniel Moyinhan. Notes taken by Norm Serge.

Office of the Prime Minister, September 26, 1979. Response to Representation by the United States Ambassador, Re the Prime Minister's Speech at the Non-Aligned Summit in Havana. Subject: The Non-Aligned Movement and Jamaica's Foreign Policy.

Office of the Prime Minister, February, 1980. Notes of discussion between President Jose Lopez Portillo of Mexico and Prime Minister Michael Manley of Jamaica, held at Cozumel, Mexico, between 4:00 p.m. and 6:00 p.m. on February 6th, 1980. Subject: Mexican-Jamaican Economic Co-operation.

Office of the Prime Minister, April 24, 1980. Letter from Prime Minister M. Manley to Carlton Alexander, President of PSOJ, Subject: "Economic Intelligence Unit."

Patterson, P. J., February 25, 1977. Minister of Foreign Affairs, Statement by The Hon. P. J. Patterson, Minister of Foreign Affairs, at News Conference. Subject: Hostility of Local and Foreign Press to Jamaica; Cuba, the C.I.A., Jamaica's National Security.

Patterson, P. J., March 29, 1977. Minister of Foreign Affairs. Letter to Prime Minister M. Manley. Subject: Jamaican-Cuban-American Relations.

Patterson, P. J., August, 1977. Minister of Foreign Affairs, "Speaking Notes for Opening Statement Heads of Mission Conference 1977." Subject: Operational and Substantive Matters Pertaining to Jamaica's Foreign Policy; Jamaica's Third World Leadership Role.

Patterson, P. J., April 28, 1979. Minister of Foreign Affairs, "Statement to Press." Subject: Jamaica's Foreign Policy.

Patterson, P. J., May 29, 1979. Minister of Foreign Affairs. Letter to Michael Harrington, President Institute of Democratic Socialism. Subject: IDS Visit to Jamaica.

Patterson, P. J., July 5, 1979. Statement by The Hon. P. J. Patterson, Deputy Prime Minister and Minister of Foreign Affairs and Vice President of the People's National Party. Subject: Response to "Allegations" of Cuban "Penetration" of Jamaica.

Patterson, P. J., September 28, 1979. Deputy Prime Minister and Minister of Foreign Affairs. Statement by The Hon. P. J. Patterson, M.P. Deputy Prime Minister and Minister of Foreign Affairs at the Meeting of the Group of Foreign Ministers of the Group of 77, New York.

Patterson, P. J., October 18, 1980. Text of Radio Broadcast by The Hon. P. J. Patterson.

PNP (Internal Document), December 19, 1974. Developments in Jamaica's Foreign Policy." Subject: International Trade Relations, Development of World Food Supplies, Environment, International Bauxite Association, Regional Relations, and Third World.

PNP (Internal Document), 1977. Report on the recent Mission to Caracas, Washington, and Ottawa. Subject: Jamaica's Foreign Policy.

PNP, "Trials and Crosses." PNP document. Subject: Policy Review.

PNP Women's Movement, 1978. Report of Visit to the Soviet Union, May 11–25, 1978.

PNP Women's Movement, June 22, 1978. Minutes of Meeting of the PNP's Women's Movement—Region 2, Held at the Casa Maria Hotel, Port Maria, Thursday, at 4:00 P.M. Subject: Addresses by Comrades— Ellington, Young, Manley, Wade, McFarcuhar, Turner, Robotham, and Pedlar.

PNP Women's Movement, July 5, 1978. Notes of the Meeting of Region 6 Delegates Held at Bay Rock Hotel. Subject: Addresses by Comrades— Manley, Reid, Fuller, Thompson, Hibbert, Stewart, Pugh, Allrington, Lyon, Codner, Ellington, Kirlew, Lyle, Hutchinson, Kalawan, Wilkinson, Stephenson, and Miller.

PNP, December 7, 1980. Women's Movement Broadcast for Sunday.

President Jimmy Carter, June 24, 1977. Letter to Prime Minister M. Manley. Subject: Mrs. Carter's Visit to Jamaica and Jamaican-American Relations.

Prime Minister M. Manley, (no date). Letter to Mr. J. M. Nkomo. Subject: Reply.

Prime Minister M. Manley (no date). Telegram to Prime Minister Forbes Burnham (Guyana). Subject: Burning of P.N.C's Headquarters.

Prime Minister M. Manley, November 20, 1974. Statement to the House of Representatives by the Prime Minister, The Hon. Michael Manley. Subject: Announcement of "Democratic Socialism."

Prime Minister M. Manley, January 6, 1976. Letter to Ramon Pez Ferro, Cuban Ambassador to Jamaica. Subject: Angola.

Prime Minister M. Manley, November 21, 1976. Prime Minister, The Hon. Michael Manley Speaks at Sam Sharps Square, Montego Bay.

Prime Minister M. Manley, November 22, 1976. Prime Minister, The Hon. Michael Manley at U.W.I.

Prime Minister M. Manley, February 22, 1977. Letter to P. J. Patterson, Minister of Foreign Affairs. Subject: Isvestia Reports.

Prime Minister M. Manley, March 8, 1977. Letter to P. J. Patterson, Minister of Foreign Affairs. Subject: "Tam Incident."

Prime Minister M. Manley, July 4, 1977. Memorandum to list attached. Subject: NIEO and the Reform of the IMF.

Prime Minister M. Manley, September 14, 1977. Letter to P. J. Patterson, Minister of Foreign Affairs. Subject: Mr. Seaga's International "Offensive" against the PNP; Korea, Libya, "Conversation with Beatrice Allende," and Conference of Communist Parties.

Prime Minister M. Manley, 21 February, 1979. Letter to PSOJ. Subject: Response to Notes of Meeting with PSOJ.

Prime Minister M. Manley, July 13, 1979. Letter to Jamaica Union of Tertiary Students. Subject: Reply.

Prime Minister M. Manley, September 10, 1979. Letter to P. J. Patterson, Deputy Prime Minister and Minister of Foreign Affairs. Subject: Request by Daniel Ortega for Visit by Mr. Manley.

Prime Minister Manley, September 26, 1979. Letter to Kiwanis Club of Kingston. Subject: Dispute surrounding Cuban Ambassador to Jamaica.

Prime Minister M. Manley, October 2, 1979. Letter to Mr. John Keller, Caribbean Holidays (New York). Subject: Jamaican Foreign Policy, Cuba, and Tourism.

Prime Minister M. Manley, November 7, 1979. Letter to Kiwanis Club of Kingston. Subject: Dispute surrounding Cuban Ambassador to Jamaica.

Prime Minister M. Manley, December 21, 1979. Letter to Dr. M. G. Lago. Subject: Jamaica's Policy, Re Anti-Fascist Struggle in Uraguay.

Prime Minister M. Manley, May 15, 1980. Letter to President Ahmed Sekou Toure (Republic of Guinea). Subject: Bauxite/Alumina Prices.

Prime Minister M. Manley, July 15, 1980. Letter to Mr. Anthony Johnson, Executive Director, PSOJ. Subject: Freedom of the Press.

Prime Minister M. Manley, July 15, 1980. Letter to Mr. W. Mahfood, Vice President, PSOJ, President, Jamaica Manufacturers' Association. Subject: JBC, CIA, *Daily Gleaner,* and Cuba.

Prime Minister and Minister of External Affairs, M. Manley, July 20, 1973. Outward Telegram to Jamaican Ambassador, Washington. Subject: Message to Secretary of State, USA, regarding U.S. Ambassador to Jamaica, Mr. Vincent deRoulet. Telegram No. 150 (10/037 II).

PSOJ, February 8, 1979. Public Statement. Subject: State Trading Corporation, Social Development Commission, Jamaica Development Bank, Peace Truce in West Kingston, Crime, Strikes, Cuban Workers in Jamaica, and the "Sudden Retirement of Major-General Green."

PSOJ, February 22, 1979. Notes of meeting at Jamaica House.

PSOJ, March 21, 1979. Letter to Prime Minister M. Manley. Subject: PNP Women's Group.

PSOJ, March 26, 1979. The Private Sector's Views on the Rationalization of Systems Controlling Jamaica's Imports and Exports. Subject: The Financial System, the Administrative System, and Physical Facilities.

PSOJ, March 27, 1979. Minutes of Meeting with the Private Sector Organization of Jamaica Held at Jamaica House. Subject: Visit to the Soviet Union, Government/Private Sector Relationship, and Rationalization of Systems Controlling Jamaica's Imports and Exports.

PSOJ, September 30, 1979. Broadcast by Mr. Abe Issa, Chairman, PSOJ Tourism Committee on RJR and JBC on Sunday, "The Future of Jamaica—2."

PSOJ, April 3, 1980. Letter to Dudley Thompson, Minister of National Security. Subject: Economic Intelligence Unit.

PSOJ, April 3, 1980. Letter to Prime Minister M. Manley. Subject: Economic Intelligence Unit.

PSOJ, April 3, 1980. Letter to Prime Minister M. Manley. Subject: IMF Negotiations.

PSOJ, April 9, 1980. Letter to Prime Minister M. Manley. Subject: Economic Intelligence Unit.

PSOJ, April 14, 1980. Letter to Prime Minister M. Manley. Subject: Jamaica's International Debt; Call for General Elections.

PSOJ, May 26, 1980. Letter from Carlton Alexander to Prime Minister Subject: The "Economic Intelligence Unit." Twenty-four other signatures attached.

PSOJ, July 7, 1980. Letter to Prime Minister M. Manley. Subject: Freedom of the Press, Jamaica's Foreign Policy, and the CIA. Signed by W. Mahfood, A. Henriques, P. Vaswani, A. Brown, and A. S. Johnson.

Report, March 5, 1977. Report on the Adventure Inn Incident of March 5, 1977. Subject: "Tam Incident." Signed by C. Bourne, L. Lindsay, L. Taylor, N. Girvan, M. Witter, G. Beckford, and H. Manhertz.

Selassie, Haile I., Theocracy Governmant (*sic*), August 22, 1979. Letter to- "His Excellency, The Governor General" (of Jamaica). Subject: "The Referral of the British High Commissioner, John Drinkall, Concerning the Obligation of the British Crown, to Repatriation; Constitutional Transferral of Authority from the British to the Ethiopian Monarchy; and Current Developments in Zimbabwe-Matebelland."

Thompson, Dudley, August, 1975. Letter—to Prime Minister M. Manley. Subject: Prime Minister Manley's Visit to the USA.

STC, December, 1977. Why a State Trading Corporation for Jamaica?

Thompson, Dudley, January 26, 1976. Minister of Foreign Affairs, Confidential letter to Prime Minister M. Manley. Subject: PNP's Political Strategies and Tactics.

United States Information Service (via Embassy of the United States of America, Kingston), Interview with Ambassador Andrew Young, the Representative of the United States of America to the United Nations.

Workers's Party of Jamaica, January, 1980. Worker's Party of Jamaica Economic Proposals to Deal with the IMF.

Young, Andrew, September 12, 1977. Representative of the USA to the UN. Letter to Prime Minister M. Manley. Subject: American-Jamaican Bilateral Relations.

## Secondary Sources

Ahmad, Aijaz. 1992. *In Theory: Classes, Nations, Literatures.* London: Verso.

Allison, Graham. 1971. *Essence of Decision: Explaining the Cuban Missile Crisis.* Boston: Little, Brown and Company.

Althusser, Louis, and E. Balibar. 1979. *Reading Capital.* London: Verso.

Ambursley, F. 1983. "Jamaica: From Michael Manley to Edward Seaga." In *Crisis in the Caribbean,* edited by F. Ambursley and R. Cohen. New York: Monthly Review Press.

Amstrup, N. 1976. "The Perennial Problem of Small States: A Survey of Research Efforts." *Cooperation and Conflict* 11.

Anderson, Benedict. 1991. *Imagined Communities.* London: Verso.

Anderson, Perry. 1976. "The Antinomies of Antonio Gramsci." *New Left Review* 100.

Anglin, D. G., and T. M. Shaw. 1979. *Zambia's Foreign Policy: Studies in Diplomacy and Dependence.* Boulder: Westview Press.

Apter, D., ed., 1964. *Ideology and Discontent.* New York: Free Press.

Armstrong, A. 1981. "The Political Consequences of Economic Dependence." *Journal of Conflict Resolution* 25, no. 3.

Arrigi, G. 1990. "The Three Hegemonies of Historical Capitalism." *Review* 13, no. 3.

Augelli, Enrico, and Craig Murphy. 1988. *America's Quest for Supremacy and the Third World: A Gramscian Analysis.* London: Pinter Publishers.

Austin-Broos, D. J. 1987. "Pentacostals and Rastafarians: Cultural, Political, and Gender Relations of Two Religious Movements." *Social and Economic Studies* 36, no. 4.

Ayoob, M. 1989. "The Third World in the System of States: Acute Schizophrenia or Growing Pains." *International Studies Quarterly* 33.

Baehr, Peter. 1975. "Small States: A Tool For Analysis." *World Politics* 27, no. 3.

Barner-Barry, C., and R. Rosenwein, 1985. *Psychological Perspectives on Politics.* Englewood Cliffs: N.J.: Prentice Hall.

Bartson, R. P. 1971. "The External Relations of Small States." In A. Schou and A. O. Brundtland, eds. *Small States in International Relations.* Stockholm: Almquist and Wiksell.

Beckford, G. 1972. *Persistent Poverty: Underdevelopment in Plantation Economies of the Third World.* London: Zed Books.

———. 1985. "Caribbean Peasantry in the Confines of the Plantation Mode of Production." *International Social Science Journal* 37, no. 3.

———. 1987. "Impact of Bauxite-Alumina on Rural Jamaica." *Social and Economic Studies* 36.

———. 1987. "The Social Economy of Bauxite in the Jamaican Man-Space." *Social and Economic Studies* 36, no. 1.

Beckford, G., and M. Witter. 1982. *Small Garden . . . Bitter Weed: Struggle and Change in Jamaica*. London: Zed Press (expanded edition).

Beckford, G., N. Girvan, L. Lindsey, and M. Witter. 1985. *Pathways to Progress: The People's Socialist Plan*. Kingston: Maroon Books.

Bell, W. 1977/1978. "Independent Jamaica Enters World Politics: Foreign Policy in a New State." *Political Science Quarterly* 92.

Bell, W., and J. W. Gibson. 1978. "Independent Jamaica Faces the Outside World: Attitudes of Elites after Twelve Years of Nationhood." *International Studies Quarterly* 22, no. 1.

Bell, W., and R. W. Robinson. 1979. "European Melody, African Rhythm, or West Indian Harmony? Changing Cultural Identity Among Leaders in a New State." *Social Forces* 58, no. 1.

Bennett, K. 1983. "Exchange Rate Policy and External Imbalance: The Jamaican Experience, 1978–1982." *Social and Economic Studies* 32, no. 4.

Bernal, R. 1984. "Foreign Investment and Development in Jamaica." *Inter-American Economic Affairs* 38, no. 2.

———. 1984. "The IMF and Class Struggle in Jamaica, 1977–1980." *Latin American Perspectives* 11, no. 3.

———. 1986. "Restructuring Jamaica's Economic Relations with Socialist Countries, 1974–1980." *Development and Change* 17, no. 4.

Biddle, W. J., and J. D. Stephens. 1989. "Dependent Development and Foreign Policy: The Case of Jamaica." *International Studies Quarterly* 33.

Block, Fred L. 1977. *The Origins of International Economic Disorder*. London: University of California Press.

Braudel, Fernand, 1980. On *History*. Translated by S. Matthews. Chicago: University of Chicago Press.

———. 1985. *Civilization and Capitalism, 15th to 18th Centuries—Volume III*. Translated by Sian Reynolds. London: Fontana.

Braveboy-Wagner, J. 1989. *The Caribbean in World Affairs: The Foreign Policies of the English-Speaking States*. Boulder: Westview Press.

Brodber, E. 1985. "Black Consciousness and Popular Music in Jamaica in the 1960s and 1970s." *Caribbean Quarterly* 31, no. 2.

Brodin, Katarina. 1972. "Belief Systems, Doctrines, and Foreign Policy." *Cooperation and Conflict* 7.

Brown, A. 1979. *Color, Class, and Politics in Jamaica*. Princeton: Princeton Transaction Books.

———. 1981. "Economic Policy and the IMF in Jamaica." *Social and Economic Studies* 30.

———. 1982. "A Comparison of the Political Style and Ideological Tendencies of Two Leaders: M. Manley and E. Seaga" *Social and Economic Studies* 31, no. 3.

———. 1982. "Issues of Adjustment and Liberalisation in Jamaica, Some Comments." *Social and Economic Studies* 31, no. 4.

Bull, Hedley. 1977. *The Anarchical Society: A Study of Order in World Politics*. New York: Macmillan.

Bull, H., and A. Watson, eds., 1988. *The Expansion of International Society*. Oxford: Clarendon Press.

Bullock, C. 1986. "IMF Conditionality and Jamaica's Economic Policy in the 1980s." *Social and Economic Studies* 35, no. 4.

Burnham, Peter, 1991. "Neo-Gramscian Hegemony and the International Order." *Capital and Class* 45.

Campbell, David. 1992. *Writing Security: United States Foreign Policy and the Politics of Identity*. Minneapolis: University of Minnesota Press.

Campbell, Horace, 1987. *Rasta and Resistance: From Marcus Garvey to Walter Rodney*. Trenton, N.J.: Africa World Press.

———. 1991. "Garveyism, Pan-Africanism and African Liberation in the Twentieth Century." In *Garvey: His Work and Impact*, edited by R. Lewis and P. Bryan Trenton. N.J.: Africa World Press.

Caporaso, J. 1978. "Dependence, Dependency, and Power in the Global System: A Structural and Behavioral Analysis." *International Organization* 32, no. 1.

Cardoso, H. 1977. "The Consumption of Dependency Theory in the United States." *Latin America Research Review* 12, no. 3.

Chase-Dunn, C. 1990. "Resistance to Imperialism: Semi-Peripheral Actors." *Review* 13, no. 1.

Chevannes, B. 1991. "Garvey Myths among the Jamaican People." In *Garvey: His Work and Impact*, edited by R. Lewis and P. Bryan. Trenton, N.J.: Africa World Press.

———. 1990. "Healing the Nation: Rastafari Exorcism of the Ideology of Racism in Jamaica." *Caribbean Quarterly* 36, nos. 1–2.

Clapham, Christopher, ed., 1977. *Foreign Policy Making in Developing Countries*. New York.

Clarke, Colin G. 1975. *Jamaica: Urban Development and Social Change: 1692–1962*. Berkeley: University of California Press.

Clarke, C., and T. Payne, eds., 1987. *Politics, Security, and Development in Small States*. London: Allen & Unwin.

Collingwood, R. G. 1956. *The Idea of History*. London: Oxford University Press.

Cooper, D. 1985. "Migration from Jamaica in the 1970s: Political Protest or Economic Pull." *International Migration Review* 19.

Cox, Robert W. 1979. "Ideologies and the New International Economic Order: Reflections on Some Recent Literature." *International Organization* 33, no. 2.

———. 1983. "Gramsci, Hegemony, and International Relations: An Essay in Method." *Millennium: Journal of International Studies* 12, no. 2.

———. 1986. "Social Forces, States, and World Orders: Beyond International Relations Theory." In *Neorealism and Its Critics*, edited by Robert Keohane. New York: Columbia University Press.

———. 1987. *Production, Power, and World Order: Social Forces in the Making of History*. New York: Columbia University Press.

———. 1992. "Toward a Post-Hegemonic Conceptualization of World Order: Reflections on the Relevancy of Ibn Khaldun." In *Governance without Government: Order and Change in World Politics*, edited by James Rosenau and Ernst-Otto Czempiel. Cambridge: Cambridge University Press.

Curtin, Philip D. 1968. *Two Jamaicas: The Role of Ideas in a Tropical Colony, 1830–1865*. Westport, Conn.: Greenwood Press.

Cuthbert, M. 1976. "Some Observations on the Role of Mass Media in the Recent Socio-Political Development of Jamaica." *Caribbean Quarterly* 22, no. 4.

Cuthbert, M., and V. Sparkes. 1978. "Coverage of Jamaica in the U.S. and Canadian Press in 1976: A Study of Press Bias and Effect (on Tourism)." *Social and Economic Studies* 27.

Daddieh, C. K., and T. M. Shaw. 1984. "The Political Economy of Decision-Making in African Foreign Policy." *International Political Science Review* 5, no. 1.

David, Steven R. 1991. "Explaining Third World Alignment." *World Politics* 43, no. 2.

Davies, O. 1986. "An Analysis of the Management of the Jamaican Economy 1972–1985." *Social and Economic Studies* 35, no. 1.

Demas, William. 1978. "The Caribbean and the New International Economic Order." *Journal of Inter-American Studies and World Affairs* 20.

Der Derian, James, and Michael J. Shapiro, eds., 1989. *International / Intertextual Relations: Postmodern Readings of World Politics*. New York: Lexington Books.

Dos Santos, T. 1970. "The Structure of Dependence." *American Economic Review* 60, no. 2.

Doty, R. L. 1993. "The Bounds of 'Race' in International Relations." *Millennium: Journal of International Studies* 22, no. 3.

Dror, Y. 1987. "High-Intensity Aggressive Ideologies as an International Threat," *Jerusalem Journal of International Relations* 9, no. 1.

East, M. A., 1973. "Size and Foreign Policy: A Test of Two Models." *World Politics* 25.

Eaton, G. 1975. *Alexander Bustamante and Modern Jamaica*. Kingston: Kingston Publishers Ltd.

———. 1984. "Jamaican Political Processes: A System in Search of a Paradigm." *Journal of Development Studies* 20, no. 4.

———. 1986. "Domestic Politics and External Relations in Jamaica under Manley 1972–1980." *Studies in Comparative International Development* 21, no. 1.

Erling, B. 1971. "The Small State in International Politics." In A. Schou and A. O. Brundtland, eds., *Small States in International Relations*. Stockholm: Almquist and Wiksell.

Eyre, L. A. 1984. "Political Violence and Urban Geography in Kingston, Jamaica." *Geographical Review* 74, no. 1.

Fanon, Frantz. 1963. *The Wretched of the Earth*. Translated by C. Farrington. New York: Grove Press.

Fauriol, Georges. 1984. *Foreign Policy Behavior of Caribbean States: Guyana, Haiti, and Jamaica.* Washington D.C.: University Press of America.

Femia, Joseph. 1981. *Gramsci's Political Thought: Hegemony, Consciousness, and the Revolutionary Process.* New York: Oxford University Press.

Feuer, C. H. 1984. "Better Must Come: Sugar and Jamaica in the 20th Century." *Social and Economic Studies* 33, no. 4.

Figueroa, M. 1988. "The Formation and Framework of Middle Strata National Leadership in Jamaica: The Crisis of the Seventies and Beyond." *Caribbean Studies* 21, nos. 1–2.

Foner, N. 1973. "Party Politics in a Jamaican Community." *Caribbean Studies* 13, no. 2.

Foucault, Michel. 1979. *Discipline and Punish.* New York: Vintage Books.

Fox, A. B. 1959. *The Power of Small States.* Chicago: University of Chicago Press.

Gafar, J. S. 1988. "Economic Growth and Economic Policy: Employment and Unemployment in Jamaica, 1972–1984." *The Journal of Developing Areas* 23.

Geertz, Clifford. 1964. "Ideology as a Cultural System." In *Ideology and Discontent,* edited by D. Apter. London: The Free Press.

George, Jim. 1994. *Discourses of Global Politics: A Critical (Re)Introduction to International Relations.* Boulder: Lynne Rienner Publishers.

Gill, Stephen R. 1989. "Global Hegemony and the Structural Power of Capital." *International Studies Quarterly* 33.

———. 1990. *American Hegemony and the Trilateral Commission.* Cambridge: Cambridge University Press.

———. 1991. "Reflections on Global Order and Sociohistorical Time." *Alternatives* 16.

———. ed. 1993. *Gramsci, Historical Materialism, and International Relations.* New York: Cambridge University Press.

Gill, Stephen R., and David Law. 1988. *The Global Political Economy: Perspectives, Problems, and Policies.* Baltimore: Johns Hopkins University Press.

Gilpin, Robert. "The Richness of the Tradition of Political Realism." In R. Keohane, ed., *Neorealism and Its Critics.* New York: Columbia University Press.

————. 1981. *War and Change in World Politics*. New York: Cambridge University Press.

Girvan, Norman. 1976. *Corporate Imperialism: Conflict and Expropriation.* New York: Monthly Review Press.

Girvan, Norman, and R. Bernal. 1982. "The IMF and the Foreclosure of Development Options: The Case of Jamaica." *Monthly Review* 33.

Girvan, Norman, and W. Hughes. 1980. "The IMF and the Third World: The Case of Jamaica, 1974–1980." *Development Dialogue* 11, no. 2.

Girvan, Norman, and O. Jefferson, eds., (No date). *Readings in the Political Economy of the Caribbean. New World Publishers.*

Goldsborough, David. 1987. "Foreign Direct Investment in Developing Countries." In T. Miljan, ed., *The Political Economy of North-South Relations.* Peterborough, Ont.: Broadview Press.

Gourevitch, P. 1978. "The Second Image Reversed: The International Sources of Domestic Politics." *International Organization* 32, no. 4.

Gramsci, Antonio. 1971. *Selections from the Prison Notebooks.* Edited and translated by Q. Hoare and G. N. Smith. New York: International Publishers.

Gray, Obika. 1991. *Radicalism and Social Change in Jamaica, 1960–1972.* Knoxville: The University of Tennessee Press.

Ground, R. L. 1982. "Jamaica: Economic Policy and Economic Performance in the 1972–1980 Period, An Interpretation." *Planning Bulletin.*

Gupta, A. 1992. "The Song of the Nonaligned World: Transnational Identities and the Reinscription of Space in Late Capitalism." *Cultural Anthropology* 7, no. 1.

Hall, Stuart. 1977. "Pluralism, Race, and Class in Caribbean Society." In *Race and Class in Post-Colonial Society: A Study of Ethnic Group Relations in the English-Speaking Caribbean, Bolivia, Chile, and Mexico.* Paris: UNESCO.

————. 1985. "Religious Ideologies and Social Movements in Jamaica." In *Religion and Ideology,* edited by R. Bobcock and K. Thompson. Manchester: Manchester University Press.

Handel, Michael. 1981. *Weak States in the International System.* London: Frank Cass.

Harrod, J. 1972. *Trade Union Foreign Policy: A Study of British and American Trade Union Activities in Jamaica.* London: Macmillan.

Hempel, C. G. 1968. "The Logic of Functional Analysis." In M. Broadbeck, ed., *Readings in the the Philosophy of Sciences.* New York: Macmillan.

Herman, M. G. 1987. "Assessing the Foreign Orientation of Sub-Saharan African Leaders." In S. G. Walker, ed., *Role Theory and Foreign Policy Analysis.* Durham: Duke University Press.

Hettne, B. 1986. "Self-Reliance and Destabilization in the Caribbean and Central America: The Cases of Jamaica and Nicaragua." *Scandinavian Journal Development Alternatives* 5.

Hickey, J. 1983. "The Stabilization Program of the U.S. in Jamaica." *Inter-American Economic Affairs* 37.

Hillman, R. S. 1979. "Legitimacy and Change in Jamaica." *Journal of Developing Areas* 13.

Holsti, K. J. 1970. "National Role Conceptions in the Study of Foreign Policy." *International Studies Quarterly* 14.

———. 1983. *International Politics: A Framework For Analysis.* Englewood Cliffs, N.J.: Prentice Hall.

Holzberg, C. S. 1977. "Social Stratification, Cultural Nationalism, and Political Economy in Jamaica: The Myth of Development and Anti-White Bias." *Canadian Review of Sociology and Anthropology* 14, no. 4.

———. 1981. "The Cultural Context of the Jamaican National System: Ethnicity and Social Stratification Reconsidered." *Anthropologica* 23, no. 2.

Huntington, Samuel P. 1993. "The Clash of Civilizations?" *Foreign Affairs,* Summer.

Jackson, R. H. 1990. *Quasi-States: Sovereignty, International Relations, and the Third World.* New York: Cambridge University Press.

Jacobs, W. R. 1973. "Appeals by Jamaican Political Parties: A Study of Newspaper Advertisements in the 1972 Jamaican General Election Campaign." *Caribbean Studies* 13, no. 2.

James, W. A. 1984. "The Decline and Fall of Michael Manley: Jamaica, 1972–1980." *Archipelage* 5.

Jervis, R. 1976. *Perception and Misperception in International Politics.* Princeton: Princeton University Press.

Johnson-Hill, J. 1981. "Unheard Voices: Jamaica's Struggle and the Multinational Media." *Caribbean Quarterly* 27, nos. 2–3.

Jones, W. O. 1968. "Plantations." in D. L. Sills, ed., *International Encyclopedia of the Social Sciences,* vol. 12.

Kaufman, Michael. 1985. *Jamaica under Manley: Dilemmas of Socialism and Democracy.* London: Zed Books.

Keeley, James F. 1990. "Toward a Foucauldian Analysis of International Regimes." *International Organization* 44, no. 1.

Kennedy, Paul. 1988. *The Rise and Fall of the Great Powers*. London: Fontana Paperbacks.

Keohane, Robert O. 1969. "Lilliputians' Dilemmas: Small States in International Politics." *International Organization* 23.

———. 1984. *After Hegemony: Cooperation and Discord in the World Political Economy*. Princeton: Princeton University Press.

———. 1986. ed., *Neorealism and Its Critics*. New York: Columbia University Press.

———. 1989. *International Institutions and State Power: Essays in International Theory*. London: Westview Press.

Kimche, David. 1973. *The Afro-Asian Movement—Ideology and Foreign Policy of the Third World*. Jerusalem: Israel Universities Press.

Kopkind, A. 1980. "Trouble in Paradise." *Columbia Journalism Review*.

Korany, Bhagat. 1974. "Foreign Policy Models and Their Empirical Relevance to Third-World Actors: A Critique and an Alternative." *International Social Science Journal* 26.

———. 1975. *Afro-Asian Non-Alignment in the Contemporary International System: A Pre-Theory*. Geneva: University of Geneva.

———. 1976. *Social Change, Charisma, and International Behavior: Toward a Theory of Foreign Policy-Making in the Third World*. Leiden, Holland: Sijthoff.

———. 1978 "Societal Variables and Foreign Policy in the Third World: Hypothesis and Data." *Journal of The Social Sciences* 6.

———. 1983. "The Take-Off of Third World Studies: The Case of Foreign Policy." *World Politics* 35.

———. 1984. "Foreign Policy Decisions in the Third World," *International Political Science Review*, January.

Krasner, Stephen D. 1985. *Structural Conflict: The Third World against Global Liberalism*. Berkeley: University of California Press.

Krasner, Stephen D., ed., 1987. *International Regimes*. Ithaca: Cornell University Press, 1983.

Kristol, I. "American Foreign Policy: A Neoconservative View." *The Jerusalem Journal of International Relations* 9, no. 1.

Kumar, Daniel K. 1988. *U.S. Policy toward Jamaica 1962–1982*. Ph.D. Dissertation, Howard University.

Kuper, Adam. 1977. "Race, Class, and Culture in Jamaica." in *Race and Class in Post-Colonial Society: A Study of Ethnic Group Relations in the English-Speaking Caribbean, Bolivia, Chile, and Mexico*. London: UNESCO.

Lacey, Terry. 1977. *Violence and Politics in Jamaica, 1960–1970: Internal Security in a Developing Country*. Manchester: Manchester University Press.

Laclau, Ernesto. 1979. *Politics and Ideology in Marxist Theory*. London: Verso.

———. 1983. "The Impossibility of Society." *Canadian Journal of Political and Social Theory* 8, nos. 1–2.

Laclau, Ernesto, and C. Mouffe. 1985. *Hegemony and Socialist Strategy: Toward a Radical Democratic Politics*. London: Verso.

Levi, Darrell. 1990. *Michael Manley: The Making of a Leader*. Athens: University of Georgia Press.

Levi, Werner. 1970. "Ideology, Interests, and Foreign Policy." *International Studies Quarterly* 14.

Levi-Strauss, Claude. 1962. *The Savage Mind*. Chicago: University of Chicago Press.

Lewis V. 1981. "Issues and Trends in Jamaican Foreign Policy 1972–1977." In C. Stone and A. Brown, eds., *Perspectives on Jamaica in the Seventies*. Kingston: Jamaica Publishing. House, 1.

———. 1983. "The Small State Alone: Jamaican Foreign Policy," *Journal of Inter-American and World Affairs*, vol. 25.

Lewis, V., ed., 1976. *Size, Self-Determination, and International Relations: The Caribbean*. Kingston, Jamaica: Institute of Social and Economic Research.

Lewis, W. F. 1986. "The Rastafari: Millennial Cultists or Unregenerative Peasants?" *Peasant Studies* 14, no. 1.

Liska, George. 1968. *Alliances and The Third World*. Baltimore Md.: Johns Hopkins Press.

Maclean, J. 1981. "Political Theory, International Theory, and Problems of Ideology." *Millennium* 10, no. 2.

Manley, Michael. 1970. "Overcoming Insularity in Jamaica." *Foreign Affairs* (October 1970).

———. 1982. *Jamaica: Struggle in the Periphery*. London: Third World Media.

———. 1987. *Up the Down Escalator: Development and the International Economy—A Jamaican Case Study*. Andre Deutsch.

Mannheim, Karl. 1985. *Ideology and Utopia: An Introduction to the Sociology of Knowledge*. New York: Harvest/NBJ Book.

Manning, B. 1976. "Goals, Ideology, and Foreign Policy." *Foreign Affairs* 54.

McBain, H. 1981. "External Financing of the Water Commission of Jamaica." *Social and Economic Studies* 30, no. 1.

———. 1981. "The Political Economy of Capital Flows: The Case of Jamaica." *Social and Economic Studies* 30.

———. 1987. "The Impact of the Bauxite/Alumina MNCs on Rural Jamaica: Constraints on Development of Small Farmers in Jamaica." *Social and Economic Studies* 36.

McGowan, P. J., and K. P. Gottwald. 1975. "Small State Foreign Policies." *International Studies Quarterly* 19.

Miliband, Ralph. 1990. "Counter-Hegemonic Struggles." In R. Miliband, J. Saville, and L. Panitch, eds., *Socialist Register*. London: Merlin Press.

Miller, Errol. 1993. "Self and Identity Problems in Jamaica: An Analysis of Attempted Solutions." *Caribbean Quarterly* 19, no. 2.

Mills, Charles. 1987. "Race and Class: Conflicting or Reconcilable Paradigms." *Social and Economic Studies* 36, no. 2.

Moon, Bruce E. 1983. "The Foreign Policy of Dependent States." *International Studies Quarterly* 27.

———. 1985. "Consensus or Compliance? Foreign-Policy Change and External Dependence." *International Organization* 39, no. 2.

Morera, Esteve. 1990. *Gramsci's Historicism: A Realist Interpretation*. New York: Routledge.

Morgenthau, Hans, J. 1973. *Politics among Nations: The Struggle For Power and Peace*. New York: Alfred A. Knopf.

Mortimer, R. A. 1980. *The Third World Coalition in International Politics*. New York: Praeger.

Moynihan, Daniel P. 1975. "The United States in Opposition." *Commentary* 59, no. 3.

Munroe, Trevor. 1972. *The Politics of Constitutional Decolonization: Jamaica, 1944–1962*. Kingston: Institute of Social and Economic Research, University of the West Indies, Jamaica.

Murphy, Craig. 1984. *The Emergence of the NIEO Ideology.* Boulder: Westview Press.

———. "What the Third World Wants: An Interpretation of the Development and Meaning of the New International Economic Order Ideology." *International Studies Quarterly* 27.

Nettleford, Rex. 1972. *Identity, Race, and Protest in Jamaica.* New York: William Morris & Co.

———. 1978. *Caribbean Cultural Identity: The Case of Jamaica.* Kingston: Institute of Jamaica.

Neufeld, Mark. 1995. *The Restructuring of International Relations Theory.* Cambridge: Cambridge University Press.

Nicholas, T. 1979. *Rastafari: A Way of Life.* New York: Anchor Press.

Nicholson, M. 1989. *Formal Theories in International Relations.* Cambridge: Cambridge University Press.

O'Flaherty, and J. Daniel. 1978. "Finding Jamaica's Way." *Foreign Policy* 31.

O'Shanghnessy, H. 1977. "Behind the Violence in Jamaica: Political and Economic Pressures on the Manley Government." *Round Table* 264.

Paul, A. H. 1983. "The Destabilization Program of the IMF in Jamaica." *Inter-American Economic Affairs* 37.

Payne A. 1976. "From Michael with Love: The Nature of Socialism in Jamaica." *Journal of Commonwealth and Comparative Politics* 14 no. 1.

———. 1983. "The Rodney Riots in Jamaica: The Background and Significance of the Events of October 1968." *Journal of Commonwealth and Comparative Politics* 21, no. 2.

———. 1988. *Politics in Jamaica.* London: C. Hurst & Co.

Payne, A., and P. Sutton, eds., 1984. *Dependency under Challenge: The Political Economy of the Commonwealth Caribbean.* Manchester: Manchester University Press.

Persaud, Randolph, B. 1995. "Social Forces and World Order Pressures in the Making of Jamaican Multilateral Policy." In *State, Society, and the UN System: Changing Perspectives on Multilateralism*, edited by K. Krause and W. A. Knight. Tokyo: United Nations University Press.

———. 1997. "Frantz Fanon, Race, and World Order." In S. Gill and J. Mittelman, eds., *Innovation and Transformation in International Studies.* Cambridge: Cambridge University Press.

Phillips, J. 1980. "Renovation of the International Economic Order: Trilateralism, the IMF, and Jamaica." In H. Sklar, ed., *Trilateralism:*

*The Trilateral Commission and Elite Planning for World Management*. Boston: South End Press.

Phillips, P. 1975. "Jamaican Foreign Relations and National Capitalism: Some Research Notes and Perspectives." *Caribbean Yearbook of International Relations*.

———. 1988. "Race, Class, Nationalism: A Perspective on Twentieth Century Social Movements in Jamaica." *Social and Economic Studies* 37, no. 3.

Pollard, V. 1982. "The Social History of Dread Talk," *Caribbean Quarterly* 28, no. 4.

Post, Ken. 1978. *Arise Ye Starvelings: The Jamaican Labor Rebellion of 1938 and Its Aftermath*. The Hague: Martinus Nijhoff.

Poulantzas, Nicos. 1978. *Political Power and Social Classes*. London: Verso.

Premdas, R., ed. 1993. *The Enigma of Ethnicity: An Analysis of Race in the Caribbean and the World*. St. Augustine, Trinidad and Tobago: University of the West Indies.

Ramsaran, R. 1989. *The Commonwealth Caribbean in the World Economy*. London: MacMillan.

Reid, G. 1974. *The Impact of Very Small Size on the International Behavior of Microstates*. Beverley Hills: Sage Publications.

Richardson, Neil. 1978. *Foreign Policy and Economic Dependence*. Austin: University of Texas Press.

Richardson, N. R., 1976. "Political Compliance and U.S. Trade Dominance." *American Political Science Review* 70.

Richardson, N., and C. Kegley. 1980. "Trade Dependence and Foreign Policy Compliance: A Longitudinal Analysis." *International Studies Quarterly* 24.

Richardson. Mary F. 1983. "Out of Many, One People—Aspiration or Reality? An Examination of the Attitudes to the Various Racial and Ethnic Groups within the Jamaican Society." *Social and Economic Studies* 32, no. 3.

Robinson, R. V., and W. Bell, 1978. "Attitudes toward Political Independence in Jamaica after Twelve Years of Nationhood." *British Journal of Sociology* 29, no. 2.

Robinson, William, I. 1996. *Promoting Polarchy: Globalization, US Intervention, and Hegemony*. Cambridge: Cambridge University Press.

———. 1999. "Latin America in the Age of Inequality: Confronting the New "Utopia," *International Studies Review*, 1, issue 3.

Rodney, Walter. *The Groundings with my Brothers.* London: Bogle-L'Ouverture, 1969.

Rosenau, James N. 1966. "The Theories of Foreign Policy." In *Approaches to Comparative and International Politics,* edited by R. B. Farell. Evanston, Ill.

———. 1971 "Pre-Theories and Theories of Foreign Policy." In *The Scientific Study of Foreign Policy,* edited by James Rosenau. New York: The Free Press.

———. 1981. "The Elusiveness of Third World Demands: Conceptual and Empirical Issues." In *World System Structure: Continuity and Change,* edited by L. Hollist and James Rosenau. Beverley Hills: Sage.

———. 1987. "Role and Role Scenarios in Foreign Policy." In *Role Theory in Foreign Policy Analysis,* edited by S. G. Walker. Durham: Duke University Press.

Rosenau, James, and E. Czempiel, eds. 1992. *Governance without Government: Order and Change in World Politics.* New York: Cambridge University Press.

Rosow, S. J. 1990. "The Forms of Internationalisation: Representation on a Global Scale." *Alternatives* 15.

Rothstein, R. L. *The Weak in the World of the Strong: The Developing Countries in the International System.* New York: Columbia University Press.

———. 1980. *The Third World and U.S. Foreign Policy: Cooperation and Conflict in the 1980s.*

Rupert, Mark. 1995. *Producing Hegemony: The Politics of Mass Production and American Global Power.* Cambridge: Cambridge University Press.

Sachak, N. 1987. "The Impact of Land Acquisition by Bauxite-Alumina Transitional Corporations on Peasants in the Bauxite Land Economy." *Social and Economic Studies* 36, no.

Said, Edward. 1979. *Orientalism.* New York: Vintage Books.

Salmon, M. G. 1987. "Land Utilization within Jamaica's Bauxite Land Economy." *Social and Economic Studies* 36, no. 1.

Sasson, S. 1987. "International Relations and the Invisibility of Ideology." *Millennium* 16, no. 3.

Semaj, Leahcim Tufani. 1980. "Rastafari: From Religion to Social Theory." *Caribbean Quarterly* 26, no. 4.

Shaw, T. M. 1985. *Toward a Political Economy of Africa: The Dialectics of Dependence.* London: Macmillan.

Shepherd, Verene, A. 1999/2000. "Poverty, Exploitation, and Agency among Indian Settlers in Jamaica: Evidence from Twentieth-Century Letters," *Journal of Caribbean Studies*, 14, nos. 1 and 2.

Singer, M. R. 1972. *Weak States in a World of Powers: The Dynamics of International Relationships*. New York: The Free Press.

Smith, M. G. 1965. *The Plural Society in the British West Indies*. Los Angeles, University of California Press.

———. 1984. *Culture, Race, and Class in the Commonwealth Caribbean*. Mona, Jamaica: Department of Extra-Mural Studies, University of the West Indies.

Smith, M. G., R. Augier, and R. Nettleford. 1967. "The Rastafari Movement in Kingston, Jamaica" (Part One). *Caribbean Quarterly* 13, no. 3.

Smith, W. S. 1982. "Dateline Havana: Myopic Diplomacy." *Foreign Policy* 47.

Snyder, R., H. W. Bruck, and B. Sapin, eds., 1962. *Foreign Policy Decision Making*. Glencoe: The Free Press.

Stephens, E. H., and J. D. Stephens. 1986. *Democratic Socialism in Jamaica: The Political Movement and Social Transformation in Dependent Capitalism*. Princeton: Princeton University Press.

———. 1987. "The Transition to Mass Parties and Ideological Politics: The Jamaican Experience Since 1972," *Comparative Political Studies* 19.

———. 1988. "Democratic Socialism in Dependent Capitalism: An Analysis of the Manley Government in Jamaica," *Politics and Society* 12, no. 3.

———. 1989. "Power, Policy, and Politics in Independent Jamaica." In *Jamaica in Independence: Essays on the Early Years*, edited by R. Nettleford. Kingston: Heinemann Publishers.

Stone, Carl. 1974. "Race and Nationalism in Urban Jamaica," *Caribbean Studies* 13, no. 4.

———1976. "Class and the Institutionalization of Two-Party Politics in Jamaica," *Journal of Commonwealth and Comparative Politics* 14, no. 2.

———. 1977. "Class and Status Voting in Jamaica," *Social and Economic Studies* 26, no. 3.

———. 1978. "Regional Party Voting in Jamaica (1959–1976)," *Journal of Inter-American Studies and World Affairs* 20, no. 4.

———. 1982. "Socialism and Agricultural Policies in Jamaica in the 1970s," *Inter-American Economic Affairs* 35, no. 4.

———. 1985. "Jamaica in Crisis: From Socialist to Capitalist Management," *International Journal* 40, no. 2.

———. 1986. *Class, State, and Democracy in Jamaica*. New York: Praeger.

Swaby, R. A. 1981. "The Rationale for State Ownership of Public Utilities in Jamaica," *Social and Economic Studies* 30, no. 1.

Taylor, Council. 1955. *Color and Class: A Comparative Study of Jamaican Status Groups*. Ph.D. dissertation, Yale University.

Thakur, Rishee. 1994. *Politics and Hegemony in Guianese Nationalism, 1945–1965*. Ph.D. dissertation, York University, Toronto.

Thomas, Clive Y. 1988. *The Poor and the Powerless: Economic Policy and Change in the Caribbean*. London: Latin American Bureau.

Thompson, W. R. 1983. "Uneven Economic Growth, Systemic Challenges, and Global Wars," *International Studies Quarterly* 27.

Thompson, W. S. 1969. *Ghana's Foreign Policy 1957–1966: Diplomacy, Ideology, and the New State*. Princeton: Princeton University Press.

Tinker, H. Race. 1977. *Conflict and the International Order: From Empire to United Nations*. New York: The Macmillan Press.

Tooze, R. 1990. "Understanding the Global Political Economy: Applying Gramsci," *Millennium: Journal of International Studies* 19, no. 2.

Vandenbosch, A. 1974. "The Small States in International Politics and Organization," *The Journal of Politics* 26.

Van Horne, W. 1981. "Jamaica: Why Manley Lost the Elections of October 1980," *World Today* (London) 37.

Vital, D. 1967 *The Inequality of States*. Oxford: Oxford University Press.

Walker, R. B. J. 1984. *Culture, Ideology, and World Order*. Boulder: Westview Press.

Walker, Stephen G., ed., 1987. *Role Theory and Foreign Policy Analysis*. Durham: Duke University Press.

Wallerstein, Immanuel. 1991. *Geopolitics and Geoculture: Essays on the Changing World-System*. New York: Cambridge University Press.

Waltz, K.. 1970. *Man, the State and War: A Theoretical Analysis*. New York: Columbia University Press.

———. 1979. *Theory of International Politics*. Reading, Mass.: Addison-Wesley Publishing Company.

Watson, Adam. 1992. *The Evolution of International Society*. New York: Routledge.

Watson, G. L. 1974. "Patterns of Black Protest in Jamaica: The Case of the Ras-Tafarians," *Journal of Black Studies* 4, no. 3.

Waxman, C., ed., 1969. *The End of Ideology Debate*. New York: Simon and Schuster.

Weinstein, B. 1972. "The Uses of Foreign Policy in Indonesia: An Approach to the Analysis of Foreign Policy in the Less Developed Countries," *World Politics*, 24, no. 3.

Williams, Gwyneth. 1987. *Third World Political Organizations*. Atlantic Highlands, N.J.: Humanities Press International.

Wish, N. 1987. "National Attributes as Sources of National Role Conceptions: A Capability-Motivation Model." In S. G. Walker, ed., *Role Theory and Foreign Policy Analysis*. Durham: Duke University Press.

Witter, M., and D. Ramjeesingh. 1986. "An Analysis of the Internal Structure of the Jamaican Economy: 1969–1974," *Social and Economic Studies* 35, no. 1.

SUNY series in Global Politics
James N. Rosenau, Editor

**List of Titles**

*American Patriotism in a Global Society*—Betty Jean Craige

*The Political Discourse of Anarchy: A Disciplinary History of International Relations*—Brian C. Schmidt

*From Pirates to Drug Lords: The Post-Cold War Caribbean Security Environment*—Michael C. Desch, Jorge I. Dominguez, and Andres Serbin (eds.)

*Collective Conflict Management and Changing World Politics*—Joseph Lepgold and Thomas G. Weiss (eds.)

*Zones of Peace in the Third World: South America and West Africa in Comparative Perspective*—Arie M. Kacowicz

*Private Authority and International Affairs*—A. Claire Cutler, Virginia Haufler, and Tony Porter (eds.)

*Harmonizing Europe: Nation-States within the Common Market*—Francesco G. Duina

*Economic Interdependence in Ukrainian-Russian Relations*—Paul J. D'Anieri

*Leapfrogging Development? The Political Economy of Telecommunications Restructuring*—J. P. Singh

*States, Firms, and Power: Successful Sanctions in United States Foreign Policy*—George E. Shambaugh

271

*Approaches to Global Governance Theory*—Martin Hewson and Timothy J. Sinclair (eds.)

*After Authority: War, Peace, and Global Politics in the 21st Century*—Ronnie D. Lipschutz

*Pondering Postinternationalism: A Paradigm for the Twenty-First Century?*—Heidi H. Hobbs (ed.)

*Beyond Boundaries? Disciplines, Paradigms, and Theoretical Integration in International Studies*—Rudra Sil and Eileen M. Doherty (eds.)

*Why Movements Matter: The West German Peace Movement and U.S. Arms Control Policy*—Steve Breyman

*International Relations—Still an American Social Science? Toward Diversity in International Thought*—Robert M. A. Crawford and Darryl S. L. Jarvis (eds.)

*Which Lessons Matter? American Foreign Policy Decision Making in the Middle East, 1979–1987*—Christopher Hemmer (ed.)

*Hierarchy Amidst Anarchy: Transaction Costs and Institutional Choice*—Katja Weber

# Index